POETRY WITH AN EDGE

NEIL ASTLEY was born in Hampshire in 1953. He worked as a journalist for four years, and was living in Darwin, Australia, when the city was destroyed by Cyclone Tracy in 1974. After reading English at Newcastle University, he founded Bloodaxe Books in Newcastle in 1978, and is now its editor and managing director. As well as editing over 300 books for Bloodaxe, he has designed all Bloodaxe's distinctive book covers.

In 1982 he received an Eric Gregory Award from the Society of Authors for a pamphlet collection, *The Speechless Act* (Mandeville Press, 1984). His first book of poems, *Darwin Survivor* (Peterloo Poets, 1988), was a Poetry Book Society Recommendation.

He has edited several anthologies for Bloodaxe, including a children's anthology, *Bossy Parrot* (1987), a critical guide, *Tony Harrison* (1991), a TV tie-in book, *Wordworks* (1992), and *Dear Next Prime Minister* (1990), a collection of open letters which may have played a small part in precipitating the fall of Margaret Thatcher. ●

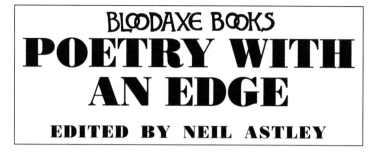

BLOODAXE BOOKS
POETRY WITH AN EDGE
EDITED BY NEIL ASTLEY

BLOODAXE BOOKS

ISBN: 1 85224 061 X

Second edition published 1993 by
Bloodaxe Books Ltd,
P.O. Box 1SN,
Newcastle upon Tyne NE99 1SN.

Second edition, second impression 1997.

First edition published 1988.

Bloodaxe Books Ltd acknowledges
the financial assistance of Northern Arts.

ACKNOWLEDGEMENTS
Acknowledgements are due to Oxford University Press
for work by Basil Bunting and the Gallery Press, Ireland,
for poems by John Hughes, Medbh McGuckian and John Montague.

For Simon and Nansi, again
(still crazy after all these years)

Cover printing by J. Thomson Colour Printers Ltd, Glasgow.

Printed in Great Britain by
Cromwell Press Ltd, Broughton Gifford, Melksham, Wiltshire.

Brief words are hard to find,
shapes to carve and discard:
Bloodaxe, king of York,
king of Dublin, king of Orkney.
Take no notice of tears;
letter the stone to stand
over love laid aside lest
insufferable happiness impede
flight to Stainmore,
to trace
lark, mallet,
becks, flocks
and axe knocks.

BASIL BUNTING
Briggflatts

Contents

Introduction

It is not easy to find out about contemporary poetry. You would expect the best starting point to be anthologies and literary magazines, but their selections are invariably partial and specialised, and their presentation often assumes a prior knowledge of modern poetry on the part of the reader.

All editors have their axes to grind. Mine would be honed on the necks of poetry publishers who alienate the very readers they should be trying to attract. The easiest way to put off potential readers is to compose a blurb as if it were a piece of literary criticism, making readers feel that they need a degree in English to understand the poems in the book. It's a common vice with poetry editors, and a lazy one. Such editors fall back on their own specialised terminology, analysing the writer's technique in technical language instead of giving a description of the book. They make no attempt to understand why a particular book might interest other readers, and in many cases they are robbing their own poets of a much wider readership.

When I started reading contemporary poetry, I nearly gave up. I'd read a few modern poets at school, and after getting hold of books by poets such as Ted Hughes and Philip Larkin, I looked around to find out what else there was. I didn't get very far.

My local bookshop didn't stock much poetry. They said there wasn't much demand for it. Browsing through the shelves, I wasn't surprised. The poetry books looked rather dull. The blurbs were written in that wooden, academic style: they didn't make me want to read the books, they put me off. Poets were called the Author: the biographical notes usually said the Author lived in London and he'd read English at Oxbridge. The Author didn't write poetry, he wrote *verse*. He was always English, and rarely female. I wasn't impressed.

This was the early 1970s, but the world of the slim volume of verse, with its dusty air of worthiness, seemed like some relic of the 1950s. This impression was reinforced when I went to a poetry reading.

The Author spent more time explaining poems than reading them. The poems were dedicated to other poets and contained many literary allusions; they often had an epigraph in Greek or Latin (which he didn't translate). For much of the time he talked about himself, and when he finally read a poem you found he wrote about himself as well. His poems left me cold, but because he was a Famous Author I gave him the benefit of the doubt, blaming my own ignorance of contemporary poetry. I was convinced that I was missing something.

His poems were all well written, but pointless. Some were called travel poems; these were descriptions in rhyming verse of places the Author had visited. If these conveyed anything more than a snapshot or postcard, I was at a loss to know what. I couldn't think of anyone who would find his work at all interesting, and couldn't understand how anyone had thought it was worth publishing; or how books like his could be produced by reputable publishers. I should have trusted my first response.

Some weeks later, I was sitting in the pub when a man came round selling copies of a poetry magazine containing work by experimental and avant-garde poets. He told me he had to produce the magazine himself on a duplicator.

The magazine's editorial struck a common chord. It was all about a new, alternative kind of poetry. The sentiments seemed admirable, but as I read on, I became suspicious. The writer talked about 'tired old forms' as though the forms themselves were tired, not the way the poets used them. Apparently, these new poets were influenced by certain American poets of the 1950s, and yet they were credited with creating a new poetic language. When I reached the poems, I found that this new poetic language was second-hand, toneless and one-dimensional. Words appeared in quotes or *italics* for no apparent reason. Lines were chopped staccato like diced vegetables, and some poems had been literally chopped up and the pieces rearranged. The ethos behind the magazine was one of self-expression, something I'd thought had gone out with the 1960s. Where the English fifties poet had been wont to quote Virgil in Latin, these humourless poets quoted equally baffling snatches from French surrealists, or grand-sounding lines from William Blake.

At first I thought there was something at fault with my response to the poets I was reading, but much as I tried I couldn't see how their work could communicate much to anyone. And it was boring.

It was either second-hand or second-rate; dull, repetitive, unimaginative, arid and wooden or self-regarding, gimmicky and pseudo-intellectual. Either way it was boring.

I wouldn't have got this far in this masochistic journey through the slough of English poetry had I not also discovered a few poets whose work I liked enormously. I remember the excitement I felt when I first came across Seamus Heaney's first book, *Death of a Naturalist*, when I discovered Derek Mahon's *Lives*, Tony Harrison's *Loiners* and Douglas Dunn's *Terry Street* in quick succession.

Someone told me about a series of mostly unobtainable books called Penguin Modern European Poets. I wasn't sure how to pro-

nounce the names of many of the writers, but that didn't matter.
Even in translation they communicated far more than most of the
English poets I'd come across. They seemed to achieve an eloquence,
a purity of utterance, which I had not experienced in my reading
of contemporary English poetry. They weren't concerned with how
things looked, but how things *were*; like the English Metaphysicals,
they were obsessed with ideas and human experience, not appear-
ances. Their names composed a litany, and became my yardstick
of literary quality: Zbigniew Herbert, Miroslav Holub, Tadeusz
Różewicz, Joseph Brodsky, János Pilinszky, Czesław Miłosz, Anna
Akhmatova, Tomas Tranströmer, Hans Magnus Enzensberger.

I couldn't reconcile a number of things. Firstly, that while many
of these outstanding European poets were no longer available in
Britain, most of the poets who were published here were producing
work which was arid and inconsequential by comparison. And if
poetry publishing had reached a dead end, where had all the readers
gone? When I showed books by these European poets to friends,
they found the writing very exciting, and wanted to get hold of
copies for themselves. Why couldn't they?

The answer seemed to lie in the economics of publishing. I dis-
covered that publishers were producing their slim volumes of verse
in short print runs. Even with a well-known poet, they would only
produce 500 or so copies. Most of the books were sold to libraries.
There was no need to make these books attractive because there was
no particular pressure to sell them. Readers didn't buy them in
bookshops because they were badly packaged and too expensive.
Most of the books were boring too, and that turned off any readers
who got as far as sneaking a look inside. For the publishers there
had been some prestige in having a poetry list, but by this time many
had found they could not rely on sales to libraries and colleges, and
they were starting to remainder their poetry books.

Through becoming involved with a literary magazine, and then
in helping to organise some readings, I came across a number of
poets who couldn't get anyone to publish their work, and not because
it wasn't any good. Some had pamphlets published by small presses,
and some produced their own pamphlets and sold them at readings.

This was how Bloodaxe began. Ken Smith sent me a typescript
collection together with a bale of paper on which to print it. When
I read the poems, I knew at once that here was a poet whose work
was so outstanding that more people ought to be able to read it. The
typescript became the first Bloodaxe title, *Tristan Crazy*, published
in October 1978. Soon I had 750 copies of *Tristan Crazy* piled on

top of the wardrobe. The printer's bill came to £230. I was doing a poorly paid temporary job, and had no money. I went to my bank manager and talked to him about my plans for Bloodaxe Books; he called it 'a speculative venture' and refused me an overdraft of £60.

Right from the beginning Bloodaxe's role has been one of working for writers and readers. There was at that time what I can only call a malaise afflicting poetry publishing. None of the publishers seemed to pay any attention to what readers wanted, and poetry was losing its readership because few people cared anything for what they were being offered by the publishers.

I saw myself as a representative reader. On the rare occasions when I discovered a book which meant something to me, I found myself feeling angry that there wasn't more good work available; I felt patronised and annoyed by the manner in which publishers presented contemporary poetry. Sean O'Brien expressed a similar dissatisfaction later when he wrote in a review of Peter Didsbury's poetry that it is 'the kind of work which makes you realise what you've been putting up with in the meantime'.

I persevered, and kept going back to the good work I was discovering as I read more widely. As the first few Bloodaxe titles started to be noticed, I began to receive some remarkable unpublished collections through the post (among them Peter Didsbury's). Like Housman, I came across poetry which was so startling that it lifted the hairs on the back of my neck. This was Housman's test of a good poem. My own test was that good poetry must *give* something to the reader. Keats said it should 'strike the reader as the wording of his own highest thoughts, and appear almost a remembrance'. This kind of response is what I'd call *edge*. A good poem will always startle the reader.

As far as the writers were concerned, there were many kinds of poets whose work I felt deserved a wider readership. Poetry publishing was so limited that it was not just the new poets who were excluded, but also some major British and Irish writers, and numerous American and European poets; and male editors and anthologists were disclaiming any preference for male poets even as they exercised blatant discrimination against women whose work was brilliantly written, powerfully balanced and *uncomfortable* to read.

Gradually, over fifteen years, Bloodaxe has published a wide range of these writers, and has itself been transformed from a kitchen-table operation run from my home in my spare time to the Bloodaxe of today. Bloodaxe's success has been created by its readers. With their support, it has gone on to become Britain's premier publisher of new poetry; only Faber, Penguin and Oxford University Press achieve higher poetry sales, buoyed up in their case by all the poets from Shakespeare to Eliot and his *Practical Cats*.

This celebratory anthology features many of the poets Bloodaxe has published in its first fifteen years, as well as some of the new poets whose books will be appearing over the next year. In order to give them adequate space, I decided to restrict the book to contemporary poetry: all the poets here were born since 1900. This meant I had to exclude some major Bloodaxe writers who would have required far too much space to do them justice, including Akhmatova, Hart Crane, Lorca, Mandelstam, Montale, Reverdy, Södergran, Tagore and Tsvetayeva. In allotting space to the various poets, I have tried to reflect their output and range.

I have made substantial changes to *Poetry with an Edge* for this new edition. To represent all the poets now published by Bloodaxe with a few poems each would have produced not an anthology but a catalogue. Instead, I have drawn *Poetry with an Edge* even closer to its title: by making it reflect Bloodaxe's international status with more poets from Europe and America; by demonstrating with the selection of poems why Bloodaxe has become Britain's leading publisher of women's poetry; and by fully representing the new generation of so-called 'Punk Modernist' poets whose work combines sophisticated technique and bizarre intelligence with humour, streetcred language and the ability to make anything a fit subject for poetry. I have had to omit many poets whose work I admire, from Jacques Dupin to David Scott, either because short extracts wouldn't work, or because I felt their poetry wouldn't sit easily in this new *Poetry with an Edge*. I think I can square this in my own mind with Bloodaxe's continuing commitment to publishing their books. Bloodaxe's range of writers is now wider than any book could properly represent, and my concern here is to produce a coherent anthology for the reader. But I have had to show the door to poets who took their books elsewhere after Bloodaxe took all the risks in launching and investing in their writing careers; we remain friends, I'm happy to say, but I have given their places in this book to poets who have moved in the opposite direction, having become unsettled by the fickleness of the big publishers.

Bloodaxe is often characterised by reviewers as having a northern bias; some have also noted that we publish black writers, and that a high proportion of our poets are women. But in building up the list, I have not consciously exercised a bias towards any kind of poetry. All I have been concerned with has been the quality of each individual book, regardless of who has written it; and most of the numerous first collections published by Bloodaxe started out as unsolicited manuscripts. Bloodaxe has been called 'anti-metropolitan', but unlike London publishers, with their parochial bias towards poets from South-East England, Bloodaxe publishes poets from throughout Britain, from London as well as the North: so this 'provincial' publisher is actually more national and international in outlook than its London counterparts. If we have exercised positive discrimination, that has been with anthologies published in order to draw attention to particular groups of poets, books which have been among our most influential, such as Jeni Couzyn's *Bloodaxe Book of Contemporary Women Poets* (1985), Adam Czerniawski's Polish anthology *The Burning Forest* (1988), E.A. Markham's *Hinterland: Caribbean Poetry from the West Indies and Britain* (1989), and the recent anthology of the new British and Irish poets of the 80s and 90s, *The New Poetry* (1993), edited by Michael Hulse, David Kennedy and David Morley. Another is Linda France's *Sixty Women Poets* (1993), an affirmative, wide-ranging selection of some of the finest poets now writing in Britain and Ireland: an anthology which is still much needed because the failure by critics and publishers to accord due recognition to women poets *make it necessary*. In publishing these kinds of anthologies, Bloodaxe is challenging the literary establishment: I don't accept that tastes and reputations should be dictated by out-of-touch professors with literary critical hang-ups or reviewers more concerned with fashion than excellence. Now that poetry is much more readily available in bookshops, it's possible to reach readers simply by putting the book in front of them.

I have written this introduction from a reader's point of view because I believe my own baffled initiation to contemporary poetry was similar to what others have gone through, and also because my own reactions and responses to contemporary poetry have been the primary influence on Bloodaxe's editorial growth. Poetry is still plagued with many mutually exclusive cliques and schools, each associated with particular magazines, presses and publishing houses, all of which serve to cosset the literary minorities and alienate the general reader. But there is a much greater variety of good poetry published today than there was fifteen years ago, and the main problem the reader has now is in knowing where to start.

I wish I could have started with *Poetry with an Edge* when I began my foray into contemporary poetry.

NEIL ASTLEY

Basil Bunting

JOANNA VOIT

Extract from part IV of
Briggflatts (1966), from the
Bloodaxe record *Basil Bunting
reads 'Briggflatts'* (1980),
reprinted here from Basil
Bunting's *Collected Poems*
(1978), published by Oxford
University Press.

BASIL BUNTING was born in 1900 in Northumberland. Yeats knew him in Paris and Italy in the 20s as 'one of Pound's more savage disciples'. His work was at first only published in America, where he built up a reputation as the best English poet of his generation, but he had to wait until the publication of his great autobiographical poem *Briggflatts* in 1966 before English critics recognised his genius. He died in 1985.

Bloodaxe's first big publishing project – in 1980 – was an LP record of the whole of *Briggflatts*. Bunting reads this section to the harpsichord accompaniment of Scarlatti's sonata in B minor, showing how closely Scarlatti's music is echoed in the poem.

The first book on his work was Victoria Forde's *The Poetry of Basil Bunting*, published by Bloodaxe in 1991. ●

From Briggflatts

As the player's breath warms the fipple the tone clears.
It is time to consider how Domenico Scarlatti
condensed so much music into so few bars
with never a crabbed turn or congested cadence,
never a boast or a see-here; and stars and lakes
echo him and the copse drums out his measure,
snow peaks are lifted up in moonlight and twilight
and the sun rises on an acknowledged land.

My love is young but wise. Oak, applewood,
her fire is banked with ashes till day.
The fells reek of her hearth's scent,
her girdle is greased with lard;
hunger is stayed on her settle, lust in her bed.
Light as spider floss her hair on my cheek which a puff scatters,
light as a moth her fingers on my thigh.
We have eaten and loved and the sun is up,
we have only to sing before parting:
Goodbye, dear love.

Her scones are greased with fat of fried bacon,
her blanket comforts my belly like the south.
We have eaten and loved and the sun is up.
Goodbye.

Applewood, hard to rive,
its knots smoulder all day.
Cobweb hair on the morning,
a puff would blow it away.
Rime is crisp on the bent,
ruts stone-hard, frost spangles fleece.
What breeze will fill that sleeve limp on the line?
A boy's jet steams from the wall, time from the year,
care from deed and undoing.
Shamble, cold, content with beer and pickles,
towards a taciturn lodging amongst strangers.

Where rats go go I,
accustomed to penury,
filth, disgust and fury;
evasive to persist,
reject the bait
yet gnaw the best.
My bony feet
sully shelf and dresser,
keeping a beat in the dark,
rap on lath
till dogs bark
and sleep, shed,
slides from the bed.
O valiant when hunters
with stick and terrier bar escape
or wavy ferret leaps,
encroach and cede again,
rat, roommate, unreconciled.

Stars disperse. We too,
further from neighbours
now the year ages.

R.S. Thomas

WELSH ARTS COUNCIL

Selection from *Selected Poems 1946-1968* (1986), first published by Hart-Davis, MacGibbon Ltd (1973).

R.S. THOMAS was born in 1913 in Cardiff, and in 1936 was ordained as a clergyman in the Church of Wales. He is 'our best living religious poet' (*Times Literary Supplement*). His *Selected Poems 1946-1968* is his own selection from his first six books; his later collections *Counterpoint* (1990) and *Mass for Hard Times* (1992) are published by Bloodaxe, and his *Collected Poems* (which excludes these) by Dent.

'His poetry is deeply coloured by his experience of working in remote rural communities, where some of the churches had tiny congregations and where life was harsh and the landscape bleak; he has created his own form of bleak Welsh pastoral, streaked with indignation over the history of Wales and the Welsh' – Margaret Drabble. ●

A Peasant

Iago Prytherch his name, though, be it allowed,
Just an ordinary man of the bald Welsh hills,
Who pens a few sheep in a gap of cloud.
Docking mangels, chipping the green skin
From the yellow bones with a half-witted grin
Of satisfaction, or churning the crude earth
To a stiff sea of clods that glint in the wind –
So are his days spent, his spittled mirth
Rarer than the sun that cracks the cheeks
Of the gaunt sky perhaps once in a week.
And then at night see him fixed in his chair
Motionless, except when he leans to gob in the fire.
There is something frightening in the vacancy of his mind.
His clothes, sour with years of sweat
And animal contact, shock the refined,
But affected, sense with their stark naturalness.
Yet this is your prototype, who, season by season
Against siege of rain and the wind's attrition,
Preserves his stock, an impregnable fortress
Not to be stormed even in death's confusion.
Remember him, then, for he, too, is a winner of wars,
Enduring like a tree under the curious stars.

Invasion on the Farm

I am Prytherch. Forgive me. I don't know
What you are talking about; your thoughts flow
Too swiftly for me; I cannot dawdle
Along their banks and fish in their quick stream
With crude fingers. I am alone, exposed
In my own fields with no place to run
From your sharp eyes. I, who a moment back
Paddled in the bright grass, the old farm
Warm as a sack about me, feel the cold
Winds of the world blowing. The patched gate
You left open will never be shut again.

On the Farm

There was Dai Puw. He was no good.
They put him in the fields to dock swedes,
And took the knife from him, when he came home
At late evening with a grin
Like the slash of a knife on his face.

There was Llew Puw, and he was no good.
Every evening after the ploughing
With the big tractor he would sit in his chair,
And stare into the tangled fire garden,
Opening his slow lips like a snail.

There was Huw Puw, too. What shall I say?
I have heard him whistling in the hedges
On and on, as though winter
Would never again leave those fields,
And all the trees were deformed.

And lastly there was the girl:
Beauty under some spell of the beast.
Her pale face was the lantern
By which they read in life's dark book
The shrill sentence: God is love.

Evans

Evans? Yes, many a time
I came down this bare flight
Of stairs into the gaunt kitchen
With its wood fire, where crickets sang
Accompaniment to the black kettle's
Whine, and so into the cold
Dark to smother in the thick tide
Of night that drifted about the walls
Of his stark farm on the hill ridge.

It was not the dark filling my eyes
And mouth appalled me; not even the drip
Of rain like blood from the one tree
Weather-tortured. It was the dark
Silting the veins of that sick man
I left stranded upon the vast
And lonely shore of his bleak bed.

Hireling

Cars pass him by; he'll never own one.
Men won't believe in him for this.
Let them come into the hills
And meet him wandering a road,
Fenced with rain, as I have now;
The wind feathering his hair;
The sky's ruins, gutted with fire
Of the late sun, smouldering still.

Nothing is his, neither the land
Nor the land's flocks. Hired to live
On hills too lonely, sharing his hearth
With cats and hens, he has lost all
Property but the grey ice
Of a face splintered by life's stone.

Reservoirs

There are places in Wales I don't go:
Reservoirs that are the subconscious
Of a people, troubled far down
With gravestones, chapels, villages even;
The serenity of their expression
Revolts me, it is a pose
For strangers, a watercolour's appeal
To the mass, instead of the poem's
Harsher conditions. There are the hills,
Too; gardens gone under the scum
Of the forests; and the smashed faces
Of the farms with the stone trickle
Of their tears down the hills' side.

Where can I go, then, from the smell
Of decay, from the putrefying of a dead
Nation? I have walked the shore
For an hour and seen the English
Scavenging among the remains
Of our culture, covering the sand
Like the tide and, with the roughness
Of the tide, elbowing our language
Into the grave that we have dug for it.

The Cry

Don't think it was all hate
That grew there; love grew there, too,
Climbing by small tendrils where
The warmth fell from the eyes' blue

Flame. Don't think even the dirt
And the brute ugliness reigned
Unchallenged. Among the fields
Sometimes the spirit, enchained

So long by the gross flesh, raised
Suddenly there its wild note of praise.

Martin Bell

Selection from: *Complete Poems* (1988), edited by Peter Porter.

MARTIN BELL was born in 1918 in Hampshire. He was a prominent member of 'The Group' in London in the 50s, and a major influence on younger poets like Peter Redgrove and Peter Porter (and later on Sean O'Brien and Peter Didsbury). His poetry reached a wide audience during the 60s through *Penguin Modern Poets*, and in 1967 he published his *Collected Poems 1937-1966*, his first and last book. He died in poverty in Leeds in 1978.

Like other "provincial" working-class contemporaries, Bell wrote fantastical, highly erudite, biting, belligerent poetry. And yet – as Philip Hobsbaum said – he also wrote 'some of the most delicate love poems of our time' as well as 'one of the major war poems in the language'. ●

Ode to Groucho

1 *Invocation*

Pindarick, a great gorblimey Ode
Soaring on buzzard wings, ornate,
Or tottering titanic on feet of clay,
It would have to be, to be adequate –
With the neo-gromboolian overtones
And the neo-classic gimmicks:
Pat gags cadenced from 'Mauberley'
In platinum-plated timing,
And tendrils convolvulating
To clutch the dirty cracks and hold the house up!

O flaking Palladian Palladium!
On a back-cloth rattled by oom-pah –
All our nostalgias, Hey there! the old vaudeville circuit.
Proscenium buttressed with brutal truths
Where sleek myths lean in manneristic attitudes,
Chalk-white in the chastest diction,
Sequined with glittering metaphysicality.
And massive ambiguities
Endlessly rocking a whole way of life.

2 *Presence*

What you had was a voice
To talk double-talk faster,
Twanging hypnotic
In an age of nagging voices -
And bold eyes to dart around
As you shambled supremely,
Muscular moth-eaten panther!

Black eyebrows, black cigar,
Black painted moustache –
A dark code of elegance
In an age of nagging moustaches –
To discomfit the coarse mayor,
Un-poise the suave headmaster,
Reduce all the old boys to muttering fury.

A hero for the young,
Blame if you wish the human situation –
Subversivest of con-men
In an age of ersatz heroes:
Be talkative and shabby and
Witty; bully the bourgeois;
Act the obvious phoney.

3 *Apotheosis*

Slickness imposed on a rough beast,
A slouching beast and hypochondriac.

Great Anarch! Totem of the lot,
All the shining rebels

(Prometheus, of course, and that old pauper
Refusing cake from Marie Antoinette,
And Baudelaire's fanatical toilette,
And Rimbaud, striding off to Africa,
And Auden, scowling at a cigarette...)

Bliss was it etc. Smartish but fair enough.
We stammered out our rudenesses

O splendid and disreputable father!

Reasons for Refusal

Busy old lady, charitable tray
Of social emblems: poppies, people's blood –
I must refuse, make you flush pink
Perplexed by abrupt No-thank-you.
Yearly I keep up this small priggishness,
Would wince worse if I wore one.
Make me feel better, fetch a white feather, do.

Everyone has list of dead in war,
Regrets most of them, e.g.

Uncle Cyril; small boy in lace and velvet
With pushing sisters muscling all around him,
And lofty brothers, whiskers and stiff collars;
The youngest was the one who copped it.
My mother showed him to me,
Neat letters high up on the cenotaph
That wedding-caked it up above the park,
And shadowed birds on Isaac Watts' white shoulders.

And father's friends, like Sandy Vincent;
Brushed sandy hair, moustache, and staring eyes.
Kitchener claimed him, but the Southern Railway
Held back my father, made him guilty.
I hated the khaki photograph,
It left a patch on the wallpaper after I took it down.

Others I knew stick in the mind,
And Tony Lister often –
Eyes like holes in foolscap, suffered from piles,
Day after day went sick with constipation
Until they told him he could drive a truck –
Blown up with Second Troop in Greece:
We sang all night once when we were on guard.

And Ken Gee, our lance-corporal, Christian Scientist –
Everyone liked him, knew that he was good –
Had leg and arm blown off, then died.
Not all were good. Gross Corporal Rowlandson
Fell in the canal, the corrupt Sweet-water,

And rolled there like a log, drunk and drowned.
And I've always been glad of the death of Dick Benjamin,
A foxy urgent dainty ball-room dancer –
Found a new role in military necessity
As R.S.M. He waltzed out on parade
To make himself hated. Really hated, not an act.
He was a proper little porcelain sergeant-major –
The earliest bomb made smithereens:
Coincidence only, several have assured me.

In the school hall was pretty glass
Where prissy light shone through St George –
The highest holiest manhood, he!
And underneath were slain Old Boys
In tasteful lettering on whited slab -
And, each November, Ferdy the Headmaster
Reared himself squat and rolled his eyeballs upward,
Rolled the whole roll-call off an oily tongue,
Remorselessly from A to Z.

Of all the squirmers, Roger Frampton's lips
Most elegantly curled, showed most disgust.
He was a pattern of accomplishments,
And joined the Party first, and left it first,
At OCTU won a prize belt, most improbable,
Was desert-killed in '40, much too soon.

His name should burn right through that monument.

No poppy, thank you.

Dorothy Hewett

VIRAGO PRESS

Selection from: *Alice in Wormland: Selected Poems* (1990), edited by Edna Longley.

DOROTHY HEWETT was born in 1923 in Perth, Western Australia, and grew up on an isolated farm. Yvonne Roberts wrote in *The Independent*: 'The purgatory and pleasures of Hewett's life have been chronicled in six books of poetry, one novel, 18 plays and four film scripts…She has lived out a soap opera of a life. Hers is a story of dips, dives and sheer good fun. If she were a man, her life would be described as Rabelaisian and she, a hell-raiser. As a woman, she has to make do with "sexually depraved": "My mother used to say: 'Women are superior to men. They can do anything.' And when I did, she punished me for it".' Her novel *Bobbin Up* and her autobiography *Wild Card* are published by Virago. ●

Legend of the Green Country

I

September is the spring month bringing tides, swilling green in the
      harbour mouth,
Turnabout dolphins rolling-backed in the rip and run, the king waves
Swinging the coast, snatching at fishermen from Leeuwin to Norah's
      Head;
A dangerous month: but I count on an abacus as befits a shopkeeper's
      daughter.
I never could keep count by modern methods, the ring of the till
Is profit and loss, the ledger, hasped with gold, sits in its heavy dust
On the counter, out front the shopkeeper's sign hangs loose and
      bangs in the wind,
The name is obliterated, the dog swells and stinks in the gutter,
The golden smell of the beer does not run in the one street, like
      water,
The windmill head hangs, broken-necked, flapping like a great plain
      turkey
As the wind rises…this was my country, here I go back for nurture
To the dry soaks, to the creeks running salt through the timber,
To the ghosts of the sandalwood cutters, and the blue breath of their
      fires,
To the navvies in dark blue singlets laying rails in the scrub.

My grandfather rode out, sawing at a hard-mouthed ginger horse,
And a hard heart in him, a dray full of rum and beer, bully-beef and
    treacle,
Flour and tea, workboots and wideawakes with the corks bobbing
    for flies;
Counting the campfires in the dusk, counting the men, counting the
    money,
Counting the sheep from the goats, and the rack-rented railway
    houses.
No wonder I cannot count for the sound of the money-changers,
The sweat and the clink, the land falling into the cash register,
Raped and eroded, thin and black as a myall girl on a railway siding.
He came back, roaring and singing up from the gullies, his beard
Smelt of rum, his money-bag plump as a wild duck under his saddle.
The old horse stumbled in the creek-bed but brought him home,
The dray rattled; as they took him down in the yard he cursed and
    swore
At the dream, and blubbered for it: next Saturday night he rode his
    horse
Up the turkey red carpet into the bar, smashing the bottles and
    glasses,
Tipping the counter, sending the barmaid screaming, her breasts
    tilting with joy.
The great horse reared and he sang and swore and flung his hat at
    the sky,
And won his bets, and rode home, satisfied, to a nagging wife and
    daughter,
Having buried his pain and his lust under the broken bottles.
The publican swept them up in the cold light next morning,
And that was the end of it, they thought, but it wasn't so easy:
There is no end to it and I stand at the mole watching the sea run out,
Or hang over the rails at the Horseshoe Bridge and listen to the tide,
Listen to the earth that pleasured my grandfather with his flocks
    and acres
Drowned under salt, his orange-trees forked bare as unbreeched
    boys.
Only the apples, little and hard, bitten green and bitter as salt,
They come up in the spring, in the dead orchard they are the fruit
Of our knowledge, and I am Eve, spitting the pips in the eye of the
    myth-makers.
This is my legend; an old man on a ginger horse who filled his till
And died content with a desert, or so they said: his stone angel

Cost a pretty penny, but the workmanship was faulty, its wings curve
In a great arc over the graveyard, it grows mildewed and dirty,
Its nose is syphilitic, its feet splay like a peasant, its hands
Clasp over its breast like the barmaid who screamed in the pub,
And kissed him, for love, not money, but only once.

II

My grandmother had a bite like a sour green apple,
Little and pitiless she kept the till,
Counted the profits, and stacked the bills of sale.
She bought the shops and the farms, the deeds were hers,
In the locked iron safe with a shower of golden sovereigns.
She never trusted the banks, they failed in the nineties,
She kept her bank notes rolled in the top of her stocking,
Caressingly, while her prices soared and dropped,
Her barometer; crops and wool and railway lines.
Each night she read the news by the hurricane lantern,
While the only child wept for love in the washing-up water.
She could argue like a man, politics, finance, banking.
In her rocking chair with her little dangling feet,
Her eyes glittered like broken beer bottle glass.
She kept one eye out for a farmer to spend his money
And a sharp tongue for a borrowing mate of my grandfather's.

Once, long ago, in Swanston Street she "made"
For fashionable ladies, their breasts half bared
And their ankles covered, pads in their hair,
Bustles, bugle beads and jet, dyed ostrich feathers,
You could see their shadows waving from hansom cabs,
And the ghostly wheels turning into Swanston Street.
She had her miracles and quoted them...
Science and Health by Mary Baker Eddy,
She read *The Monitor* while the dust storms whirled,
And marvelled that God was love; it was all clear profit.
She wet the bagging to filter the westerlies,
Planted geraniums and snowdrops under the tank,
And squashed black caterpillars on moonlit forays.
She balanced the ledger and murmured, 'God is love,'
Feeling like God, she foreclosed on another farm.

She never read for pleasure, or danced or sang,
Or listened with love, slowly life smote her dumb,
Till she lay in the best bedroom, pleating the quilt,
In a fantasy of ball dresses for Melbourne ladies.
Her eyes were remote as pennies, her sheets stank,
She cackled and counted a mythical till all her days.

III

My father was a black-browed man who rode like an Abo.
The neighbours gossiped, 'A touch of the tarbrush there.'
He built the farm with his sweat, it lay in the elbow
Of two creeks, thick with wattle and white ti-tree.
At night he blew on the cornet; once, long ago, he'd played
On the pleasure cruises that went up the Yarra on Saturday nights;
The lights bobbed in the muddy water, the girls in white muslin sang
    Tipperary.
Now he played in the lonely sleepout, looking out over the flat,
With the smell of creekwater, and a curlew crying like a murdered gin,
Crying all night, till he went out with a shotgun and finished its
        screaming,
But not his own... he, the mendicant, who married the storekeeper's
        daughter.

My mother was a dark round girl in a country town,
With down on her lip, her white cambric blouse
Smelt of roses and starch, she was beautiful,
Warm, and frigid in a world of dried-up women,
Aborting themselves with knitting needles on farms.
She wept in the tin humpy at the back of the store,
For the mother who hated, the father who drank
And loved her; then, sadly, she fell in love
And kissed the young accountant who kept the books,
Behind the ledgers, the summer dust on the counters.
He was on the booze, broke all his promises,
Went off to the city and sang in an old spring cart,
'Bottle-oh, Bottle-oh' till his liver gave out
And he died; she married in arum lilies, satin, tulle,
Under the bell that tolled for the storekeeper's daughter.
Men shot themselves in the scrub on her wedding day.
My father brought her wildflowers, rode forty miles,
But he never kissed like the beautiful bottle-oh,
Boozing in the pub like a fly caught in its amber.

The roof of the hospital cracked like purgatory,
At sunset the birth blood dried on the sheets,
Nobody came to change them, the sun went down,
The pain fell on her body like a beast and mauled it.
She hated the farm, hated the line of wattles
Smudging the creek, kept her hands full of scones,
Boiled the copper, washing out sins in creek water,
Kept sex at bay like the black snake coiled in the garden,
Burning under the African daisies and bridal creeper,
Took her children to bed, he lay alone in the sleep-out,
With a headache and *The Seven Pillars of Wisdom*.
The girls in their picture hats came giggling and singing,
Trailing their hands like willows from the Yarra launches,
Till the dream was nightmare and all his life a regret,
Bought and gelded in an old grey house by a creek-bed.

IV

My grandfather rode round the sheep in leggings, and fed the calves,
He mended the gates, once a month he drove into town to his "lodge",
A white carnation picked at dusk from my grandmother's garden,
A dress suit with a gold watch, a chain looped over his belly,
Magnificent!...but my father only grinned sourly and read Remarque's
All Quiet on the Western Front, while my mother polished his medals
For Anzac Day. They never understood him, none of the
        shopkeepers' breed,
Christ! how could they? They only had a copy of the Bible,
My grandmother quoted it (mostly wrong), and Tennyson bound
        in morocco,
The Stag at Bay on the sitting-room wall, two elephants from Bombay,
Spoil from the trip they took "home"...was it a century ago?
The piano where, once a year, we sang hymns, when the minister
        came.
They had no religion, they believed in themselves, no other,
Self-made men and women who sat round their groaning table,
While all the no-hopers were taken over by the banks,
Or walked off, and took up dead-end jobs in the city;
The farms lay at their boundaries breeding dust and rabbits.
They breasted it all, the waves of drought and depression,
Of flood and fire, sown in sparks from the black steam trains
Roaring through wheat and the dead white grass by the sidings.
Their haystacks burnt as gold as their money bags, their till
Was full of horses drooling on oats and rock salt, of cows

With udders streaming white milk in the frosty mornings,
Of roosters crowing their triumph from the stable roof, and orchards,
Green as their hopes, tangy with peach, cradled with quail and
        oranges.
Only the sheep bleating their thin cry on the winter evenings,
Echoed the crows, the scavengers that were our kinsmen.
The woolly ghosts cropped the grass to its roots; the hard hoofs
Beat a track to the end of a world where the creeks ran dry,
The lambs lay blind while the crows ate their eyes in the salmon
        gums,
And the timberless paddocks blew in dust as far as the sea.

        V

Only the man with the cornet, who rode with Remarque
Across his saddle bows, only he loved the soil,
Running it through his fingers he sensed its dying,
Its blowing away on the winds of time and cut timber,
He saw the salt of its death rising.
He said, 'I have a plan', and rode with it into the cities,
A plan for trees, acres of trees blowing by creekbeds,
Forests marching in long green lines to save a country,
Picking up their roots and digging them into the earth,
Holding it fast against the salt and the wind tides.
But the laughter rose in gales from the men in cities,
Their desks shook, their papers scattered like almond blossom in
        storm,
'Visionary'…'Dreamer…go back to the bend in two creeks,
Thick with wattle and ti-tree you have grown to love,
Go back and wait for the trees to wither, the creek to run,
Drowned in salt, for this is your heritage…'
'Years from now we will not be sitting here, we will be gone',
And where will you go, man the great Dreamer…dead and the land
        dead,
Only your ghost will ride like an Abo, crying *Trees* through the
        corrugated iron
Of the sidings, where the rails buckle with heat and men sit smoking
And brooding on a green world, as you once dreamed of Gippsland,
Under the fern-choked water, falling, falling: you tried to give us
A vision of greenness and water, who were bred out of desert and
        scrub
And sheep crying and crow…our father whispered *Trees* as he blew
        Tipperary.

VI

The women were strong and they destroyed the men,
Lying locked and cold in their sexless beds,
Putting greed in their men's fingers instead of love.
They drove them from the earth, left them derelict,
Dead mutton hanging on hooks on the verandahs.
For them the curlew wailed, the old horse lay
Trapped in the paddock all night with rheumaticky haunches.
My grandfather wept, 'Whoa back there Ginger, whoa back,'
Till the glasses winked in the bar like barmaids' eyes,
The virgins in muslin, the pretty French girls from Marseilles,
And a little whore in the rain on Princess Bridge.
Where would they go, rich, gelded and blind,
Tugging their old mad women with them to their graves?

VII

This land is not mine to give or trade,
I have no lien on these sad acres,
Where the crow flies home,
A solitary reaper.
The milky creek runs death,
The wattle and the ti-tree are all gone.
My father went, exiled himself in cities,
Sour as a green apple, his tap-root broken.

The orchard lies a nameless graveyard
Behind the farm, stripped of its flowers and fruit,
Its trees, its birds, its bees murmuring.
Only the skull of a sheep dropped at the cross-roads,
And the rattling dray in the scrub on the empty skyline,
My grandfather yelling, 'Whoa back there Ginger, whoa back,
While I carry my money bags home through the heart of this country.'
The wheels of the old dray turning, bring us full circle,
Death whirls in the wind, the old house hunches in on itself
And sleeps like the blind, *The Stag at Bay* hangs skewed
On the wall, the elephants from Bombay are chipped by the children,
Nobody plays *Rock of Ages* on the untuned piano now.
But the crows cry over my salty acres, scavengers come home
To roost and foul their nests in the creaking gum trees.

VIII

Who rises from the dead each spring must pay the cost.
How shall I pay living at the harbour's mouth
Where my father's ghost sits mumbling over breakfast,
Nodding at headlines, full of strikes and wool boards,
Tariffs to sink his teeth into, wars for his grandsons,
Where's Remarque now! His medals on the wall blink
Their derision, his heart's grown crooked, out of season.
He forgets how to sink a well or plant a tree.
His back's like sandalwood, his smell is sweet with death.
He crumbles where he sits, the tide rises to his lips.
Mother to daughter the curse drops like a stone.
My mother sits silent with nothing to remember.

Yet sometimes in the dark I come upon him in his chair,
A book lying open on his knees, his eye turned inward,
And then he sings old songs of Bendigo and windlasses,
And tells me tales of Newport railway workers, Nellie Melba
Singing High Mass, and how he read all night in Collingwood,
Voted for Labor and fell in love with Nellie Stewart.
But never a word of that far green country of his spirit,
Where the trees grow greener than the Gippsland grass.
All this is locked away in grief and salt.
Maybe, in death, his lips will whisper it,
And the green vision that gave sap to all his days
Will rise again and give him back his country.

IX

This is *my* truth, a grandfather boozed with guilt
And gold, who got free kisses from a barmaid for his gift,
And a great horse that swung its rump and tilted the world down.
A man rides through the windmill country like an Abo,
Blowing his cornet in a wail of *Trees*, bewitched
By Gippsland fern and luminous girls mirrored in the Yarra.
I will pay this debt, go back and find my place,
Pick windfalls out of the grass like a mendicant.
The little sour apples still grow in my heart's orchard,
Bitten with grief, coming up out of the dead country.
Here I will eat their salt and speak my truth.

Miroslav Holub

VOJTECH PISARIK

MIROSLAV HOLUB was born in 1923. He is not only the Czech Republic's most important poet, but also a leading scientist, working as a research immunologist in Prague. His witty newspaper pieces are published in *The Jingle Bell Principle* (Bloodaxe, 1992). Ted Hughes regards him as 'one of the half dozen most important poets writing anywhere'. A. Alvarez has called him 'one of the sanest voices of our time'.

Selection from: *Poems Before & After: Collected English Translations* (1990), translated by Ewald Osers, George Theiner and Ian and Jarmila Milner.

'Looking at his characteristic poetic manner, it would be tempting to say that Holub brings a scientist's dispassionate eye to bear upon history and contemporary life. In fact he is as passionate as any other poet, but chooses a cool, understated, astringent rhetoric to make his mordant comments on human needs and pretensions' – William Scammell.   ●

Conversation with a poet

Are you a poet?
　　Yes, I am.
How do you know?
　　I've written poems.
If you've written poems it means you *were* a poet. But now?
　　I'll write a poem again one day.
In that case maybe you'll be a poet again one day. But how will you know it is a poem?
　　It will be a poem just like the last one.
Then of course it won't be a poem. A poem is only once and can never be the same a second time.
　　I believe it will be just as good.
How can you be sure? Even the quality of a poem is for once only and depends not on you but on circumstances.
　　I believe that circumstances will be the same too.
If you believe that then you won't be a poet and never were a poet. What then makes you think you are a poet?
　　Well – I don't rightly know. And who are you?

[EO]

The corporal who killed Archimedes

With one bold stroke
he killed the circle, tangent
and point of intersection
in infinity.

On penalty
of quartering
he banned numbers
from three up.

Now in Syracuse
he heads a school of philosophers,
squats on his halberd
for another thousand years
and writes:

one two
one two
one two
one two

[IM/JM]

A helping hand

We gave a helping hand to grass –
    and it turned into corn.
We gave a helping hand to fire –
    and it turned into a rocket.
Hesitatingly,
cautiously,
we give a helping hand
to people,
to some people...

[GT]

The fly

She sat on a willow-trunk
watching
part of the battle of Crécy,
the shouts,
the gasps,
the groans,
the tramping and the tumbling.

During the fourteenth charge
of the French cavalry
she mated
with a brown-eyed male fly
from Vadincourt.

She rubbed her legs together
as she sat on a disembowelled horse
meditating
on the immortality of flies.

With relief she alighted
on the blue tongue
of the Duke of Clervaux.

When silence settled
and only the whisper of decay
softly circled the bodies

and only
a few arms and legs
still twitched jerkily under the trees,

she began to lay her eggs
on the single eye
of Johann Uhr,
the Royal Armourer.

And thus it was
that she was eaten by a swift
fleeing
from the fires of Estrées.

[GT]

The door

Go and open the door.
  Maybe outside there's
  a tree, or a wood,
  a garden,
  or a magic city.

Go and open the door.
  Maybe a dog's rummaging.
  Maybe you'll see a face,
or an eye,
or the picture
              of a picture.

Go and open the door.
  If there's a fog
  it will clear.

Go and open the door.
  Even if there's only
  the darkness ticking,
  even if there's only
  the hollow wind,
  even if
          nothing
                  is there,
go and open the door.

At least
there'll be
a draught.

[IM]

The end of the world

The bird had come to the very end of its song
and the tree was dissolving under its claws.

And in the sky the clouds were twisting
and darkness flowed through all the cracks
into the sinking vessel of the landscape.

Only in the telegraph wires
a message still
crackled:

C·—·—·o———m——e· h···o———m——e·
y—·——o———u···— h···a·—v···—e·
a·— s···o———n—.

[EO]

The Prague of Jan Palach

And here stomp Picasso's bulls.
And here march Dalí's elephants on spidery legs.
And here beat Schönberg's drums.
And here rides Señor de la Mancha.
And here the Karamazovs are carrying Hamlet.
And here is the nucleus of the atom.
And here is the cosmodrome of the Moon.
And here stands a statue without the torch.
And here runs a torch without the statue.
And it's all so simple. Where
Man ends, the flame begins –
And in the ensuing silence can be heard the crumbling
of ash worms. For
those milliards of people, taken by and large,
are keeping their traps shut.

[GT]

Brief reflection on accuracy

Fish
   always accurately know where to move and when,
   and likewise
   birds have an accurate built-in time sense
   and orientation.

Humanity, however,
   lacking such instincts resorts to scientific
   research. Its nature is illustrated by the following
   occurrence.

A certain soldier
   had to fire a cannon at six o'clock sharp every evening.
   Being a soldier he did so. When his accuracy was
   investigated he explained:

I go by
   the absolutely accurate chronometer in the window
   of the clockmaker down in the city. Every day at seventeen
   forty-five I set my watch by it and
   climb the hill where my cannon stands ready.
   At seventeen fifty-nine precisely I step up to the cannon
   and at eighteen hours sharp I fire.

And it was clear
   that this method of firing was absolutely accurate.
   All that was left was to check that chronometer. So
   the clockmaker down in the city was questioned about
   his instrument's accuracy.

Oh, said the clockmaker,
   this is one of the most accurate instruments ever. Just imagine,
   for many years now a cannon has been fired at six o'clock sharp.
   And every day I look at this chronometer
   and always it shows exactly six.

So much for accuracy.
   And fish move in the water, and from the skies
   comes a rushing of wings while

Chronometers tick and cannon boom.

[EO]

Half a hedgehog

The rear half had been run over,
leaving the head and thorax
and the front legs of the hedgehog shape.

A scream from a cramped-open
jaw. The scream of the mute is
more horrible than the silence after a flood,
when even black swans float
belly upwards.

And even if some hedgehog doctor were
to be found in a hollow trunk or under the leaves
in a beechwood there'd be no hope
for that mere half on Road E12.

In the name of logic,
in the name of the theory of pain,
in the name of the hedgehog god the father, the son
and the holy ghost amen,
in the name of games and unripe raspberries,
in the name of tumbling streams of love
ever different and ever bloody,
in the name of the roots which overgrow
the heads of aborted foetuses,
in the name of satanic beauty,
in the name of skin bearing human likeness,
in the name of all halves
and double helices, or purines
and pyrimidines

we tried to run over
the hedgehog's head with the front wheel.

And it was like guiding a lunar module
from a planetary distance,
from a control centre seized
by cataleptic sleep.

And the mission failed. I got out
and found a heavy piece of brick.
Half the hedgehog continued screaming. And now
the scream turned into speech,

prepared by
the vaults of our tombs:
Then death will come and it will have your eyes.

[EO]

Distant howling

In Alsace,
on 6th July 1885,
a rabid dog knocked down
the nine-year-old Joseph Meister
and bit him fourteen times.

Meister was the first patient
saved by Pasteur
with his vaccine, in thirteen
progressive doses
of the attenuated virus.

Pasteur died of ictus
ten years later.
The janitor Meister
fifty-five years later
committed suicide
when the Germans occupied
his Pasteur Institute
with all those poor dogs.

Only the virus
remained above it all.

[EO]

Denise Levertov

DAVID GEIER

Selection from: *Selected Poems* (1986).

DENISE LEVERTOV was born in 1923 and grew up in Ilford, Essex. In 1948 she moved to the States, and established herself as 'America's foremost contemporary woman poet' (*Library Journal*). She also became a prominent political activist, campaigning for civil rights, against the Vietnam War, against the Bomb, and against US-backed régimes in Latin America. 'We are living our whole lives in a *state of emergency*,' she wrote in 1967.

Her books are published by New Directions in America. In Britain Bloodaxe has published her *Selected Poems* (1986) and her later collections *Oblique Prayers* (1986), *Breathing the Water* (1988) and *A Door in the Hive / Evening Train* (1993). ●

Living

The fire in leaf and grass
so green it seems
each summer the last summer.

The wind blowing, the leaves
shivering in the sun,
each day the last day.

A red salamander
so cold and so
easy to catch, dreamily

moves his delicate feet
and long tail. I hold
my hand open for him to go.

Each minute the last minute.

The Ache of Marriage

The ache of marriage:

thigh and tongue, beloved,
are heavy with it,
it throbs in the teeth

We look for communion
and are turned away, beloved,
each and each

It is leviathan and we
in its belly
looking for joy, some joy
not to be known outside it

two by two in the ark of
the ache of it.

The Mutes

Those groans men use
passing a woman on the street
or on the steps of the subway

to tell her she is a female
and their flesh knows it,

are they a sort of tune,
an ugly enough song, sung
by a bird with a slit tongue
but meant for music?

Or are they the muffled roaring
of deafmutes trapped in a building that is
slowly filling with smoke?

Perhaps both.

Such men most often
look as if groan were all they could do,
yet a woman, in spite of herself,

knows it's a tribute:
if she were lacking all grace
they'd pass her in silence:

so it's not only to say she's
a warm hole. It's a word

in grief-language, nothing to do with
primitive, not an ur-language;
language stricken, sickened, cast down

in decrepitude. She wants to
throw the tribute away, dis-
gusted, and can't,

it goes on buzzing in her ear,
it changes the pace of her walk,
the torn posters in echoing corridors

spell it out, it
quakes and gnashes as the train comes in.
Her pulse sullenly

had picked up speed,
but the cars slow down and
jar to a stop while her understanding

keeps on translating:
'Life after life after life goes by

without poetry,
without seemliness,
without love.'

Talk in the Dark

We live in history, says one.
We're flies on the hide of Leviathan, says another.

Either way, says one,
fears and losses.

And among losses, says another,
the special places our own roads were to lead to.

Our deaths, says one.
That's right, says another,
now it's to be a mass death.

Mass graves, says one, are nothing new.
No, says another, but this time there'll be no graves,
all the dead will lie where they fall.

Except, says one, those that burn to ash.
And are blown in the fiery wind, says another.

How can we live in this fear? says one.
From day to day, says another.

I still want to see, says one,
where my own road's going.

I want to live, says another, but where can I live
if the world is gone?

Elizabeth Bartlett

ELIZABETH BARTLETT was born in 1924. She worked as a medical secretary for 16 years, and later in the home help service and as a tutor. Her powerfully evocative poems are remarkable for their painfully truthful insights into people's lives.

'The deprivations of childhood become the deprivations of adulthood and then the disappointments and loneliness of middle age. But Ms Bartlett is captain of her own soul and has, in addition, a rocketing forthrightness of expression. She has served and survived the Welfare State and her poems should be force-fed to Tories who think the workers get too much coddling' – Peter Porter. ●

Selection from: *New &
Selected Poems* (1994),
edited by Carol Rumens.

Of This Parish

Very ladylike, she couldn't bear a hair
unwittingly strayed upon her curling tongue.
Fastidious to an obsessional degree, she
polished her furniture to a high patina,
reflecting her anxious countenance too well.
The phone accentuated her carefully modulated
voice, but picked up a cracked and frantic note
which was not in keeping with the rest of her.
In drawers, her underwear lay neat and still,
well-ironed, aired and diligently mended.
Money was tight, and meals were very frugal,
but set nicely on a tray, cooked to a turn.
The neighbours laughed behind their hands,
not unkindly, you understand, but were not
surprised when the police and the ambulance
arrived together, one removing her correct
thin body, the other a coil of knotted rope
which they carelessly flung in the back of the car
leaving her front door locked, and picking up
a small stool which lay on its side in the hall.

In Memory of Steve Biko

Somehow the drains of feeling were blocked that week.
Biko died, and also a giraffe called Victor who was thought
To be mating at the time, and fell and couldn't get up again.
For Biko, also, it was a fall into death, the cause
Unknown, but guessed at, something far more disturbing
Than a very large animal, hauled to his feet, and perhaps
One day to be stuffed. We all know who hogged the news,
A simple but prolonged death, a pretty girl keeper,
Not a young black man.

We who mourned him were not the giraffe mourners,
And we measure with our eyes the space he died in,
And the means that brought his life to an end,
And the fact that good does not triumph over evil,
If indeed it ever did. Cradled in soft arms
With a girl's hair on his cheek he would never
Have believed his luck, but thought it one more
Trick in a diabolical game of cards.
Steve Biko, the sweet voice cries, lie here
Against this bale of straw. You were said
To have died on hunger strike
But this was not the case.

There will obviously be very little left
Of you to stuff as a memorial in King Williams Town,
And your mating days are over now
All your days are over now, for good and all.

As the news came in the following weeks
It seemed he died, as they say, under interrogation,
Said to have laughed at his keepers, said to have
Died of brain damage, naked and manacled.
He was careless enough to have injured himself,
Or so it would appear. The animal died
Like a man, the man like an animal,
As the drains of feeling gradually unblocked,
The canvas hoists were folded away,
The manacles were shown in the courts.
No one was to blame, was the verdict.

In two minutes flat.

Themes for women

There is love to begin with, early love,
painful and unskilled, late love for matrons
who eye the beautiful buttocks and thick hair
of young men who do not even notice them.

Parturition, it figures, comes after, cataclysmic
at first, then dissolving into endless care
and rules and baths and orthodontic treatment,
Speech days, Open days, shut days, exams.

There are landscapes and inscapes too, sometimes tracts
of unknown counties, most often the one great hill
in low cloud, the waterfall, the empty sands, the few
snowdrops at the back door, the small birds flying.

Politics crop up at election time and ecology
any old time, no ocelot coats, no South African
oranges, a knowledge of the Serengeti
greater than the positioning of rubbish dumps
here in this off-shore island in hard times.

Seasons never go out of fashion, never will,
the coming of Spring, the dying fall
of Autumn into Winter, fine brash summers,
the red sun going down like a beach ball
into the sea. These do not escape the eyes
of women whose bodies obey the tides
and the cheese-paring sterile moon.

As you might expect, death hangs around a lot.
First ageing mothers, senile fathers; providing
the ham and sherry when the show is over,
examining stretched breasts to catch the process
of decay in time. In farmhouse kitchens they make
pigeon pies, weeping unexpectedly over
curved breasts among the floating feathers.
The men tread mud in after docking lambs' tails,
and smell of blood.

Lauris Edmond

ROBERT CROSS

Selection from: *New and
Selected Poems* (1992).

LAURIS EDMOND was born in 1924. She is now
one of New Zealand's leading poets, but did
not publish her first book until 1975. Since
then she has published ten other collections
in New Zealand, as well as a three-volume
autobiography. In 1985 she won the Common-
wealth Poetry Prize.

'A remarkable warmth and humanity shines
through all her poetry. She deals with topics
people care about – love of all kinds, family
relationships, loss, ageing, the fragility of
happiness – and writes of them with courage,
candour, and a maturity of perception which
amounts to wisdom' – Fleur Adcock. ●

A Difficult Adjustment

It takes time, and there are setbacks;
on Monday, now, you were all ennui
and malice; but this morning I am
pleased with my handiwork: your
stick figure moves, your two eyes
are large and dark enough, your
expression is conveniently mild.
You have begun to disagree with me,
but weakly, so that I can easily prove
you wrong. In fact you are entirely
satisfactory.
                I suppose, really, you are
dead. But someone silently lies down
with me at night and shows a soothing
tenderness. I have killed the pain
of bone and flesh; I suffer no laughter
now, nor hear the sound of troubled
voices speaking in the dark.

Cows

I followed the by-pass road behind Woodville
the sky as clean as a cut apple
around me the milky and putrid smell of cows
– in the rise of the dew, cows steaming
and wandering, slung from the frames
like black and white blankets
hung out to dry. They do say
you can make milk from grass, without cows
and their warm galumphing machinery
and tunnelly stomachs... Bah! at the thought
steam bursts in an angry spiral
straight up from a cake of shit
and the small ears twitch and shudder
above the luminous heads.

Or so I say. But these are the real,
the solid cows that cannot quarrel
or kill, have never fallen in love
and could not defend the dumb expertise
of their milk-making, which they did not invent
and do not observe with the least interest,
any more than they remember in autumn
how they roared all night in the spring
when their calves were taken away.

They do not suppose this matters,
nor that anything else does – indeed,
they do not suppose. Their time is entirely
taken up with the delicious excruciating
digestion of existence
and if they please me on the by-pass road
in the ripening sun this morning
that is wholly my affair.

At Bywell

This earth is dense with days, lived through
and left behind in long-repeated seasons.
We read of villagers who 'in these parts'
received the travellers who walked
the Roman Bridge across the Tyne
a thousand years ago, bringing
Border gossip, news no doubt of
the murdering Scots not sixty miles away.

Hushed on this later summer afternoon
by their remote yet homely presences,
we walk the spongy grass with some idea,
I think, of treading lightly on a soil
so pungently composed; passing each other
heads down pondering our closeness
above the churchyard ground to those
who've gone within with all their gear –

the woven tunics, mantles, breeches,
heel-less shoes, the treasured oxen, children's
breakfast bowls, the sunlit harvestings
of barley, groats, round smoky kitchens
jumpy with tallow flames, their bright
or clouded eyes...foolish to think we hear them
in the shadow of the limes – and yet
they do speak, for a moment, when we stand

by the north wall, close enough to touch
the dusty stone, mellow as trapped sunlight
– surely it's their prayers we hear, as in
the squat Saxon tower we see their knuckling down
to the severer ecstasies of God. In the nave
I touch with a kind of shyness the frosterly
marble column – black sheen with grey
stone flowers alive, alight within it.

G.F. Dutton

Selection from: *Squaring the Waves* (1986) and *The Concrete Garden* (1991).

G.F. DUTTON was born in 1924. He has spent most of his life in Scotland, whose passionate austerities, urban or otherwise, edge much of his poetry. His numerous books cover many subjects, from enzymology to mountaineering. A lifetime of sea and river swimming inspired his poem sequence *How Calm the Wild Water* (from which the first two poems are taken).

'Over a huge landscape – recognisably Scotland and its border of cold ocean – Dutton's strong, clean poems strike like shafts of light through rolling clouds. They are illuminations. Each poem exists in an enormous perspective of time...I think he is one of the finest poets of our time' – Anne Stevenson. ●

How calm the wild water

how calm the wild water
when you are riding it
when you are stroking

the high white haunches,
when you are in control;
the little while

you are deciding it.
the rocks' howl
quiet at your heel.

when you have thrust
to the silent centre,
where the heart would burst.

Storm

however far down
on the sea floor:
you hear the storm.

in the moving silence
of fragments to and fro,
in the slow resistance

of the great stem
you are clinging to.
but nothing more.

and the small fish
look up as they pass
at the desperate visitor.

The high flats at Craigston

the high flats at Craigston stand
rawboned in a raw land,
washed by thunderstorm and sun
and cloud shadows rolling on

from the bare hills behind, each one
out-staring the wind;
that every night
cling together and tremble with light.

The Concrete Garden

It takes time
to become set. Before that

you spread it out
smack it, thrust

bright-eyed advances
about the agglomerate, sow

whatever is new,
is bound to grow,

push through
rise to you there – you

regarding from heaven
before the streets stiffen.

Even then, they swear, one mushroom
can break up a pavement.

Bulletin

The glaciers have come down,
dead white
at the end of the street. All over town

cold mist of their breath,
and along gutters
water runs

freezing beneath. But
the machines are out, lined up,
beautiful, their great lights

tossing back darkness. And the engineers
have promised to save us,
they have left their seats

for a last meal, when they return
all will be well, under control,
it is their skill, listen –

already upstairs
they are teaching their children
to sing like the ice.

Pamela Gillilan

SIMON THIRSK

Selection from: *All-Steel Traveller: New & Selected Poems* (1994).

PAMELA GILLILAN was born in London, married in 1948 and moved to Cornwall in 1951. When she sat down to write her poem *Come Away* after the death of her husband David, she had written no poems for a quarter of a century. Then came a sequence of incredibly moving elegies.

Other poems followed, and two years after starting to write again, she won the Cheltenham Festival poetry competition. Her first collection *That Winter* (Bloodaxe, 1986) was shortlisted for the Commonwealth Poetry Prize. Her second book, *The Turnspit Dog* (Bloodaxe, 1993), is a collaboration with artist Charlotte Cory. ●

Come Away

His name
filled my scream
I ran barefoot down the stairs
fast as the childhood dream

when lions follow;
up again I ran,
the stairs a current of air
blew me like thistledown.

I laid my palm on his calf
and it was warm and muscled
and like life.

Come away said the kind doctor.
I left the body there
lying straight, our wide bed
a single bier.

All night I watched
tree branches scratch the sky,
printed another window-frame
for ever on my eye.

When I came home in the morning
all the warmth had gone.
I touched his useless hand.
Where his eyes had shone
behind half-lifted lids were grown
cataracts of stone.

When You Died

1

When you died
I went through the rain
Carrying my nightmare
To register the death.

A well-groomed healthy gentleman
Safe within his office
Said – Are you the widow?

Couldn't he have said
Were you his wife?

2

After the first shock
I found I was
Solidly set in my flesh.
I was an upright central pillar,
The soft flesh melted round me.
My eyes melted
Spilling the inexhaustible essence of sorrow.
The soft flesh of the body
Melted onto chairs and into beds
Dragging its emptiness and pain.

I lodged inside holding myself upright,
Warding off the dreadful deliquescence.

3

November.
Stooping under muslins
Of grey rain I fingered
Through ribbons of wet grass,
Traced stiff stems down to the wormy earth
And one by one snapped off
The pale surviving flowers; they would ride
With him, lie on the polished plank
Above his breast.

People said – Why do you not
Follow the coffin?
Why do you not
Have any funeral words spoken?
Why not
Send flowers from a shop?

4

When you died
They burnt you.
They brought home to me
A vase of thin metal;
Inside, a plastic bag
Crammed, full of gritty pieces.
Ground bones, not silky ash.

Where shall I put this substance?
Shall I scatter it
With customary thoughts
Of nature's mystical balance
Among the roses?

Shall I disperse it into the winds
That blow across Cambeake Cliff
Or drop it onto places where you
Lived, worked, were happy?

Finally shall I perhaps keep it
Which after all was you
Quietly on a shelf
And when I follow

My old grit can lie
No matter where with yours
Slowly sinking into the earth together.

    5

When you died
I did not for the moment
Think about myself;
I grieved deeply and purely for your loss,
That you had lost your life.
I grieved bitterly for your mind destroyed,
Your courage thrown away,
Your senses aborted under the amazing skin
No one would ever touch again.

I grieve still
That we'd have grown
Even more deeply close and old together
And now shall not.

Two Years

When you died
All the doors banged shut.

After two years, inch by inch,
They creep open.
Now I can relish
Small encounters,
Encourage
Small flares of desire;
Begin to believe as you did
Things come right.
I tell myself that you
Escaped the slow declension to old age
Leaving me to indulge
This wintry flowering.

But I know
It's not like that at all.

Four Years

The smell of him went soon
From all his shirts.
I sent them for jumble,
And the sweaters and suits.
The shoes
Held more of him; he was printed
Into his shoes. I did not burn
Or throw or give them away.
Time has denatured them now.

Nothing left.
There never will be
A hair of his in a comb.
But I want to believe
That in the shifting housedust
Minute presences still drift:
An eyelash,
A hard crescent cut from a fingernail,
That sometimes
Between the folds of a curtain
Or the covers of a book
I touch
A flake of his skin.

Mairi MacInnes

Selection from: *Elsewhere & Back: New & Selected Poems* (1993).

MAIRI MacINNES was born in 1925 in County Durham. She lived in America from 1959 to 1985, and now lives in north Yorkshire.

'She demonstrates a tough, noble appetite for place, for nature and its creatures, in a rugged language that accurately matches its occasions as her heart and her mind inform her senses and her words' – Theodore Weiss. 'A quality of visionary realism, of narrative freedom harkening to things seen and considered...Mairi MacInnes is a true poet who, in accepting the challenge of major themes, shows herself to be equal to them, technically, emotionally and above all, humanly, in the subtle resonances of her compassion' – Anne Stevenson. ●

The Old Naval Airfield

I looked out Henstridge lately,
  somewhere where it always was,
even then, without maps or signs,
  and thought of Philip, chief flying instructor,
brave Philip, who soon was dead –
  long ago, though, many years ago.
Pretty old, bosky old, footpath
  country, and nothing was familiar
till suddenly the dull lane
  roused me. A humpbacked bridge
over a disused railway led me
  to B Camp that was: now a wood and a shed.
Opposite, the Wessex Grain Company –
  storage silos that hummed
in the afternoon air like planes.
  On the edge of the field, a bunker gradually
took my eye. A well-turfed barrow?
  No, dear God, the rusted roof of a hangar
half-fallen in! And over the field, look,
  Philip's control tower, a tall wreck
marooned in breaking waves of grass!

Survival is a form of murder.
    My father ran round the garden in the dark
shouting, 'She's dead, and I could've
        done more for her. I could have, and I didn't.'
She'd said earlier, 'He couldn't do more,
        that man, best man who ever lived.'
Truth is, you can always do more.
    You have to survive, that too, but it's murder.
He lived on, as you do if you can.

The Groundhog
FROM *The House on the Ridge Road*

Dark: a grinding and gnawing.
Leprous buildings coming alight.
Stink of blood.

Click of the ready: ratchet of the clock,
scurry and plink of a blind going up.

On the grass by the barn, a working, a lump:
rawhead and bloodybones.
And when the gun went off, pandemonium.

Something hurried to the wall
dragging its heavy furs.
Out of a door at a run, thick with desire
for its ancient barbarous flesh,
its huge teeth, its stupidity,
the man caught it, clubbed it till it was limp,
humped it to the wall
and dumped it over. Back in the kitchen
the house dog nosed his hand.
The children pointed: 'Blood! Blood!'
as he took off his boots. Fear,
fear and laughter made them choke.

As they wheezed and screamed, he felt again
tremors in his fingertips where the dog's tongue worked,
beast sighs in their small pink mouths,
hatred in their wrong hysteria.

The Cave-In

What did he say, that blinded dusty boy,
when he was dug out?
                                  – That first the darkness
of the cave-in lay identical, outside and in,
across his eyelids; that the cries
he shrilled met stone and cried back to him
as echoes. He was imprisoned by an entire hill.
So humble and colossal it was, he cried until
the cold stationed in his boots wormed up
to his armpits, and threaded itself on vertebrae
and folded round his belly in a web.
So his tears dried up in convulsive shivers;
the taste of salt and tannin dried out his head.

When he came to, he heard thumps –
his heart, perhaps, or a pavement tamper,
and increasingly nearer, a flutter of water,
a streaming, pounding, a clatter of hoofs
that halted almost on top of him. He knew the advance
of a heavy animal, he smelled sweet grass
on its breath, and acrid hairiness of hide,
before he felt on his ears the bloom
of huge warm lips, tenderly, curiously applied,
and the nudge of damp nostrils on his neck,
and recognised the pushiness of a great beast
used to its own success.
                                  He got up (he said)
oh, joyfully, and touched the warm and rounded moleskin
which shut in tons of brilliant flesh,
and felt it glide under his hands, and twitch, ticklish,
till in a gigantic snatch it bolted off
slap into the rock, and there the skull and skeleton
sparked like a lode, or a luminous fossil,
the bones of a horse running; while he heard,
a good way off, the noise of hoofs.

What a horse was doing there, what it meant,
he'd no time to wonder before the rescuers
broke through the rockfall and found him.

James Wright

Selection from: *Above the
River: Complete Poems* (1992).

JAMES WRIGHT was born in 1927. He is one of
the most significant, most enduring figures
in modern American poetry. Whether he
was writing about his native Ohio, the nat-
ural world, love lost and found, or the lum-
inous resonant Italy of his later work, his
mastery of language and his powerful,
haunting voice marked him out as one of
the finest writers of his time, a poet whose
work caught the spirit of America's anxious
yet hopeful post-war years. Helen Vendler
called him 'one of the few poetic voices of
the American midwest – the gritty, bleak
and depressed places of his youth.'

James Wright won the Pulitzer Prize for
his poetry in 1972. He died in 1980. ●

A Note Left in Jimmy Leonard's Shack

Near the dry river's water-mark we found
    Your brother Minnegan,
Flopped like a fish against the muddy ground.
Beany, the kid whose yellow hair turns green,
Told me to find you, even in the rain,
    And tell you he was drowned.

I hid behind the chassis on the bank,
    The wreck of someone's Ford:
I was afraid to come and wake you drunk:
You told me once the waking up was hard,
The daylight beating at you like a board.
    Blood in my stomach sank.

Beside, you told him never to go out
    Along the river-side
Drinking and singing, clattering about.
You might have thrown a rock at me and cried
I was to blame, I let him fall in the road
    And pitch down on his side.

Well, I'll get hell enough when I get home
        For coming up this far,
Leaving the note, and running as I came.
I'll go and tell my father where you are.
You'd better go find Minnegan before
        Policemen hear and come.

Beany went home, and I got sick and ran,
        You old son of a bitch.
You better hurry down to Minnegan;
He's drunk or dying now, I don't know which,
Rolled in the roots and garbage like a fish,
        The poor old man.

Saint Judas

When I went out to kill myself, I caught
A pack of hoodlums beating up a man.
Running to spare his suffering, I forgot
My name, my number, how my day began,
How soldiers milled around the garden stone
And sang amusing songs; how all that day
Their javelins measured crowds; how I alone
Bargained the proper coins, and slipped away.

Banished from heaven, I found this victim beaten,
Stripped, kneed, and left to cry. Dropping my rope
Aside, I ran, ignored the uniforms:
Then I remembered bread my flesh had eaten,
The kiss that ate my flesh. Flayed without hope,
I held the man for nothing in my arms.

Autumn Begins in Martins Ferry, Ohio

In the Shreve High football stadium,
I think of Polacks nursing long beers in Tiltonville,
And gray faces of Negroes in the blast furnace at Benwood,
And the ruptured night watchman of Wheeling Steel,
Dreaming of heroes.

All the proud fathers are ashamed to go home.
Their women cluck like starved pullets,
Dying for love.

Therefore,
Their sons grew suicidally beautiful
At the beginning of October,
And gallop terribly against each other's bodies.

Lying in a Hammock at William Duffy's Farm in Pine Island, Minnesota

Over my head, I see the bronze butterfly,
Asleep on the black trunk,
Blowing like a leaf in green shadow.
Down the ravine behind the empty house,
The cowbells follow one another
Into the distances of the afternoon.
To my right,
In a field of sunlight between two pines,
The droppings of last year's horses
Blaze up into golden stones.
I lean back as the evening darkens and comes on.
A chicken hawk floats over, looking for home.
I have wasted my life.

A Blessing

Just off the highway to Rochester, Minnesota,
Twilight bounds softly forth on the grass.
And the eyes of those two Indian ponies
Darken with kindness.
They have come gladly out of the willows
To welcome my friend and me.
We step over the barbed wire into the pasture
Where they have been grazing all day, alone.
They ripple tensely, they can hardly contain their happiness
That we have come.
They bow shyly as wet swans. They love each other.
There is no loneliness like theirs.
At home once more,
They begin munching the young tufts of spring in the darkness.
I would like to hold the slenderer one in my arms,
For she has walked over to me
And nuzzled my left hand.
She is black and white,
Her mane falls wild on her forehead,
And the light breeze moves me to caress her long ear
That is delicate as the skin over a girl's wrist.
Suddenly I realise
That if I stepped out of my body I would break
Into blossom.

The Art of the Fugue: A Prayer

Radiant silence in Fiesole
And the long climb up a hill which is only one feather
Of the sky, and to set out within the sky,
As the dark happy Florentine would surely gather
All that he had to gather and every night set forth
And enter the pearl.

Florence below our hands, the city that yielded
Up the last secret of Hell.
Fiesole below me and around me and the wings
Of the invisible musician Brother Esposito folded
Around me and my girl.

And the organ
Silent in its longing for the only love.
And Bach and Dante meetings and praying
Before the music began.

And a little bell ringing halfway down the hill.

And me there a long way from the cold dream of Hell.
Me, there, alone, at last,
At last with the dust of my dust,
As far away as I will ever get from dying,
And the two great poets of God in the silence
Meeting together.

And Esposito the organist waiting to begin.
And a little bell halfway down delicately drifting off.

And Florence down there darkening, waiting to begin.

And me there alone at last with my only love,
Waiting to begin.

Whoever you are, ambling past my grave,
My name worn thin as the shawl of the lovely hill town
Fiesole, the radiance and silence of the sky.
Listen to me:

Though love can be scarcely imaginable Hell,
By God, it is not a lie.

John Cassidy

SHIRLEY BAKER

Selection from: *Night Cries*
(1982).

JOHN CASSIDY was born in 1928, and lives in Bolton, Lancashire. His pamphlets *Changes of Light* and *The Fountain* (1979) were two of Bloodaxe's first publications. His second book-length collection, *Night Cries*, was given a Poetry Book Society Recommendation in 1982, the first major literary honour won by a Bloodaxe author. His third collection, *Walking on Frogs*, was published by Bloodaxe in 1989.

Cassidy's poetry has been much admired by the critics. Dick Davis liked its 'wary ease' and 'placid surfaces that mask a buried violence'. Terry Eagleton called *Night Cries* 'a strong, delicate volume of nature poetry …a kind of *Lyrical Ballads* of our time'. ●

Defining an Absence

This is to walk squinting into a sun
   which edges everything wintrily
with incredible hardness, even
   grass-stalks frosted into still
sabres bristling at the bottoms of walls,
   the walls themselves given
such uncompromising presence
   their weight is known as never before.

And never before have footsteps
   been like the tapping of a door
someone has gone out through and left loose
   in a cool wind, defining an absence
no sun will ever do anything to
   but sharpen like the sabres of the grass,
or plant as firmly in the early light
   as these blank formidable walls.

Disturbance

I woke when a magpie hammered
Its machine-gun voice from close range
Into my ear as if in the same room.
A sharp light marked the first break
Of the first morning in June, the sky
A whole smooth eggshell.

The magpie was smashing a sparrow's nest
Above the window, pick-axing through
To the bald, reptilian young.
Three days hatched, they were spiked
Out of that lined, close world by a black
Bill and an implacable eye.

All their last energy went in a frenzy
Of wheezing. One was lifted fifty yards
Away to a bough and banged and broken
And gulped. It was there to be seen but I saw
In my mind and lay close under blankets
Unmoving, thinking of instability

And how it seems to live in another
Medium, unseen, unknown, outside,
Till the great beak crashes in.
Knowing it is no benefit. I hear
The black-white-black flap of that magpie
Come chattering back for the next grab.

Overhearing

The loneliest voice I heard as a child
was the moaning of telegraph poles
on a two-mile stretch of road, white
and straight as a taut string,
a road lying over a wild
gorse-cluttered common, between low walls.

The multiple hum, the packed chord
of the poles and the pots seemed, were,
had to be the milling conversations
of the communicators, town to town,
spilling into the wind each stretched word
out of the loops of swinging wire.

The summer wind pushed back and forth up there
between the poles. Its warmth curled
over the electric voices, but would not
smother the cries of the desolate callers
yearning from town to town. The air
trembled with all the agonies of the world.

The wind was in the end the stronger,
turning explanatory, blowing chill.
The squeezed allowances of speech
leaking from within the thin wire links
cooled to simple movements of the air:
themselves more primitive, and lonelier still.

Connie Bensley

CONNIE BENSLEY was born in 1929 in London. Her poems are sharply satirical, often poking fun at social pretence and suburban pretension. They present a black comedy of manners in which her hapless characters are bounced between love, death and the local supermarket.

'Her language is uncluttered, slightly tight-lipped, but clear and direct. She can be funny and frightening at the same time' – George Szirtes. 'Her poems are sharp, intelligent, vulnerably immaculate, and they make much of their impact by pulling the shreds of whatever carpet remains from under your feet' – John Mole. ●

Selection from: *Central Reservations* (1990) and *Choosing To Be a Swan* (1994).

She's Nothing But Trouble

If she smiles, don't smile back.
But of course you will, like an electrician
taking chances with the wiring
on a dull Tuesday afternoon.

Desires

Newly shaven, your eyes only slightly bloodshot,
Your rat-trap mouth smiling up at the corners,
You remind me of the Head Girl
I used to be in love with.

It's something about your sporty build,
The way you seem to be counting the people in the café
With a view to lining them up in teams.

It's quite set me in the mood for the evening,
And I follow you alertly through the door,
Hoping you'll turn and snap at me
To pick my feet up, and not to slouch.

Choice

You're the one I boned up mah jongg for
You're the one I bought the chaise longue for
You're the one I yearn to go wrong for.

You're the one I'll garden my plot with
You're the one I'll throw in my lot with
You're the one I'll find my G spot with.

You're the one I've had my teeth capped for
You're the one my scruples were scrapped for
You're the one I get all unwrapped for:
                              You're the one.

A Friendship

He made restless forays
into the edge of our marriage.
One Christmas Eve he came late,
his dark hair crackling with frost,
and ate his carnation buttonhole
to amuse the baby.

When I had a second child
he came to the foot of my bed at dusk
bringing pineapples and champagne,
whispering 'Are you awake?' –
singing a snatch of opera.
The Nurse tapped him on the shoulder.

At the end, we took turns at his bedside.
I curled up in the chair; listened to each breath
postponing itself indefinitely.
He opened his eyes once and I leaned forward:
'Is there anything you want?'
'Now she asks,' he murmured.

Visiting Time

In the ward, after the stroke,
he could not remember whom he liked
and whom he disliked.

A young man with reddened eyes
held his hand. He could not name him
though the tie seemed familiar.

When a woman swept in with flowers
and seemed to assume intimacy
he feigned sleep.

The Star and the Birds

In the New Year, it starts with
a star. They point to it on her X-ray –
white, fragile, filamented,
sinister as a footstep in a dark alley.

She packs a bag, reads her horoscope.
On the ward the trolleys come and go
freighted with figures,
white-capped, whey-faced, dopey.

Taking his coarse pen (*Excuse* me)
the houseman draws an arrow
on her breast. It points to her heart
like some ironic early Valentine.

The ceiling of the anaesthetic room
is painted – its theme is zoological.
She watches the tropical birds
blur in a melée of bright wings.

At home her kitchen,
under its fine frost of dust,
listens to the answering machine
whirring and parroting.

Cars

Beside the railway lines
cars are waiting – metal pets
parked in abutting flocks
cooled by absence: witnesses
to strife, aggrandisement, love,
adultery, death.

They die too. In car graveyards
they lie jumbled, piled,
like animals awkwardly mating,
waiting to be transmuted,
crushed to metallic essence,
finally overtaken.

The Idea

Standing idly at the window, she decides
to introduce her two friends, A and B
to each other. They are sure to get on.

At first they do not;
and then they do – warming
to badinage over the ratatouille.

Weeks later, someone remarks:
A and B are on holiday together.
A postcard arrives, signed by both,

funny and silly, with a view of a lake.
She stands at the window, chipping away
at the flaking paint for something to do.

Hans Magnus Enzensberger

ANDREAS POHLMANN

Selection from: *Selected Poems* (1994), translated by Hans Magnus Enzensberger and Michael Hamburger.

HANS MAGNUS ENZENSBERGER was born in 1929 in Bavaria and grew up in Nazi Nuremberg. His poetry's social and moral criticism of the post-war world owes much to Marxism, yet insists on the freedoms which have often been denied by Communist governments: like Orwell he maintains that satire and criticism should not be party-political.

As well as being Germany's most important poet, he is a provocative cultural essayist and one of Europe's leading political thinkers. No British poet can match him in his range of interests and his moral passion. 'We hear in Enzensberger the human voice amongst human voices, feel the extraordinariness of ordinary men' – George Szirtes. ●

Rondeau

It's easy to talk.

But you can't eat words.
So bake bread.
It's hard to bake bread.
So become a baker.

But you can't live in a loaf.
So build houses.
It's hard to build houses.
So become a bricklayer.

But you can't build a house on a mountain.
So move the mountain.
It's hard to move mountains.
So become a prophet.

But you can't hear thoughts.
So talk.
It's hard to talk.
So become what you are

and keep on muttering to yourself,
useless creature.

Purgatorio

Woe the earth is tiny in the brochures
to the snackbar waddle development experts
enveloped in travel cheques
the quarantine flag has been hoisted

Will Herr Albert Schweitzer
please go to Transit Information

Booked out book-keepers paddle
through glass-lined corridors
to the last judgement
Last call for Nagasaki

Will Herr Adolf Eichmann
please go to Transit Information

On account of fog the world is closed
On pedal trolleys brides arrive
in shrouds that trail in the wind
The plane is ready to take off.

Will Monsieur Godot
please go to Transit Information

Exit B Channel thirty-two
The nylon voice cries woe upon us
Funeral processions flood the runways
Sirens blaze in the dark

Concert of Wishes

Sanad says: Give me my daily pita
Fräulein Brockmann looks for a comfortable little flat not too ex-
    pensive with a cooking recess and a broom cupboard
Véronique longs for world revolution
Dr Luhmann desperately needs to sleep with his mum
Uwe Köpke dreams of a perfect specimen of Thurn and Taxis seven
    silbergroschen pale blue imperforated
Simone knows exactly what she wants: to be famous Simply famous
    no matter what for or at what price

If Konrad had his way he'd simply lie in bed for ever
Mrs Woods would like to be tied up and raped quite regularly but
    only from behind and by a gentleman
Guido Ronconi's only desire is the unio mystica
Fred Podritzke would love to work over all those crackpot lefties with
    a length of gas piping until not one of them so much as twitches
If someone doesn't give him his steak and chips this minute Karel
    will blow his top
What Buck needs is a flash and nothing else

And peace on earth and a ham sandwich and the uncensored dia-
    logue and a baby and a million free of tax and a moaning that
    gives way to the familiar little breathless shrieks and a plush
    poodle and freedom for all and off with his head and that the
    hair we have lost will grow again overnight

[MH]

Vending Machine

He puts four dimes into the slot
he gets himself some cigarettes

He gets cancer
he gets apartheid
he gets the King of Greece
federal tax state tax sales tax and excise

he gets machine guns and surplus value
free enterprise and positivism
he gets a big lift big business big girls
the big stick the great society the big bang
the big puke
king size extra size super size

He gets more and more
for his four dimes
but for a moment all the things he is getting himself
disappear

even the cigarettes

He looks at the vending machine
but he doesn't see it
he sees himself
for a fleeting moment
and he almost looks like a man

Then very soon he is gone again
with a little click
there are his cigarettes

He has disappeared
it was just a fleeting moment
some kind of sudden bliss

He has disappeared
he is gone
buried under all the stuff he has gotten
for his four dimes

Clothes

Here they lie, still and cat-like
in the sun, in the afternoon,
your clothes, baggy,
undreaming, as if by chance.
They smell of you, faintly,
they almost take after you,
give away your dirt,
your bad habits,
thr trace of your elbows.
They take their time, don't breathe,
are left over, limp, full of buttons,
properties, stains.
In the hands of a policeman,
a dressmaker, an archaeologist
they would reveal their seams,
their idle secrets. But where you are,
whether you suffer, what
you had always wanted to tell me
and never did, whether
what happened has happened

for love's sake or from need
or from negligence, and why
all this has come about as it did
when it was a question
of saving our skin,
whether you are dead by now
or have gone to wash your hair,
they do not tell.

Old Revolution

A beetle lying on its back.
The old bloodspots are still on show
in the museum. Decades playing dead.
A sour smell from the mouth of thirty ministries.
At the Hotel Nacional four deceased musicians
are playing night by night the tango from '59:
Quizás, quizás, quizás.

By the murmur of a tropical rosary
History is taking a nap. Only those
who long for toothpaste, light bulbs
and spaghetti are tossing sleeplessly
between the damp bedsheets.

A sleepwalker in front of ten microphones
is preaching to his tired island:
After me nothing will follow.
It is finished.
The machine guns glisten with oil.
The shirts are sticky with cane-juice.
The prostate has had it.

Wistfully the aged warrior
scans the horizon for an aggressor.
There is no one in sight. Even the enemy
has forgotten about him.

[HME]

John Montague

GALLERY PRESS

Selection from: *New Selected Poems* (1990).

JOHN MONTAGUE was born in 1929. Derek Mahon calls him 'the best Irish poet of his generation'. He commands a pivotal place in contemporary Irish poetry: a vital link between the generation of Patrick Kavanagh and younger poets like Heaney, Mahon and Muldoon, whose style and internationalism owe much to his example. He is one of the most prophetic, generous and moving voices of our time. 'John Montague is the Éluard of Ireland, a craftsman of great subtlety and a highly sensitive student of people and things' – Derek Mahon.

His *New Selected Poems* (1990) is a sampler of work from eight collections, including *The Rough Field* and *Mount Eagle*, which are available separately from Bloodaxe in Britain and Gallery in Ireland. ●

Like Dolmens Round My Childhood, the Old People

Like dolmens round my childhood, the old people.

Jamie MacCrystal sang to himself,
A broken song without tune, without words;
He tipped me a penny every pension day,
Fed kindly crusts to winter birds.
When he died, his cottage was robbed,
Mattress and money-box torn and searched.
Only the corpse they didn't disturb.

Maggie Owens was surrounded by animals,
A mongrel bitch and shivering pups,
Even in her bedroom a she-goat cried.
She was a well of gossip defiled,
Fanged chronicler of a whole countryside;
Reputed a witch, all I could find
Was her lonely need to deride.

The Nialls lived along a mountain lane
When heather bells bloomed, clumps of foxglove.
All were blind, with Blind Pension and Wireless,
Dead eyes serpent-flicked as one entered
To shelter from a downpour of mountain rain.
Crickets chirped under the rocking hearthstone
Until the muddy sun shone out again.

Mary Moore lived in a crumbling gatehouse,
Famous as Pisa for its leaning gable.
Bag-apron and books, she tramped the fields
Driving lean cattle from a miry stable.
A by-word for fierceness, she fell asleep
Over love stories, *Red Star* and *Red Circle*,
Dreamed of gypsy love rites, by firelight sealed.

Wild Billy Eagleson married a Catholic servant girl
When all his Loyal family passed on:
We danced round him shouting 'To Hell with King Billy',
And dodged from the arc of his flailing blackthorn.
Forsaken by both creeds, he showed little concern
Until the Orange drums banged past in the summer
And bowler and sash aggressively shone.

Curate and doctor trudged to attend them,
Through knee-deep snow, through summer heat,
From main road to lane to broken path,
Gulping the mountain air with painful breath.
Sometimes they were found by neighbours,
Silent keepers of a smokeless hearth,
Suddenly cast in the mould of death.

Ancient Ireland, indeed! I was reared by her bedside,
The rune and the chant, evil eye and averted head,
Fomorian fierceness of family and local feud.
Gaunt figures of fear and of friendliness,
For years they trespassed on my dreams,
Until once, in a standing circle of stones,
I felt their shadows pass

Into that dark permanence of ancient forms.

The Hill of Silence

1

From the platform
of large raised stones

lines appear to lead us
along the hillside

bog tufts softening
beneath each step

bracken and briar
restraining our march

clawing us back, slowing
us to perception's pace.

2

A small animal halts
starts, leaps away

and a lark begins
its dizzy, singing climb

towards the upper skies
and now another stone appears

ancient, looming, mossed
long ago placed,

lifted to be a signpost
along the old path.

3

Let us climb further.
As one thought leads
to another, so one lich-

ened snout of stone
still leads one on,
beckons to a final one.

4

Under its raised slab
thin trickles of water

gather to a shallow pool
in which the head stone

mirrors, and rears
to regard its shadow self,

and a diligent spider weaves
a trembling, silver web

a skein of terrible delicacy
swaying to the wind's touch

a fragile, silken scarf
a veined translucent leaf.

5

This is the slope of loneliness.
This is the hill of silence.
This is the winds' fortress.
Our world's polestar.
A stony patience.

6

We have reached a shelf
that surveys the valley

on these plains below
a battle flowed and ebbed

and the gored, spent warrior
was ferried up here

where water and herbs
might staunch his wounds.

7

Let us also lay ourselves
down in this silence

let us also be healed
wounds closed, senses cleansed

as over our bowed heads
the mad larks multiply

needles stabbing the sky
in an ecstasy of stitching fury

against the blue void
while from clump and tuft

cranny and cleft, soft footed
curious, the animals gather around.

Kamau Brathwaite

JULIAN STAPLETON

Selection from:
MiddlePassages (1992).

KAMAU BRATHWAITE was born in 1930 in Barbados. He is Professor of Comparative Literature at New York University.

He reversed the Middle Passage of slavery when he exiled himself to Ghana, where he re-discovered his African roots. Returning home, he charted a second discovery, that of Africa in the Caribbean through two trilogies of interconnected books (published by OUP), the first from the 1960s which turned into *The Arrivants* (1973) and a second (Bajan) trilogy comprising *Mother Poem* (1977), *Sun Poem* (1982) and *X/Self* (1987). His Bloodaxe book *MiddlePassages* (1992) is an offshoot of the second trilogy. ●

Stone

for Mikey Smith (1954-1983),
stoned to death on Stony Hill, Kingston

W hen the stone fall that morning out of the johncrow sky

it was not dark at first . that opening on to the red sea humming
but something in my mouth like feathers . blue like bubbles
carrying signals & planets & the sliding curve of the
world like a water pic. ture in a raindrop when the pressure. drop

W hen the stone fall that morning out of the johncrow sky

I couldn't cry out because my mouth was full of beast & plunder
as if I was gnashing badwords among tombstones
as if the road up stony hill . round the bend by the church
yard . on the way to the post office . was a bad bad dream

& the dream was like a snarl of broken copper wire zig
zagging its electric flashes up the hill & splitt. ing spark & flow.
ers high. er up the hill. past the white houses & the ogogs bark.
ing all teeth & fur. nace & my mother like she up. like she up.

like she up. side down up a tree like she was scream.
like she was scream. like she was scream. ing no & no.
body i could hear could hear a word i say. ing . even though
there were so many poems left & the tape was switched on &

runn. ing & runn. ing &
the green light was red & they was stannin up there &
evva. where in london & amsterdam & at unesco in paris &
in west berlin & clapp. ing & clapp. ing & clapp. ing &

not a soul on stony hill to even say amen

& yet it was happening happening happening .
the fences begin to crack in i skull .
& there was a loud booodooooooooooooooooogs like
guns goin off . them ole time magnums .

or like a fireworks a dreadlocks was on fire .
& the gaps where the river comin down
inna the drei gully where my teeth use to be smilin .
& i tuff gong tongue that use to press against them & parade

pronunciation . now unannounce & like a black wick in i head & dead

& it was like a heavy heavy riddim low down in i belly . bleedin dub .
& there was like this heavy heavy black dog thump. in in i chest &
pump. in

murdererrrrrrrrrrrrrrrrrrrrrrrrrrrrrrrrrrrrrrrrrrrrrrrrrrrrrrrrrrrrrrrrr

& i throat like dem tie. like dem tie. like dem tie a tight tie a.
round it. twist. ing my name quick crick. quick crick .
& a nevva wear neck. tie yet .

& a hear when de big boot kick down i door . stump
in it foot pun a knot in de floor. board .
a window slam shat at de back a mi heart .

de itch & ooze & damp a de yaaad
in mi sil. ver tam. bourines closer & closer .
st joseph marching bands crash. ing & closer .

bom si. cai si. ca boom ship bell . bom si. cai si. ca boom ship bell

& a laughin more blood & spittin out

lawwwwwwwwwwwwwwwwwwwwwwwwwwwwwwwwwwwwwwwd

i two eye lock to the sun & the two sun starin back black
from de grass

& a bline to de butterfly fly. in

•

& it was a wave on stony hill caught in crust of sun. light

•

& it was like a matchstick schooner into harbour muffled in the
silence of of it wound

•

& it was like the blue of speace was filling up the heavens
with it thunder

& it was like the wind was grow. ing skin
the skin had hard hairs . hardering

•

it was like marcus garvey rising from his coin .
stepping towards his people crying dark

& every mighty word he trod. the ground fall dark & hole
be. hine him like it was a bloom x. ploding sound .

my ears were bleed. ing sound

•

& I was quiet now because i had become that sound

the sun. light morning washed the choral limestone harsh
against the soft volcanic ash. i was

& it was slipping past me into water. & it was slipping past me
into root. i was

& it was
slipping past me into flower. & it was ripping upwards

into shoot. i was

& every politrician tongue in town was lash.
ing me with spit & cut. rass wit & ivy whip & wrinkle jumbimum

it was like warthog . grunt. ing in the ground

& children running down the hill run right on through the spash
of pouis that my breathe. ing make when it was howl & red &

bubble
& sparrow twits pluck tic & tap. worm from the grass

as if i man did nevva have no face . as if i man did nevva in this place

■

W hen the stone fall that morning out of the johncrow sky

i could not hold it brack or black it back or block it off or limp
away or roll it from me into memory or light or rock it steady
into night. be

cause it builds me now with leaf & spiderweb & soft & crunch &
like the pow.
derwhite & slip & grit inside your leather. boot &

fills my blood with deaf my bone with hobbledumb & echo.
less neglect neglect neglect neglect &

lawwwwwwwwwwwwwwwwwwwwwwwwwwwwwwwwwwwwwww

•

i am the stone that kills me

Tomas Tranströmer

K.G. SVENSSON

Selection from: *Collected Poems* (1986), translated by Robin Fulton.

TOMAS TRANSTRÖMER was born in 1931 in Stockholm. He is Sweden's most important poet. Also a professional psychologist, Tranströmer has been called a 'buzzard poet' in Sweden, because he sees the world from a height, in a mystic dimension, but brings every detail of the natural world into sharp focus – as at the end of *The Journey's Formulae*.

In his early work he drew on the aesthetic traditions of Swedish nature poetry. His poetry then became more personal, open and relaxed. 'A single-minded, obstinate search back to a pristine sensibility that actually belongs in childhood' – Joanna Bankier. ●

The Journey's Formulae
(from the Balkans, 1955)

1

A murmur of voices behind the ploughman.
He doesn't look round. The empty fields.
A murmur of voices behind the ploughman.
One by one the shadows break loose
and plunge into the summer sky's abyss.

2

Four oxen come, under the sky.
Nothing proud about them. And the dust thick
as wool. The insects' pens scrape.

A swirl of horses, lean as in
grey allegories of the plague.
Nothing gentle about them. And the sun raves.

3

The stable-smelling village with thin dogs.
The party official in the market square
in the stable-smelling village with white houses.

His heaven accompanies him: it is high
and narrow like inside a minaret.
The wing-trailing village on the hillside.

4

An old house has shot itself in the forehead.
Two boys kick a ball in the twilight.
A swarm of rapid echoes. – Suddenly, starlight.

5

On the road in the long darkness. My wristwatch
gleams obstinately with time's imprisoned insect.

The quiet in the crowded compartment is dense.
In the darkness the meadows stream past.

But the writer is halfway into his image, there
he travels, at the same time eagle and mole.

Allegro

I play Haydn after a black day
and feel a simple warmth in my hands.

The keys are willing. Soft hammers strike.
The resonance green, lively and calm.

The music says freedom exists
and someone doesn't pay the emperor tax.

I push down my hands in my Haydnpockets
and imitate a person looking on the world calmly.

I hoist the Haydnflag – it signifies:
'We don't give in. But want peace.'

The music is a glass-house on the slope
where the stones fly, the stones roll.

And the stones roll right through
but each pane stays whole.

Alone

I

One evening in February I came near to dying here.
The car skidded sideways on the ice, out
on the wrong side of the road. The approaching cars –
their lights – closed in.

My name, my girls, my job
broke free and were left silently behind
further and further away. I was anonymous
like a boy in a playground surrounded by enemies.

The approaching traffic had huge lights.
They shone on me while I pulled at the wheel
in a transparent terror that floated like egg white.
The seconds grew – there was space in them –
they grew as big as hospital buildings.

You could almost pause
and breathe out for a while
before being crushed.

Then something caught: a helping grain of sand
or a wonderful gust of wind. The car broke free
and scuttled smartly right over the road.
A post shot up and cracked – a sharp clang – it
flew away in the darkness.

Then – stillness. I sat back in my seat-belt
and saw someone coming through the whirling snow
to see what had become of me.

II

I have been walking for a long time
on the frozen Östergötland fields.
I have not seen a single person.

In other parts of the world
there are people who are born, live and die
in a perpetual crowd.

To be always visible – to live
in a swarm of eyes –
a special expression must develop.
Face coated with clay.

The murmuring rises and falls
while they divide up among themselves
the sky, the shadows, the sand grains.

I must be alone
ten minutes in the morning
and ten minutes in the evening.
– Without a programme.

Everyone is queuing at everyone's door.

Many.

One.

From March 1979

Weary of all who come with words, words but no language
I make my way to the snow-covered island.
The untamed has no words.
The unwritten pages spread out on every side!
I come upon the tracks of deer's hooves in the snow.
Language but no words.

Jenny Joseph

SIMON THIRSK

Selection from: *Selected Poems* (1992).

JENNY JOSEPH was born in 1932 in Birmingham. Her Bloodaxe *Selected Poems* (1992) draws on four previous collections. Bloodaxe also publishes *Persephone* (1986), a fiction in prose and poetry; a new book, *Extended Similes*, is due out in 1994.

'She mixes mystery and plain statement in a wholly original way...Clear observation, bold aphorisms and sharp unhappiness are woven together in her poems. The end product feels like joy' – Peter Porter. 'Like Emily Dickinson, a domestic poetry, but a philosophical domestic poetry from a private house and a back garden, again like Dickinson, which have room in them for most of what one can find to think about the world' – Robert Nye. ●

Dawn walkers

Anxious eyes loom down the damp-black streets
Pale staring girls who are walking away hard
From beds where love went wrong or died or turned away,
Treading their misery beneath another day
Stamping to work into another morning.

In all our youths there must have been some time
When the cold dark has stiffened up the wind
But suddenly, like a sail stiffening with wind,
Carried the vessel on, stretching the ropes, glad of it.

But listen to this now: this I saw one morning.
I saw a young man running, for a bus I thought,
Needing to catch it on this murky morning
Dodging the people crowding to work or shopping early.
And all heads stopped and turned to see how he ran
To see would he make it, the beautiful strong young man.
Then I noticed a girl running after, calling out 'John'.
He must have left his sandwiches I thought.
But she screamed 'John wait'. He heard her and ran faster,
Using his muscled legs and studded boots.
We knew she'd never reach him. 'Listen to me John.

Only once more' she cried. 'For the last time, John, please wait,
    please listen.'
He gained the corner in a spurt and she
Sobbing and hopping with her red hair loose
(Made way for by the respectful audience)
Followed on after, but not to catch him now.
Only that there was nothing left to do.

The street closed in and went on with its day.
A worn old man standing in the heat from the baker's
Said 'Surely to God the bastard could have waited'.

Warning

When I am an old woman I shall wear purple
With a red hat which doesn't go, and doesn't suit me.
And I shall spend my pension on brandy and summer gloves
And satin sandals, and say we've no money for butter.
I shall sit down on the pavement when I'm tired
And gobble up samples in shops and press alarm bells
And run my stick along the public railings
And make up for the sobriety of my youth.
I shall go out in my slippers in the rain
And pick the flowers in other people's gardens
And learn to spit.

You can wear terrible shirts and grow more fat
And eat three pounds of sausages at a go
Or only bread and pickle for a week
And hoard pens and pencils and beermats and things in boxes.

But now we must have clothes that keep us dry
And pay our rent and not swear in the street
And set a good example for the children.
We must have friends to dinner and read the papers.

But maybe I ought to practise a little now?
So people who know me are not too shocked and surprised
When suddenly I am old, and start to wear purple.

Stephen Berg

COPPER CANYON PRESS

Selection from: *New & Selected Poems* (1992).

STEPHEN BERG was born in 1934. He is one of the most original and vital American poets of his generation. William Arrowsmith has called his poems 'all risk, with the courage of their own miraculous compassion and truth'.

'Berg's is a unique, powerful voice in American poetry. Passionate and audacious, elequent and zany, his poems deal with the most raw and emotionally rending themes, while maintaining a startling forthrightness of vision and a remarkable elegance of tone ...This is the lyric striving to extend itself, and the human soul struggling to come to terms with all the lost and lonely corners of its mansion' – C.K. Williams. 'A poet (and translator and editor) of energy, range, intimacy, daring, narrative and evocative authority' – W.S. Merwin. ●

Lament

My mother wants to be burned, she told me
last night stretched out watching TV
after I told her what the doctor said.
'Don't put me anywhere, either,' she added.
I left the room, came back
and found her leaning out a window,
fondling, whispering to the slick branches
of the cherry tree, freshly budded,
shiny after rain,
that brushed the front of my house,
pulling them against her naked breasts
to soothe herself with the cool leafy wood,
to feel something other than her own hands
touch the nipples.

Eating Outside

Fat pine boughs
droop over the vegetable garden's
sticks and leaves
the moon's hazy face comes and goes
in the heat.
Beautiful women,
your skin can barely be seen.
The moon's gone. Clouds everywhere.
A pale hand curls
on the tabletop next to mine,
there's talk about work and love.
We're like the moon at this hour
as clouds swallow it or dissolve so
it glides through the shaggy limbs,
full, like the grief inside us,
then floats off by itself
beyond the last tips of the needles.
The trees are quiet. In the house
my daughters play the piano and laugh.
The family dog races in and out howling.
The candles on the table have blown out.
I keep trying to explain
but when I go back, like now, there's
the red hammock, the barbecue guarding
the lit back wall like a dwarf,
the self, awed by changes,
motioning to us as it leaves.
Deep among those arms, it pauses
clear, white and unseen.

Self-Portrait at Six

My wife hung it there, on the wall on the way to our bedroom.
When you take the five steps up to the landing in front of our
door, it's on your left, usually in shadow in a gold-rimmed, oval
mat. Victorian oval walnut molding frame, the eyes already hurt,
defensive in the way we think 'open' means but is, actually, only a
form of wariness. No steadiness, no self-assurance, no clarity of
mind influence the fact yet. The thick brown hair is mine, but the
mouth is all wonder in a kind of sullen trance and pleads not to
be wounded more. He fears the world can kill him, and will, the
world is always mysterious, like disease. Being alone attacks him
from the outside, saddening his look, he can't ignore it by simply
playing. Instead it seems he can't defend himself, there's no cour-
age of acceptance in his gaze. At my age now, I've come to imag-
ine my mother, at the beginning of my life, as a young lovely
woman, baffled by her pain, who found my helplessness too much
like her own to let her simply reflect my emerging self. So, to
extend the thought, my face on the stairwall, then, was already
trapped in the battles of identity and self-denial, of believing that
freedom is impossible because another feels nearly like who one is.
Isn't that what our first taste of death is – invasion of another's
pain? Isn't that how we first split ourselves into good and bad?
Think of any awareness that lets you act without even a shade of
sensing others are watching you, judging you, caring about you,
so that desire and action fuse, and there's no gap, no hint of pain
that slows you. But this is memory, interpretation, the two great
dangers of the mind. What it is I'm getting at, what it is that brings
that picture back and stirs my ideas is the gnawing aloneness of
people, of all things, of consciousness itself, and the opposite –
that each of us lives in others' minds, as they live in ours, some-
times flaring in images, sometimes engrossed in each others' flesh.
Each night before I go to bed I pass myself on the stairs, eternally
helpless, caught with an early madness crossing my face, and it
seems, as I tuck myself in, trying not to be seen or heard, that the
entire universe is the dark fetal mound breathing on one side of
our bed, that everything flows from it, everything returns.

Gösta Ågren

GÖSTA ÅGREN was born in 1936 in Ostrobothnia, the Swedish-speaking part of northern Finland. He has developed an intellectually austere form of aphorism-lyric, which in its concentration and imagistic density looks both inwards to the metaphysical traditions of Finland-Swedish modernism, and outwards to contemporary English-language poetry. 'An Ostrobothnian quasi-separatist, Marxist, he is heavily influenced by R.S. Thomas, but his taut, muscley, short lines remind me, too, of Edward Bond, prismed through a totally Finland-Swedish consciousness... tough, but compassionate...abstract and imagistic and sensual. He feels like a major poet' – Adam Thorpe. ●

Selection from: *A Valley in the Midst of Violence: Selected Poems* (1992), translated by David McDuff.

Childhood Summer

Through the slow shadows
the cows approach, warm
evening mothers, that rather
stay than go. Their eyes
are great flowers, their bodies
are full of grass. Almost plants
they are, groping their way home
on gently walking roots.

It was summer. Summer.

Stress

The mail falls like severed wings to the floor.
On the calendar you write down times and days.
Your life slowly becomes more important than you.

Death's Secret

It is not true
that death begins after life.
When life stops
death also stops.

Block

I, who do not understand
the answer, commit it
to the darkness inside this
precise block of words.
It is after all none the less
the answer that is needed, not
the wording.

Bird

Real birds
can fly, and therefore have
no need of doing it.
They even lack wings.

The Day

That morning, when he at last
woke up and rose from
the mist of his bed, the world had
cleared to heraldry.
Lions with naked faces
contemplated their souls, cloudy
with winter streets. Matter
condensed to ecstasy while

the everyday, sword of the archangel,
slowly passed through the room.
Bound in ropes of blood
an immense being sank in the west.
And night came, as night
always will come.

Thesis

If definitions were possible no one would need to make them,
but every meaning ends in silence
and life and death are wings of the same bird.

At Last

It is a matter of scouring away
layer upon layer of form.
When only the content remains
the poem is finished.

Brendan Kennelly

IAN GROUND

Selection from: *A Time for Voices* (1989), *Cromwell* (1983/1987) and *The Book of Judas* (1991).

BRENDAN KENNELLY was born in 1936 in Co. Kerry, and is now Professor of Modern Literature at Trinity College, Dublin. He has published over 20 books, and edited the *Penguin Book of Irish Verse*.

In Ireland his poetry is rated as highly as Heaney's, and many Irish critics regarded Kennelly's *Cromwell* as the most important work in Irish literature since Kavanagh's *The Great Hunger* – until Kennelly followed it with *The Book of Judas*, a 400-page epic poem in which he allows another reviled figure his voice: 'The great theme of the book is betrayal; betrayal of others but ultimately of oneself' – Anthony Roche. 'Moral terrorism, a modern sensibility struggling with medieval demons' – Augustine Martin. ●

Poem from a Three Year Old

And will the flowers die?

And will the people die?

And every day do you grow old, do I
grow old, no I'm not old, do
flowers grow old?

Old things – do you throw them out?

Do you throw old people out?

And how you know a flower that's old?

The petals fall, the petals fall from flowers,
and do the petals fall from people too,
every day more petals fall until the
floor where I would like to play I
want to play is covered with old
flowers and people all the same
together lying there with petals fallen
on the dirty floor I want to play
the floor you come and sweep
with the huge broom.

The dirt you sweep, what happens that,
what happens all the dirt you sweep
from flowers and people, what
happens all the dirt? Is all the
dirt what's left of flowers and
people, all the dirt there in a
heap under the huge broom that
sweeps everything away?

Why you work so hard, why brush
and sweep to make a heap of dirt?
And who will bring new flowers?
And who will bring new people? Who will
bring new flowers to put in water
where no petals fall on to the
floor where I would like to
play? Who will bring new flowers
that will not hang their heads
like tired old people wanting sleep?
Who will bring new flowers that
do not split and shrivel every
day? And if we have new flowers,
will we have new people too to
keep the flowers alive and give
them water?

And will the new young flowers die?

And will the new young people die?

And why?

The Visitor

He strutted into the house.

Laughing
He walked over to the woman
Stuck a kiss in her face.

He wore gloves.
He had fur on his coat.
He was the most confident man in the world.
He liked his own wit.

Turning his attention to the children
He patted each one on the head.
They are healthy but a bit shy, he said.
They'll make fine men and women, he said.

The children looked up at him.
He was still laughing.
He was so confident
They could not find the word for it.
He was so elegant
He was more terrifying than the giants of night.

The world
Could only go on its knees before him.
The kissed woman
Was expected to adore him.

It seemed she did.

I'll eat now, he said,
Nothing elaborate, just something simple and quick –
Rashers, eggs, sausages, tomatoes
And a few nice lightly-buttered slices
Of your very own
Home-made brown
Bread.
O you dear woman, can't you see
My tongue is hanging out
For a pot of your delicious tea.
No other woman in this world
Can cook so well for me.

I'm always touched by your modest mastery!

He sat at table like a king.
He ate between bursts of laughter.
He was a great philosopher,
Wise, able to advise,
Solving the world between mouthfuls.
The woman hovered about him.
The children stared at his vital head.
He had robbed them of every word they had.
Please have some more food, the woman said.
He ate, he laughed, he joked,
He knew the world, his plate was clean
As Jack Spratt's in the funny poem,
He was a handsome wolfman,
More gifted than anyone
The woman and children of that house
Had ever seen or known.

He was the storm they listened to at night
Huddled together in bed
He was what laid the woman low
With the killing pain in her head
He was the threat in the high tide
At the back of the house
He was a huge knock on the door
In a moment of peace
He was a hound's neck leaning
Into the kill
He was a hawk of heaven stooping
To fulfil its will
He was the sentence tired writers of gospel
Prayed God to write
He was a black explosion of starlings
Out of a November tree
He was a plan that worked
In a climate of self-delight
He was all the voices
Of the sea.

My time is up, he said,
I must go now.

Taking his coat, gloves, philosophy, laughter, wit,
He prepared to leave.
He kissed the woman again.
He smiled down on the children.
He walked out of the house.
The children looked at each other.
The woman looked at the chair.
The chair was a throne
Bereft of its king, its visitor.

A Glimpse of Starlings

I expect him any minute now although
He's dead. I know he has been talking
All night to his own dead and now
In the first heart-breaking light of morning
He is struggling into his clothes,
Sipping a cup of tea, fingering a bit of bread,
Eating a small photograph with his eyes.
The questions bang and rattle in his head
Like doors and cannisters the night of a storm.
He doesn't know why his days finished like this
Daylight is as hard to swallow as food
Love is a crumb all of him hungers for.
I can hear the drag of his feet on the concrete path
The close explosion of his smoker's cough
The slow turn of the Yale key in the lock
The door opening to let him in
To what looks like release from what feels like pain
And over his shoulder a glimpse of starlings
Suddenly lifted over field, road and river
Like a fist of black dust pitched in the wind.

Horsechestnuts

Everything in the room was too clean.
The boy watched the old priest nod over his crossword.
The pencil slipped from his grip, rolled on the floor.
Once or twice, the boy felt he was smothering.
All the words flew off into the darkness
Like frightened birds whose wings obscured the stars.
The boy said goodnight to the old man's silence,
Picked his way in blackness between two lines of trees,
Horsechestnuts rising beneath him, crowding about him.
They were coming alive, soon their loneliness would cry out.
He started to kick them though he couldn't see.
He picked them up and threw them at the night.
These were men's hearts he was flinging about
As if the flinging might set them free.
He threw hearts at the darkness till he came
To the gate and the first shocking timid light.

Manager, Perhaps?
FROM *Cromwell*

The first time I met Oliver Cromwell
The poor man was visibly distressed.
'Buffún' says he, 'things are gone to the devil
In England. So I popped over here for a rest.
Say what you will about Ireland, where on
Earth could a harassed statesman find peace like
This in green unperturbed oblivion?
Good Lord! I'm worn out from intrigue and work.
I'd like a little estate down in Kerry,
A spot of salmon-fishing, riding to hounds.
Good Lord! The very thought makes me delighted.
Being a sporting chap, I'd really love to
Get behind one of the best sides in the land.
Manager, perhaps, of Drogheda United?'

Nails

The black van exploded
Fifty yards from the hotel entrance.
Two men, one black-haired, the other red,
Had parked it there as though for a few moments
While they walked around the corner
Not noticing, it seemed, the children
In single file behind their perky leader,
And certainly not seeing the van
Explode into the children's bodies.
Nails, nine inches long, lodged
In chest, ankle, thigh, buttock, shoulder, face.
The quickly-gathered crowd was outraged and shocked.
Some children were whole, others bits and pieces.
These blasted crucifixions are commonplace.

A Running Battle

What are they doing now? I imagine Oliver
Buying a Dodge, setting up as a taxi-driver
Shunting three dozen farmers to Listowel Races.
I see Ed Spenser, father of all our graces
In verse, enshrined as a knife-minded auctioneer
Addicted to Woodbines and Kilkenny beer,
Selling Parish Priests' shiny furniture
To fox-eyed housewives and van-driving tinkers.
William of Orange is polishing pianos
In convents and other delicate territories,
His nose purple from sipping turpentine.
Little island is Big, Big Island is little.
I never knew a love that wasn't a running battle
Most of the time. I'm a friend of these ghosts. They're mine.

Under the Table
FROM *The Book of Judas*

There was a bomb-scare at the Last Supper.
We were tucking into the bread and wine
When the phone rang in an abrasive manner
And someone said in a Cork accent at th'other end of the line

Dat dere was a big hoor of a bomb in de room, boy.
Unpardonable, I thought. Nothing excused it.
Zebedee found the bomb in a bag under the table.
Jesus defused it.

After that opening shock the evening went well.
Peter got sloshed and showed his old
Tendency to pull rank.

I told him, in the vaults of my mind, to go to hell
And brooded on my tentative efforts to open
An account in a Swiss Bank.

The First Time

The first time I kissed The Church
Was at a party in Clonmacnoise.
We were both slightly pissed and lurched
Towards the base of a Celtic Cross
Where the kiss took place. It was a French one,
Sloppy, germful, yet dexterous and long.
'That was refreshing' smiled The Church 'You're a gas man.
Now do sing an Irish song.'

I obliged with The Rose of Tralee,
A harmonious rendering of that difficult air
So frequently murdered by drunken women and men.

'That was beautiful' smiled The Church 'I see
No singer in Ireland who can compare
With you. You're pure music, Judas. Kiss me again.'

Ottó Orbán

LÁSZLÓ CSIGÓ

Selection from: *The Blood of the Walsungs* (1993), translated by George Szirtes and others.

OTTO ORBAN was born in 1936. He had his baptism of fire as a child in Hungary under German rule, and war has been one of his abiding themes. His dizzy, argumentative poems are alive with danger, humanity and his own inimitably grim high-spirits.

Having translated Ginsberg's *Howl*, Orbán was regarded for a while as Hungary's own Beat poet, but he is an extremely versatile writer, and arguably his greatest achievements have been with the prose poem and the 14-line unrhymed (often dactylic) "sonnet", in which he admits his debt to Lowell and Berryman. But Orbán never really sounds like any other poet... ●

A Small Country: 1

I too was duped about poetry being omnipotent...We have no ocean? Let's invent one. The Danube glinted green. Viki listened ecstatically to my latest adolescent poem. I expected the melon rind to float past me as it did for Attila József. But time only vomited flames and the metallic clicking so characteristic of an earlier age. Years later we met again at the Lukacs pool in Budapest. One couldn't detect on her the prison years. She's all right, she said. Got married. They erased her criminal record, at least promised that. We have one life and one death. This means in a small country: *one* pool, *one* authority and *one* projection room where the film profession congregates. And the film on the screen is a study of a family tree where everybody is related to everybody and the concepts ABOVE and BELOW are provisional because an unforeseeable change could come and make everything stand on its head and reveal the fact that there has been no change. In the treadmill meanwhile ample blood splashes – well, we're gathering grapes...A few photos with black borders: souvenirs, epitaphs. We quickly forget them and sunbathe on the rim of a volcano. HOWDY, HOW THE HECK ARE YOU?...THANKS, I'M FINE...Should I have said that there's still time to remedy things?...I stopped reading poems to women. I don't believe that poetry is a care package dropped from a helicopter among those in a bad way. The poem, like a bloodhound, is driven by its instincts after the wounded prey.

But the latter will change form and essence on the run: go ahead, catch the real anguish in the act! You follow the trail of probability's interstellar Mafia, the trail of the Black Hand, who had spun a gas cloud (torn from the sun) as if it were a lottery wheel – this way inside the cloud, a massacre and a tourist path could intersect. It cajoles, with a reasonable image of the future, a passion for gambling.

(translated by Nicholas Kolumban)

A Small Country: 2

A Central European hell. None of Dante's Latin exaggeration; even though some sort of juice bubbles in the basin between the great mountain ranges, it's a geyser, not a tar pool. Instead of demons turning spits, merely a troop of globetrotting tourists gushes from the bus. Yes, some scraping of brakes and teeth. Otherwise the arrangement's first-class. And the view's perfect for a picture postcard, no fooling; cliffs here, undulations there, a plain beyond, and on them always the particular century's props: castle, clay-and-wattle church, TV tower. And people lying atop each other like rocks. Deep drilling's a favourite amusement, to demonstrate which stratum was laid down earliest. Aside from that, the main business is keeping accurate accounts, newborns to be later transferred from the *Income* column to other columns, depending on what turns out to be necessary just then: heroes, victims, et cetera. Note: it's easier for the bookkeepers if each generation's placed, when it comes to the bottom line, under *Loss*. Furthermore, note that the small country's panther doesn't give birth to a mouse; she delivers a panther, which for economy's sake is as small as a mouse. Still, there's no economising on one thing, and, as all visitors agree, the bloodied clouds offer marvellous vistas at sunset. Especially when, staring into the objective of the coin-binoculars, we observe that Caraffa, a Generalissimo of Italian lineage and Grand Marshal of the Imperial Army garrisoned on the high ground, writes a letter on a flying desk made out of a puff of haze ruffled in the Baroque manner, to Baron Jacob Julius Haynau: 'Greetings, dear cuz! I hear you've had them hanged. Wonderful! I myself prefer using tongs...'

(translated by Jascha Kessler)

The Spirit of the Age

I saw a beggar. Recognised him. Knew him instinctively. 'You have
a damned nerve,' I cried and shook his shoulders in cold fury.
'You dare to poke your nose in here! Aren't you the liar who told
us this would be positively the last struggle? Wasn't it you who
promised every poet a redhead or red way ahead – to each accord-
ing to his need?' I stood there for a long time screaming furiously
...eventually he raised his hooded head and I saw he had no eyes.
His hollow sockets were a keyhole opening on to a smooth and
endless plain where fire and smoke mingled, and invisible feet
pounded over a few exposed bones. It might have been cavalry or
fugitives. There was the dreadful constant sound of something
grinding. I couldn't tell whether it was a loose axle or a human cry,
or if it was the earth scratching its bloody surface in the eternal
drought that follows tears of suffering. Then he addressed me in a
flat exhausted voice as if talking down a microphone. 'You think
yourself a seer because you've been disappointed. And in your
infinite wisdom you bawl at me like some cheap whore. You come
back with your dowry, your naive ideas, your bloody revolution!
Bring back God, the family, tradition, and kick me out! But are
we not one person? And isn't your imagination the whole problem?
The wheel of time remains indifferent, you are the squirrel in the
cage rushing round on the wheel which like a lathe turns out the
centuries.' He fell quiet and the wind dispersed him and nothing
remained of him except the cooling ground where he had sat, and
fire and smoke and dust.

(translated by George Szirtes)

Before the Autumn Cull

Why should a bull suffer all these fancy diseases,
when his peasant mind cannot cope with abstractions?
Both heaven and hell for him are merely fields,
one grows fine grass, the other burning thistles...

It makes me laugh when I consider my beliefs,
the great humane ideals, sheer nineteenth-century,
and for all my reservations and parentheses
they are essentially blind, incurable.
I'm of that parting generation whose baptism of fire
bequeathed them epilepsy and a sense of solid values;
The moderns in their screaming nosedive showered us
with cream-puffs that exploded. I tasted them
and have been this way since, standing by the cellar,
light, light, infinite light and a fluttering, the wrecked yard.

(translated by George Szirtes)

A Visit to Room 104

I saw how death pursued its calling in peacetime;
carving fine detail, a vigilant minor craftsman:
one lump on the thighbone, one on the brain, one by the eyes –
he worked in fine temper and whistled a tune down the oxygen tube...
All our lives we prepare for the great Titus Dugovic scene
where we perform a spectacular double-twist dive off the castle
          ramparts
and make an impression on our descendants –
a downbeat ending comes as a surprise...
We're not prepared for the fact that our bodies pack up –
that we find no space in bed for our hands or our legs,
that we spend the whole night on a bed of sharp nails, tossing and
          turning...
mud then or spirit? The choice of the romantic,
of the archer with one eye shut, of the eschatologist –
from death's point of view all things are mud, even the spirit.

(translated by George Szirtes)

The Exploded Treadmill

Should I trust in history, that elusive old harridan?
The past is idiotic and tells lies;
I was sitting by the bedside of my dying friend
smiling encouragement at him: everything's fine...
The present at least is certain. Certain intense schizophrenia –
in childhood I was an old man, now I long to recover
my mad adolescence as an ethical yardstick...
Sooner or later we grasp that our fickle companion for life, our talent
has rented its studio on that plot of land between bull and red rag,
and that patience in real life does not bear roses
but a heap of embers on the frame of a hospital bed...
There's nothing to trust in but my idle improvisations,
up to my neck in the grease, I pimple the world with a verse,
once in God's likeness, now a rattling and clattering old wreck...

(translated by George Szirtes)

The Beauty of War

War's for the conquerors, for Alexander the Great,
the scoutmaster gazing with pleasure on his warriors warming
each other, stuck in life's freezer at that jamboree in Macedon.
They share their last fag, he brags to the Chronicle
though he heartily despises the liberal press
because they create such a stink at each piffling court-martial,
when even a blind man can see that civilisation's at stake...
What's done is done, always look on the bright side!
Alas, the barbed wire has a circular section, all sides are bright;
war is the thing that Pilinszky saw, at the age of twenty-four:
time spinning according to the law of the camera
a frozen frame from an accelerated film of mad alternatives,
a cage that preserves the glow of damnation, the smoke and the heat,
the victims like poultry waiting for slaughter, caught on the wire.

(translated by George Szirtes)

Marin Sorescu

MOIRA CONWAY

Selection from: *Selected Poems* (1983), translated by Michael Hamburger, and *The Biggest Egg in the World* (1987), translated by Ioana Russell-Gebbett with other poets.

MARIN SORESCU was born in 1936 in the village of Bulzesti, in Dolj, Romania, the fifth child of a family of peasants. In Romania he is now so popular that his readings have to be held in football stadiums and his books sell 100,000 copies on publication day.

When Bloodaxe published his *Selected Poems* in 1983, he was tipped in the *Sunday Times* as a future Nobel prizewinner: 'His poems, however, have crowned him with the only distinction that matters. If you don't read any other new book of poetry this year, read this one.' His latest collection, *The Biggest Egg in the World*, is translated by eight leading British and Irish poets, including Ted Hughes and Seamus Heaney. ●

Friends

Come on, let's kill ourselves, I say to my friends.
Today we communicated so well,
we were all so sad,
never again shall we rise to
that point of perfection together;
to hesitate now would be a sin.

In the bath, I believe, it's most tragic,
so let's do it the way the enlightened Romans did it,
opening their veins
while discoursing on the nature of love.
Friends, the water's been heated,
let's begin, I will count: one, two, three...

Not without astonishment I noted in Hell
that I was on my own.
For some it's harder, I told myself,
some have all sorts of ties;
it can't be that they were making a fool of me: a man's word counts
        for something,
but the passage of time...

True enough, Hell wasn't a bed of roses for me,
especially at first, with nobody about
I could really talk to,
but gradually I found company, made friends.

A circle quite extraordinarily close-knit.
We discussed a number of theories,
felt in excellent spirits
and even got as far as suicide.

...And again I found myself alone, in Purgatory.
Looking around, for a kindred soul or two,
and yet, although the occupants of Purgatory,
in their inter-territorial uncertainty,
are very prone to suspicion –
a girl is fond of me, she loves me, she's good-looking,
we have moments of great ecstasy. It's incredible, marvellous!

I'm about to propose...
Knowing better now, I leave it to her,
before taking the plunge.
The girl does what she does, and is alive again –
and I'm alone in Heaven.
Never has anyone got this far,
I am the first, the world exists as a project;
a very vague affair
in the mind of God,
with whom meanwhile I have made friends.

On all levels, it seems, there is sadness.
God is in despair,
I gaze into his empty eyes and lose myself.
He whirls into the chasms of my deaths.
We understand each other splendidly,
my God, I believe it couldn't be better.
It's your turn. Or what do you say
to leaving it all in the dark?

(translated by Michsel Hamburger)

The Thieves

One of my poems kept me awake at night,
so I sent it into the country
to a grandfather.

After that I wrote another
and sent it to my mother
to store in her attic.

I still wrote several more
and with misgivings entrusted them to relations
who promised to keep them with care.

And so forth; for every new poem
there was someone to take it in.
Since each of my friends
in his turn has
a friend he keeps quiet about.

And now even I don't remember
where this and that line might be,
and if I were to fall among thieves
and they tortured me too, the most I could tell them
is that those dubious things
are somewhere in the country
and safe.

Superstition

My cat washes
with her left paw,
there will be another war.

For I have observed
that whenever she washes
with her left paw
international tension grows
considerably.

How can she possibly keep her eye
on all the five continents?
Could it be
that in her pupils
that Pythia now resides
who has the power
to predict
the whole of history
without a full-stop or comma?

It's enough to make me howl
when I think that I
and the Heaven with its souls I have
shouldered
in the last resort
depend
on the whims of a cat.

Go and catch mice,
don't unleash
more world wars,
damned
lazybones!

(translated by Michael Hamburger)

Destiny

The hen I'd bought the night before,
Frozen,
Had come to life,
Had laid the biggest egg in the world
And had been awarded the Nobel Prize.

The phenomenal egg
Was passed from hand to hand,
In a few weeks it had gone round the world,
And round the sun
In 365 days.

The hen had received who knows how much strong currency
Valued in pails of grain
Which she never managed to eat

Because she was invited everywhere,
Gave lectures, granted interviews,
Was photographed.

Often the reporters insisted
That I should be there too
In the photograph
Beside her.

And so, after having served Art
All my life

Suddenly I'm famous
As a poultry-breeder.

(translated by Ted Hughes & Ioana Russell-Gebbett)

The sentence

Each new passenger, on the tramcar,
is a carbon-copy of the one who occupied
the seat before him.

Either we're moving too fast
or the world's too small.

Everyone's neck is chafed
by the newspaper whoever's behind him's reading.
If I turned round right now
I'd be cutting
my own throat.

(translated by Paul Muldoon & Ioana Russell-Gebbett)

Stewart Conn

GLASGOW HERALD

Selection from: *In the Kibble Palace: New & Selected Poems* (1987).

STEWART CONN was born in 1936 in Glasgow, and grew up in Ayrshire. His early poems draw on memories of his farming background, the people looking larger than life in stories of their near heroic deeds – as seen through the child's (or poet's) eye. 'They become figures in a private mythology,' Dannie Abse has written, 'they are figures caught up heroically in elemental violence' (as in the poem *Ferret*).

Edward Morgan describes his main qualities as 'celebration of characters and subtle probing of family relationships. The sense of menacing subterranean forces, in nature or in the mind, is persuasively conveyed.' His most recent collection is *The Luncheon of the Boating Party* (1992). ●

Driving through Sutherland

Here too the crofts were burned
To the ground, families stripped
And driven like cattle to the shore.
You can still hear the cursing,
The women shrieking.

            The duke
And his lady sipped port, had
Wax in their ears. Thatch
Blazed. Thistles were torn up
By the root.

            There are men
In Parliament today who could
Be doing more.

            With these thoughts
In mind we drive from Overscaig
To Lairg, through a night as blue
As steel. Leaving Loch Shin behind
We find facing us an even colder
Firth, and a new moon rising
Delicately over a stubble field.

Ferret

More vicious than stoat or weasel
Because caged, kept hungry, the ferrets
Were let out only for the kill:
An alternative to sulphur and nets.

Once one, badly mauled, hid
Behind a treacle-barrel in the shed.
Throwing me back, Matthew slid
The door shut. From outside

The window, I watched. He stood
Holding an axe, with no gloves.
Then it sprang; and his sleeves
Were drenched in blood

Where the teeth had sunk. I hear
Its high-pitched squeal,
The clamp of its neat steel
Jaws. And I still remember

How the axe flashed, severing
The ferret's head,
And how its body kept battering
The barrels, long after it was dead.

Tremors

We took turns at laying
An ear on the rail –
So that we could tell
By the vibrations

When a train was coming.
Then we'd flatten ourselves
To the banks, scorched
Vetch and hedge-parsley,

While the iron flanks
Rushed past, sending sparks
Flying. It is more and more
A question of living

With an ear to the ground:
The tremors, when they come,
Are that much greater –
For ourselves, and others.

Nor is it any longer
A game, but a matter
Of survival: each explosion
Part of a procession

There can be no stopping.
Though the end is known,
There is nothing for it
But to keep listening.

Visiting Hour

In the pond of our new garden
were five orange stains, under
inches of ice. Weeks since anyone
had been there. Already by far
the most severe winter for years.
You broke the ice with a hammer.
I watched the goldfish appear,
blunt-nosed and delicately clear.

Since then so much has taken place
to distance us from what we were.
That it should come to this.
Unable to hide the horror
in my eyes, I stand helpless
by your bedside and can do no more
than wish it were simply a matter
of smashing the ice and giving you air.

Under the Ice

Like Coleridge, I waltz
on ice. And watch my shadow
on the water below. Knowing that
if the ice were not there
I'd drown. Half willing it.

In my cord jacket
and neat cravat, I keep
returning to the one spot.
How long, to cut
a perfect circle out?

Something in me
rejects the notion.
The arc is never complete.
My figures-of-eight
almost, not quite, meet.

Was Raeburn's skating parson
a man of God, poised
impeccably on the brink;
or his bland stare
no more than a decorous front?

If I could keep my cool
like that. Gazing straight ahead,
not at my feet. Giving
no sign of knowing
how deep the water, how thin the ice.

Behind that, the other
question: whether the real you
pirouettes in space,
or beckons from under the ice
for me to come through.

C.K. Williams

BRUCE DAVIDSON

Selection from: *Flesh and Blood* (1987/1988), *Poems 1963-1983* (1988) and *A Dream of Mind* (1992).

C.K. WILLIAMS was born in 1936 in Newark, New Jersey, and now lives in Paris. He is the most challenging American poet of his generation, a poet of intense and searching originality who makes lyric sense out of the often brutal realities of everyday life. Stanley Kunitz calls him 'a wonderful poet in the authentic American tradition of Whitman and W.C. Williams who tells us on every page what it means to be alive in our time.'

Poems 1963-1983 draws on his first four books. His fifth collection, *Flesh and Blood*, shows him whittling down complex narrative to short, arresting nodes of intense observation, perception and reflection. The poems of his latest book *A Dream of Mind* explore jealousy, psychology, states of consciousness and family relationships. ●

The Mistress

After the drink, after dinner, after the half-hour idiot kids' cartoon special on the TV,
after undressing his daughter, mauling at the miniature buttons on the back of her dress,
the games on the bed – 'Look at my pee-pee,' she says, pulling her thighs wide, 'isn't it pretty?' –
after the bath, pajamas, the song and the kiss and the telling his wife it's her turn now,
out now, at last, out of the house to make the call (out to take a stroll, this evening's lie),
he finds the only public phone booth in the neighborhood's been savaged, receiver torn away,
wires thrust back up the coin slot to its innards, and he stands there, what else? what now?
and notices he's panting, he's panting like an animal, he's breathing like a bloody beast.

The Lover

When she stopped by, just passing, on her way back from picking up
    the kids at school,
taking them to dance, just happened by the business her husband
    owned and her lover worked in,
their glances, hers and the lover's, that is, not the husband's, seemed
    so decorous, so distant,
barely, just barely touching their fiery wings, their clanging she thought
    so well muffled,
that later, in the filthy women's bathroom, in the stall, she was hor-
    rified to hear two typists
coming from the office laughing, about them, all of them, their boss,
    her husband, 'the blind pig,'
one said, and laughed, 'and her, the horny bitch,' the other said, and
    they both laughed again,
'and *him*, did you see *him*, that sanctimonious, lying bastard – I
    thought he was going to *blush*.'

Kin

'You make me sick!' this, with rancor, vehemence, disgust- again,
    'You hear me? *Sick!*'
with rancor, vehemence, disgust again, with rage and bitterness,
    arrogance and fury –
from a little black girl, ten or so, one evening in a convenience
    market, to her sister,
two or three years younger, who's taking much too long picking out
    her candy from the rack.
What next? Nothing next. Next the wretched history of the world.
    The history of the heart.
The theory next that all we are are stories, handed down, that all we
    are are parts of speech.
All that limits and defines us: our ancient natures, love and death
    and terror and original sin.
And the weary breath, the weary going to and fro, the weary always
    knowing what comes next.

Philadelphia: 1978

I'm on my way to the doctor to get the result of chest X-rays because
    I coughed blood
a few weeks ago while we were still in California; I am more or less
    a wreck of anxiety
and just as I turn the corner from Spruce Street onto Sixteenth
    where my doctor's is,
a raggedy-looking guy coming toward me on the sidewalk yells to me
    from fifty feet away:
'I know that walk! I sure know *that* walk!' smiling broadly, with
    genuine good feeling.
Although I don't recognise him – he looks druggy, wasted – I smile
    back, then, as we come closer,
he suddenly seems dubious, asking, 'Don't I know you?' 'Maybe not.'
    'Weren't you in 'Nam?'
and before I can answer, 'Shit!' he spits out, 'shit!' furious with me:
    'You fucking *shit*!'

The Dream

How well I have repressed the dream of death I had after the war
    when I was nine in Newark.
It would be nineteen-forty-six; my older best friend tells me what
    the atom bomb will do,
consume me from within, with fire, and that night, as I sat, bolt
    awake, in agony, it did:
I felt my stomach flare and flame, the edges of my heart curl up and
    char like burning paper.
All there was was waiting for the end, all there was was sadness, for
    in that awful dark,
that roar that never ebbed, that frenzied inward fire, I knew that
    everyone I loved was dead,
I knew that consciousness itself was dead, the universe shucked clean
    of mind as I was of my innards.
All the earth around me heaved and pulsed and sobbed; the orient
    and immortal air was ash.

Bob

If you put in enough hours in bars, sooner or later you get to hear
every imaginable kind of bullshit.
Every long-time loser has a history to convince you he isn't living at
the end of his own leash
and every kid has some pimple on his psyche he's trying to com-
pensate for with an epic,
but the person with the most unlikely line I'd ever heard – he told
me he'd killed, more than a few times,
during the war and then afterwards working for the mob in Philadel-
phia – I could never make up my mind about.
He was big, bigger than big. He'd also been drinking hard and
wanted to be everyone's friend
and until the bartender called the cops because he wouldn't stop
stuffing money in girls' blouses,
he gave me his life: the farm childhood, the army, re-upping, the
war – that killing –
coming back and the new job – that killing – then almost being
killed himself by another hood and a kind of pension,
a distributorship, incredibly enough, for hairdresser supplies in the
ward around Passyunk and Mifflin.
He left before the cops came, and before he left he shook my hand
and looked into my eyes.
It's impossible to tell how much that glance weighed: it was like
having to lift something,
something so ponderous and unwieldy that you wanted to call for
someone to help you
and when he finally turned away, it wouldn't have bothered me at
all if I'd never seen him again.

This is going to get a little nutty now, maybe because everything was
a little nutty for me back then.
Not a little. I'd been doing some nice refining. No work, no woman,
hardly any friends left.
The details don't matter. I was helpless, self-pitying, angry, inert,
and right now
I was flying to Detroit to interview for a job I knew I wouldn't get.
Outside,
the clouds were packed against our windows and just as I let my
book drop to look out,

we broke through into a sky so brilliant that I had to close my eyes
        against the glare.
I stayed like that, waiting for the stinging after-light to fade, but it
        seemed to pulse instead,
then suddenly it washed strangely through me, swelling, powdering,
and when my sight came back, I was facing inwards, into the very
        center of myself,
a dark, craggy place, and there was a sound that when I blocked the
        jets,
the hiss of the pressurisation valves and the rattling silverware and
        glasses, I realised was laughter.
The way I was then, I think nothing could have shocked me. I was
        a well, I'd fallen in,
someone was there with me, but all I did was drift until I came to
        him: a figure, arms lifted,
he was moving in a great, cumbersome dance, full of patience, full
        of time, and that laughter,
a deep, flowing tumult of what seemed to be songs from someone
        else's life.
Now the strange part. My ears were ringing, my body felt like water,
        but I moved again,
farther in, until I saw the face of who it was with me and it was Bob,
        the drunk,
or if it wasn't him, his image filled the space, the blank, the template,
        better than anyone else,
and so, however doubtful it seems now, I let it be him: he was there,
        I let him stay.
Understand, this happened quickly. By that night, home again, I was
        broken again,
torn, crushed on the empty halves of my bed, but for that time, from
        Pittsburgh, say,
until we braked down to the terminal in Detroit, I smiled at that self
        in myself,
his heavy dance, his laughter winding through the wrack and detritus
        of what I thought I was.

Bob, I don't know what happened to. He probably still makes the
        circuits of the clubs and corner bars,
and there must be times when strangers listen and he can tell it, the
        truth or his nightmare of it.
'I killed people,' the secret heart opening again, 'and Jesus God, I
        didn't even know them.'

The Idyll

*I just don't want to feel put down; if she decides she wants to sleep with
  someone, listen,*
*great, go ahead, but I want to know about it and I want the other guy
  to know I know;*
*I don't want some mother sliming in her sack, using her and thinking he's
  one up me.*

She's always touching men, she sort of leans *at them, she has to have
  them* notice *her,*
want to grab *her: it's like she's always telling me she's on the lookout
  for some stud,*
*some gigantic sex-machine who's going to get it on with her a hundred
  times an hour.*

*Once it really happened: she looked me in the eye and said 'I balled
  someone else last night.'*
Christ, I felt these ridges *going up and down my jaw, I thought my teeth
  were going to break.*
*What'd I do? I took her home, we made out like maniacs. What else was
  I supposed to do?*

Sometimes I wonder if I need *it. I mean, she'll be coming onto somebody,
  as usual,*
*I'll want to crack her head for her, but if I think about it, I might get
  a buzz from it,*
*it must be what going into battle's like: sometimes I think going nuts from
  her is my religion.*

*I don't know if she fools around much now; I guess I'm not a whole lot
  into other women either.*
*The last time I was with another chick – she was a little knockout, too
  – I wasn't hardly there.*
I realised who I want to be with was her. *I turned off. Hell, is that how
  you get* faithful.

Sylvia Kantaris

SYLVIA KANTARIS was born in 1936 in Derby-shire, lived in Australia for some years, and now lives in Cornwall. She has published three books with Bloodaxe: *The Air Mines of Mistila*, an extraordinary fable written with Philip Gross, a Poetry Book Society Choice in 1988; *Dirty Washing: New & Selected Poems* (1989), which draws on four other collections; and *Lad's Love* (1993), a book-length sequence tracing the stormy course of a relationship between a middle-aged woman and her young lover (from which the last two poems here are taken).

Selection from: *Dirty Washing* (1989) and *Lad's Love* (1993).

'Kantaris writes clearly, frankly, movingly and humorously about a wide variety of human relationships' – Peter Reading. ●

Watercolours, Cornwall

You grow dependent on the weather's moods,
living by courtesy of wind and water
between constraining seas, although sometimes,
in summer, it seems you could slide out easily
across the line where the light blue thickens,
like a colour-wash, before you're beaten back
to shelter by squalls of rain spreading a grey
stain inland. In such weather the peninsula
holds you in small focus. It is a place
for mannikins – their salty, patchwork fields,
their bent shrubs and squat houses huddled away
from the sea's edge, although some stragglers stick
it out too long on sand-cliffs which crumble bit
by bit, under assault, and leave them hanging,
flimsy in the wind like empty matchboxes
until, another day, there's no trace left –
as when a painter thinks maybe he'd rather
not have any hint of humans even half-
way in the picture, and moves the sea up
by an inch or two, to wipe them off.

Windy Monday

FROM *Dirty Washing*

The wind billows like a stuffed shirt this washday.
I spin the man and peg him on my line to bloat and puff out
with the full authority of wind, like bladderwrack.

It is a pumped-up Dunlopillo president of no parts,
portly with nothingness, his flap a clackety-clack
of digits at the laundromat. O windy diplomat,

keeping up your sleeve an aftershave of sundry secrets
like a Company Director of the Stock Exchange,
your pockets stuffed with wads of air like multiple zeros.

Magnate of the wrangled fleet of sheets and honourable
Fellow of the Faithful Flock of Pillowslips,
you lord it in full sail of pomp and circumstance.

Our man of wind is tested by the whiteness test
of God's own cleanliness and rinsed in *Comfort* –
full-blown representative of earthly windbags.

In consequence whereof (and so forth) drizzle is undiplomatic.
It winds him. Now he sags and blusters, breathless.
I am not sad to see him shrink like that,

cuddling his own flatness in his flattened arms, like flatness,
or a little flag of little consequence,
soggy with such sadness like a dishrag.

I'll leave him there all night to hang and ghost it
in the moonlight and get bleached (whiter than white).
Why should I let a Man of Consequence drip dry like cuckoo-spit
            on my hearth?

Jane Fonda, your mother, and me

It wasn't out of fear of your mother
that I wouldn't meet her. On my own I'd dare,
since she said over the phone she didn't care
about my age, just wanted you out of *her* hair.
It was the memory of the jeans I used to wear
before they shrank on me that was the matter.
You said you'd have them but had given them to her
I noticed when I saw them on the chair
by her bed that afternoon when we lay there
(nothing Freudian, you said, just comfier)
and I cast your mother in the image of Jane Fonda.
So since I couldn't equal *her* now, either –
same vintage as myself but shapelier, leaner –
how could I let you see all three together?

'Domestic'

'We see dozens of domestics every week,'
one of the cops said, reassuringly.
Seems I was lucky that I hadn't snuffed it
totally – just throttled and my head and face bashed up.
Oh, we were growing more domestic by the minute
since grants and housing-benefit were cut
and my lover had nowhere else but here to live
so he said I had to die 'because of poll tax'.

'Is this man your son?' they'd asked.
Final irony. Pity I couldn't laugh.
He used to joke: 'If anybody ever asks you that,
say I'm your dad.' I saw him out in handcuffs.
If it's true that each man kills the thing he loves
it was himself he really meant to finish off.

Matt Simpson

SHIRLEY BAKER

Selection from: *An Elegy for the Galosherman: New & Selected Poems* (1990).

MATT SIMPSON was born in 1936 in Bootle, and in many of his poems looks back at his upbringing there, at family tensions in a close-knit Merseyside comunity with strong seafaring traditions.

'What Simpson gives us is something entirely his own, a unified dockland reverie that interweaves family history, an elliptical narrative of childhood and adolescence in a sharply realised place and time, war, street wisdoms and the trades of the sea. It's done by anecdote, by portrait, by quizzical meditation…and more than anything else, by elegy' – Kit Wright. 'A special individual voice speaking from an interesting place…a good hardness coming out of family values and physical working objects…a real special poet' – W.S. Graham. ●

My Grandmother's African Grey

My father's brother brought it home,
madcap Cliff, a 'case', with wit as wild
as erotic dreams. It was his proof
of Africa and emblem of the family pride
in seamanship.
                    But the parrot quickly sensed
our pride was ragged. Perverse, it
nipped its feathers out
with tar-black pincering beak, until,
baring a stubbly breast, it looked
like poultry obscenely undead.

A gift to grandma and to Auntie Bell
who lived together, two odd shoes
inside a wardrobe of a house, it learnt
to parody my grandma's Liverpudlian
wash-house talk, her lovely common-
as-muck, which it counterpointed faithfully
with Auntie Bell's posh how-d'you-do's
that froze you to politeness:
Sunday Best, with little finger cocked.

The bird survived them both, lost all sense
of Africa, one quarter of a century on a perch.
Shabby slate-grey feathers came to mean
my grandmother; its tail's red splash
was Auntie Bell – their stout and brandy accents
jangling on inside the cage.

Homecoming

Due on the tide, my father's rusted hulk,
weary from landings at Sicily, sailed
into blitzed Liverpool under the waving swords
of searchlights, into the flash and batter of
the ack-ack guns. Under a sky in panic,
into the erupting port, up-river he came
urging home his helpless and unspeaking love.

Next morning, docked, he slung his canvas bag
about his shoulders like a drunken mate, himself
unsteady in the smoking, settling air, and walked
into our street, turning the corner by
the foundry. The street was flattened – brick and wood
in scorched disorder. 'I thought that you were goners,'
he afterwards said, finding us safe up-town
at my grandma's house.

And I remember the last few days,
the quivering run-up hours to that street's death:
a five-year-old and his mother hunched
under the stairs, with the fat chrome springs
of an obsolete pram jigging over my head
and plaster puffing white dust in our hair,
the sky droning and tingling blasts
as a neighbouring street went down.

'We moved that day,' my mother used to say,
'and that same night your dad came home.'
She prized the weird coincidence. It was
as if someone had given her flowers.

The Ghost of My Mother

What of her history when all the traces
are of him: his hair bunched in the nose,
the excremental wax that clogs my ears,
a moody sea at work in the veins?
Her death alone was memorable,
a blood-burst in the mouth.
She was his victim – much as I
still carting round his blustering ghost
that beat her down. What of her
when I revamp his tantrums
and sudden shamefaced tenderness
that buys back love with promises,
embittered dreams of something good?
Ghosts are rarely charitable.
And now she nudges me,
with frightened, loving eyes.

Dead Ringer

I've tried, dad, talking you round,
needing your thumbs up. But now
I'm past it and, in any case,
you've been dead too long. It's just
that sometimes at the mirror you
stare through me with something
quizzical that I've no answer to.

Easy for you, you joked your way
out of almost everything. That night
I'm in the bath and you burst in:
'Swap,' you said, 'a tanner and
my owld one for that?'

Still can't get over your lying there
that way. A breathless mirror,
your gawping and unfunny mouth.

Tony Harrison

MOIRA CONWAY

Selection from: *The Gaze of the Gorgon* (1992).

TONY HARRISON was born in 1937 in Leeds. He is the most important poet writing in Britain today, as well as Britain's leading theatre and film poet – writing for the BBC, Channel Four and the National Theatre. His *Selected Poems* is published by Penguin, and he has published several books with Bloodaxe, including his latest collection *The Gaze of the Gorgon* (1992), winner of the Whitbread Poetry Award. Bloodaxe publishes a critical anthology on his work, *Tony Harrison*, edited by Neil Astley (1991).

In much of his recent work, he confronts the unspeakable terrors of the 20th century, forging his own response to these dark times through the element of fire, seeking – in the source of terror itself – the heart of eloquence and celebratory love. ●

A Cold Coming

'A cold coming we had of it.'
T.S. ELIOT
Journey of the Magi

I saw the charred Iraqi lean
towards me from bomb-blasted screen,

his windscreen wiper like a pen
ready to write down thoughts for men,

his windscreen wiper like a quill
he's reaching for to make his will.

I saw the charred Iraqi lean
like someone made of Plasticine

as though he'd stopped to ask the way
and this is what I heard him say:

'Don't be afraid I've picked on you
for this exclusive interview.

Isn't it your sort of poet's task
to find words for this frightening mask?

If that gadget that you've got records
words from such scorched vocal chords,

press RECORD before some dog
devours me mid-monologue.'

So I held the shaking microphone
closer to the crumbling bone:

'I read the news of three wise men
who left their sperm in nitrogen,

three foes of ours, three wise Marines
with sample flasks and magazines,

three wise soldiers from Seattle
who banked their sperm before the battle.

Did No. 1 say: God be thanked
I've got my precious semen banked.

And No. 2: O praise the Lord
my last best shot is safely stored.

And No. 3: Praise be to God
I left my wife my frozen wad?

So if their fate was to be gassed
at least they thought their name would last,

and though cold corpses in Kuwait
they could by proxy procreate.

Excuse a skull half roast, half bone
for using such a scornful tone.

It may seem out of all proportion
but I wish I'd taken their precaution.

They seemed the masters of their fate
with wisely jarred ejaculate.

Was it a propaganda coup
to make us think they'd cracked death too,

disinformation to defeat us
with no post-mortem millilitres?

Symbolic billions in reserve
made me, for one, lose heart and nerve.

On Saddam's pay we can't afford
to go and get our semen stored.

Sad to say that such high tech's
uncommon here. We're stuck with sex.

If you can conjure up and stretch
your imagination (and not retch)

the image of me beside my wife
closely clasped creating life...

(I let the unfleshed skull unfold
a story I'd been already told,

and idly tried to calculate
the content of ejaculate:

the sperm in one ejaculation
equals the whole Iraqi nation

times, roughly, let's say, 12.5
though that .5's not now alive.

Let's say the sperms were an amount
so many times the body count,

2,500 times at least
(but let's wait till the toll's released!).

Whichever way Death seems outflanked
by one tube of cold bloblings banked.

Poor bloblings, maybe you've been blessed
with, of all fates possible, the best

according to Sophocles i.e.
'the best of fates is not to be'

a philosophy that's maybe bleak
for any but an ancient Greek

but difficult these days to escape
when spoken to by such a shape.

When you see men brought to such states
who wouldn't want that 'best of fates'

or in the world of Cruise and Scud
not go kryonic if he could,

spared the normal human doom
of having made it through the womb?)

He heard my thoughts and stopped the spool:
'I never thought life futile, fool!

Though all Hell began to drop
I never wanted life to stop.

I was filled with such a yearning
to stay in life as I was burning,

such a longing to be beside
my wife in bed before I died,

and, most, to have engendered there
a child untouched by war's despair.

So press RECORD! I want to reach
the warring nations with my speech.

Don't look away! I know it's hard
to keep regarding one so charred,

so disfigured by unfriendly fire
and think it once burned with desire.

Though fire has flayed off half my features
they once were like my fellow creatures',

till some screen-gazing crop-haired boy
from Iowa or Illinois,

equipped by ingenious technophile
put paid to my paternal smile

and made the face you see today
an armature half-patched with clay,

an icon framed, a looking glass
for devotees of "kicking ass",

a mirror that returns the gaze
of victors on their victory days

and in the end stares out the watcher
who ducks behind his headline: GOTCHA!

or behind the flag-bedecked page 1
of the true to bold-type-setting SUN!

I doubt victorious Greeks let Hector
join their feast as spoiling spectre,

and who'd want to sour the children's joy
in Iowa or Illinois

or ageing mothers overjoyed
to find their babies weren't destroyed?

But cabs beflagged with SUN front pages
don't help peace in future ages.

Stars and Stripes in sticky paws
may sow the seeds for future wars.

Each Union Jack the kids now wave
may lead them later to the grave.

But praise the Lord and raise the banner
(excuse a skull's sarcastic manner!)

Desert Rat and Desert Stormer
without scars and (maybe) trauma,

the semen-bankers are all back
to sire their children in their sack.

With seed sown straight from the sower
dump second-hand spermatozoa!

Lie that you saw me and I smiled
to see the soldier hug his child.

Lie and pretend that I excuse
my bombing by B52s,

pretend I pardon and forgive
that they still do and I don't live,

pretend they have the burnt man's blessing
and then, maybe, I'm spared confessing

that only fire burnt out the shame
of things I'd done in Saddam's name,

the deaths, the torture and the plunder
the black clouds all of us are under.

Say that I'm smiling and excuse
the Scuds we launched against the Jews.

Pretend I've got the imagination
to see the world beyond one nation.

That's your job, poet, to pretend
I want my foe to be my friend.

It's easier to find such words
for this dumb mask like baked dogturds.

So lie and say the charred man smiled
to see the soldier hug his child.

This gaping rictus once made glad
a few old hearts back in Baghdad,

hearts growing older by the minute
as each truck comes without me in it.

I've met you though, and had my say
which you've got taped. Now go away.'

I gazed at him and he gazed back
staring right through me to Iraq.

Facing the way the charred man faced
I saw the frozen phial of waste,

a test-tube frozen in the dark,
crib and Kaaba, sacred Ark,

a pilgrimage of Cross and Crescent
the chilled suspension of the Present.

Rainbows seven shades of black
curved from Kuwait back to Iraq,

and instead of gold the frozen crock's
crammed with Mankind on the rocks,

the congealed geni who won't thaw
until the World renounces War,

cold spunk meticulously jarred
never to be charrer or the charred,

a bottled Bethlehem of this come-
curdling Cruise/Scud-cursed millenium.

I went. I pressed REWIND and PLAY
and I heard the charred man say:

Josef Hanzlík

J. NIKODYM

Selection from: *Selected Poems* (1993), translated by Ewald Osers and Jarmila & Ian Milner.

JOSEF HANZLÍK was born in 1938. He is one of the leading middle-generation Czech poets. However veiled, the driving force of his poetry has always been an obsession with political violence. After 1968, the savagery of his language and imagery became internalised; forced to write less aggressively, he was able to achieve greater philosophical depth in his poetry.

'Hanzlík's poetry, more particularly his early poetry, is characterised by controlled savagery, by a smouldering anger, though balanced and held in check by a note of lyricism and often indeed of tenderness… Hanzlík's unmistakable individual voice, bruising though it may be, is refreshingly new' – Ewald Osers. ●

Variation XVII
(Abductions)

Wolves carry off affectionate children
the river the clay of the dead
fire a letter with a lock of hair

The stone runs with a broken bone
Teeth carry off deceived intestines
The dog hides out with a severed glass eye

The belly carries off the gums and a foot
glass grips grazed skin
raw liver makes off with mildew

The whitewash hides a purloined sleep
The brine has trapped two spiders and some plumage
grass conceals tetanus

Puss mixes with Cinnamon
oil reaches out for oats
the whip carries the window-frames away

Concrete swallows urine
the handkerchief bites the lung
typhoid carries off armpit hair

The bed denies the nail-marks on the neck
crying carries off nocturnal gloves and sorrow
the wardrobe has slammed shut on sister's shirt

The morning rips the tongues out of love's shoes
The wind from the slaughter-house snaps the umbrella's ribs
The violin carries the rope away and with it everything else

[EO]

Vengeance

The night bird beats against the bolted door
Unless you've smeared the handle with the blood
of a sacrificed lamb
he will smash the first-born's head against the door-post

But woe unto you if you are marked with blood
having sacrificed your neighbour
in the insolent error
that he is less than you

for then the night bird
will reward your house
with the mark of his friendship

and there will be no grief but you will taste it
there'll be no death
but you will die it

[EO]

The Postilion

In a ringing frosty night the postilion arrives in a blue and white
     piped coat and a tricorn hat rich with tassels

And the postilion blows his horn and the eight pairs of horses which
     draw his fabulous sleigh ring with silver

And the postilion comes to the villages where live the Anxious and
     the Fearful and those Waiting for Grace and at each sound of his
     horn and each note of his silver bell the Anxious and the Fear-
     ful and those Waiting for Grace run out into the street for the
     postilion is bringing them Grace

And the postilion places Grace into their outstretched hands and as
     soon as an outstretched hand catches hold of Grace the postilion
     cuts it off with an axe right up to the shoulder and flings it into
     his sleigh

And thus he distributes Grace and thereafter cuts off the hands
     clutching Grace – the hands of the Anxious and the Fearful and
     those Waiting for Grace down to the last man in the village for
     he too believes that for him an exception will be made

And only in the forest behind the village does the postilion sling out
     all those severed arms from his sleigh removing from them those
     decorative wrappers with the unmarked paper so that provided
     they are not too badly blood-stained he can use them for others

[EO]

In the Heavenly Darkness over the Town X

It is 20 hours Central European Time
Above the town an empty leaden sky
in the first third of October
Night is descending on the streets
the night of lovers stray cats and hotel bars

or murderers and police patrols
In the streets of the town
eyes blinded by neon
and the glitter of shop windows
cannot see as far as the starless October sky
they don't perceive the little red coral
winking solitarily like blood
intravenously trickling drop by drop and hastening
to prolong someone's unique event

The little coral is urgently winking
Its flashes tread on the darkness
like children's bare feet tip-toeing
The aircraft is on a scheduled flight
and the air hostess announces in broken English:
'We're overflying the town X'

Ah yes in the town's streets
in corners in the parks in back seats of cars
in borrowed bachelor flats
and under the arches of the bridges
lovers are writing the Stories of Countless Nights
murderers are testing their razors on a hair
and junkies with ampules and powders
crawl out of their holes

Ah yes in the aircraft
which hums softly like a summer meadow
people with a glass of Ballantine coffee and a cigarette
are watching the town below them
those clumps and cascades of light
exploding shining spreading like a bursting supernova
in the Great Magellan Nebula

Ah yes
in the soft town streets
and in the airliner's seats
a lover of unquiet turns on a tape recorder
and a Belgian girl with a Dürer wig
sings like an angel with a childish voice
'Mama can I have that big elephant
over there?'

But of course darling
you can have that big elephant
you can have anything
so long as I am
so long as you are

So long as the lights of town X are there

And while the hostess's public address system
effortlessly crosses the state frontier
the passengers still see the lights of town X
they have not gone out they have not vanished into the irretrievable
the outskirts of town X have passed on the baton
to the outskirts of another town X
the haloes of their lights are gently touching
light holding light
as people hold hands

in this Europe overcrowded with neighbours
like a summer beach
upon this beautiful inhabited Earth

whose nights do not belong to murderers
but to lovers
and dreams

[EO]

Ken Smith

MOIRA CONWAY

Selection from: *The Poet Reclining: Selected Poems 1962-1980* (1982), *Terra* (1986), *Wormwood* (1987) and *Tender to the Queen of Spain* (1993).

KEN SMITH was born in 1938 in Rudston, the son of an itinerant farm labourer. He grew up in rural Yorkshire (page 158), was uprooted to Hull (155-6), and spent some years in America. He now lives in London, the setting of his major long poem *Fox Running* and much of *Terra* and *Wormwood* (see pages 160-62). He was writer-in-residence for two years at Wormwood Scrubs prison. As well as poetry, he has published *Inside Time* and *Berlin: Coming in from the Cold*.

His Selected Poems *The Poet Reclining* includes *Fox Running* and *Tristan Crazy* (the first book published by Bloodaxe). His other Bloodaxe titles are *Burned Books* (1981), his collected prose, *A Book of Chinese Whispers* (1987), *The heart, the border* (1990) and *Tender to the Queen of Spain* (1993). ●

Family Group

He also was a stormy day: a squat mountain man
smelling of sheep and the high pasture, stumping
through pinewoods, hunched and small, feeling
the weather on him. Work angled him.
Fingers were crooked with frost, stiffened.

Ploughing he would fix his eye on the hawthorn,
walking firm-booted, concerned for the furrow.
Horse and man in motion together, deliberate,
one foot put before the other, treading cut clay.
He would not see the bird perched on the plough.
He would not chase the plover limping over stubble.

He was my father who brought in wood and lit
the hissing lamp. And he would sit, quiet
as moor before the fire. She drew him
slowly out of silence. She had a coat
made from a blanket and wore boys' shoes.
She was small and had red hands, firm-boned,
and her hair was greying. The house was stone
and slate. It was her house, his home,
and their family, and they quarrelled often.

She churned butter, baked, and scrubbed floors,
and for forty years he laboured the raw earth
and rough weather. In winter we made mats
from rags with pegs. We guarded ourselves
and were close. We were poor and poorer banking
each pound saved. Each year passed slowly.

Now he lives in the glass world of his shop,
and time is grudged. Ham and tinned meat
and vegetables are his breathing day.
He works harder and is unhappy. She too
stoops through the labouring year, is greyer
and grumbles. Nothing gets made any more
but money that cannot be made. Nothing
means happiness. The light comes down wires,
water through tubes. All is expensive, paid.

Silence is gone from their lives, the city
has taken that poised energy. Violence
is articulate. The deliberate motion is gone
and he moves with pain through time that is work
that is cash. He will not notice the crashed
gull fallen in the storm, the grabbing sparrows.
She cannot ease him into speech, or be content
before the broody fire. She is in fashion now.
But seasons pass them without touching.
They will not feel the winter when it comes.

Eli's poem

I met a woman from the sea coast,
she took me aside in the bushes
and wrapped me around and said *we are alone
as the moon up there is with just two sides.*
I did what was to be done and came away with her.

Now I am with a crazy woman
who hurts herself with ashes and briars
running in the scrub. She takes blankets
and stuffs them under her skirt for a child.
She takes out the blanket and croons on it,
washes it, beats it with sticks till it cries
and tears it to pieces. Her lament
goes down the street on cut feet in the gravel.
She runs in a nightgown thinking she's the police
and charges anyone with ridiculous crimes
like wearing a hat sideways and walking wrong.
The people here know her and smile and say
yes they will come to the court to answer.
She writes everything down in her book.
In bed she's like trying to catch a hare.
She wants to sleep with me all night
till my back breaks, if I doze off
she wakes me crying for love.
I married a crazy woman for her brown hair.
At first I thought she was pregnant
but her blood runs, the doctor shakes his head at me.
I tell her your child is in the other country
and will not come here because of your frenzy.
She runs to the church crying she's evil,
the priest holds out his god's battered arms
and says *come child everyone's evil.*
I cool her with my breath, I cool her with water.
She's insatiable as the river, like winds
she has no place to go and runs
from whatever does not move. She's holding a wooden knife
and staring it down till it becomes pure menace
and I fear it myself. I sleep with her
because then I control her and know where she is,
but I don't know what runs in her.
Now she is out on the hill wailing
cutting her flesh on the stiff grass
where I go to her lamenting.

Being the third song of Urias

Lives ago, years past generations
perhaps nowhere I dreamed it:
the foggy ploughland of wind
and hoofprints, my father
off in the mist topping beets.

Where I was eight, I knew nothing,
the world on a cold winter light
on half a dozen fields, then
all the winking blether of stars.

Before like a fool I began
explaining the key in its lost locked box
adding words to the words to the sum
that never works out.

                Where I was
distracted again by the lapwing,
the damp morning air of my father's
gregarious plainchant cursing
all that his masters deserved
and had paid for.
                Sure I was
then for the world's mere being
in the white rime on weeds
among the wet hawthorn berries
at the field's edge darkened by frost,
and none of these damned words to say it.

I began trailing out there in voices,
friends, women, my children,
my father's tetherless anger, some
like him who are dead who are
part of the rain now.

From Tristan Crazy
Four, being a prayer to the western wind

Without you:
the moon's failed waters,
lost wheats of the Sahara.

A woman hides in these syllables.
She goes singing and dancing
through fields of tall yellow to the sea.

But the pastures are an old grit in my teeth,
the eastern forests an ash and smoke.

I pick among shrubs
for one leaf of you. On the sea
or high in the treeless upland
where I almost hear you
the wind whines to itself
be thou with me love
the corn in its chaff, or where
have I heard it?

Ships, ports, wharves, men
leaning on the cathedral stones,
I've been everywhere talking to everyone,
no one has seen you. In the snowy north,
in Germany and on the Atlantic
amongst men who are gulls' feasts
and the dreams of carrion it's your face
I fail to find in mirrors and water.

Asleep I see you
walking as once you were by the river,
but awake sleep has kept you,
I'm miles away where I barely think
how your sounds are, and must come
round the world's other side
finding again the same strangeness
opens your face in the gates of the city,
the wanderer home in his bed again.

Let us consider the chicken

Lately I've been thinking about the chickens,
clucking their peevish lives out in the long batteries,
where the lights shorten the days, nothing changes,
it's hell on earth and every one in here is loo-loo.

Even in a yard they fret, always at the edge,
suspicious, laying the great egg, staring, watching,
wary for the cockbird or pecking at their dinners
or asleep dreaming worms, slugs, fat maggots.

And then they die, all of them without names,
numbers, without biographies, votes, pension rights,
their throats routinely cut, stripped, chopped up,
cooked in a pot with onions and peppers and devoured.

Chuck. Chuck. The Hungarians, who got them
from the Bulgarians, they say *tyuk. Tyuk tyuk tyuk.*
Comrades, clearly this is not in the chickens' interest.
Our feathered friends are manifestly at a disadvantage.

And no one protests, no one gives a gipsy's gob
for all their aspirations, dreams, their brief itchy lives
scratching and complaining, part of the food chain.

   Save the chicken. Save the chicken.

After Mr Mayhew's visit

So now the Victorians are all in heaven,
Miss Routledge and the young conservatives
chatting with the vicar, visiting again
the home for incurables who never die.

The old damp soaks through the wallpaper,
there's servant trouble, the cook
fighting drunk at the sherry, and Edith
coughing and consumptive, fainting away.

Only this time it never ends: the master
continually remarking how the weather bites cold,
the brandy flask stands empty, and the poor
are pushing to the windows like the fog.

Encounter at St Martin's

I tell a wanderer's tale, the same
I began long ago, a boy in a barn,
I am always lost in it. The place
is always strange to me. In my pocket

the wrong money or none, the wrong paper,
maps of another town, the phrase book
for yesterday's language, just a ticket
to the next station, and my instructions.

In the lobby of the Banco Bilbao
a dark woman will slip me a key, a package,
the name of a hotel, a numbered account,
the first letters of an unknown alphabet.

The Botanic Garden Oath

Each of us, with a tale to tell,
each one starring in the scenario called *me*,
sad for all the little of our lives
and all the short days of our loving.

But today I leave that out and take a train.
I've joined the Rupert Bear School of Poetry
and I'll not say anything controversial.
Here there's peace, the traffic tuned to a blur

and only the flightpath of the great planes
to disturb this fuchsia magellanica.
Especially I love the tropical conservatories,
their great ferns and the hot air full as sex.

From As It Happens

the remembered city

Camberwell Clerkenwell Muswell a haze,
glassy steel etched on tile was the city,
its traffic clear over to Canning Town
where I don't want to go as it happens
by wheel or by water. Wind blows there
through the towers, the spraycan sneers
this is white man's land and the shadow
on scrapyards is soon rain, it's forever
the mean meridian of Greenwich, coming in
off the flyover to Rathbone and Silvertown:
all the lost boys hunched on their knives –
the Posse, the Firm, the Little Silver Snipers

in the flats, flat voices

betwixt traffic and trains, boats on the tide,
dog grunts and the midnight rain between blocks –
upright streets as it happens, the lift shrieks
at the seventeenth floor in the airshaft
the wind hunts ruins to howl through,
the doors open on blue video voices.

You hear glass split, long clatter of heels
on the stairwell, a man's shout and a slam
all the way to the street where a car
coughs like a baby.
                            Later you hear
through the breezeblock *it's not her
car as it happens, it's not his baby.*

Frances Horovitz

MIKE GOLDING

Selection from: *Collected Poems* (1985), edited by Roger Garfitt.

FRANCES HOROVITZ was born in 1938 in London. Many of her poems were inspired by the remote Cotswold valley where she lived for ten years; others by the border country of Cumbria and the Welsh Marches. The first five poems here, from *Snow Light, Water Light* (1983), came out of two winters spent in a farmhouse on Hadrian's Wall – near the Roman fort of Birdoswald, and Camboglanna (or the Crooked Glen), reputed site of Arthur's last battle. She died in 1983, after a long illness. *Evening* was one of the last poems she wrote.

'She has perfect rhythm, great delicacy and a rather Chinese yet very locally British sense of landscape...her poetry does seem to me to approach greatness' – Peter Levi. ●

Rain – Birdoswald

I stand under a leafless tree
more still, in this mouse-pattering
        thrum of rain,
than cattle shifting in the field.
        It is more dark than light.
A Chinese painter's brush of deepening grey
        moves in a subtle tide.

        The beasts are darker islands now.
Wet-stained and silvered by the rain
        they suffer night,
marooned as still as stone or tree.
        We sense each other's quiet.

        Almost, death could come
inevitable, unstrange
        as is this dusk and rain,
and I should be no more
        myself, than raindrops
glimmering in last light
        on black ash buds

or night beasts in a winter field.

January

A sealed stillness
– only the stream moves,
tremor and furl of water
under dead leaves.

In silence
the wood declares itself:
angles and arabesques of darkness,
branch, bramble,
tussocks of ghost grass
– under my heel
ice shivers
frail blue as sky
between the runes of trees.

Far up
rooks, crows
flail home.

The Crooked Glen

I saw nothing but waves and winds

…the moon resting in a broken apple tree
an ushering wind shake ash and alder
by the puckered river.
Lightly, like boats, the thin leaves rock and spin.

Blood-dark berries stir; above my head the thorn trees lean.
In their black pools the moon fragments herself.

Ghost dry the unquiet reeds…

I saw nothing but the waters wap
and waves wan

For Stephen Procter

on seeing his exhibition of forms in glass

Perfected whiteness
– a stellar littoral, bright
beyond bone or pearl.

Spiral chambers sing of
sea's breath, the curve
and fall of flowers.

Cave within a cave
of quiet, thought becomes music;
litanies of light resolve

in gathering trance.
A whorl of shadow
trembles, brims.

Oh wave and silence,
breaking still
in shining arcs of air.

Sightings

Flake on flake, snow
packed light as ash
                or feather,
shavings of crystal.
By moonlight
stars pulse underfoot.

The burning fox ran here,
his narrow print
        under gate
                and over wall
diagonal across the field;
        skeining of rabbit tracks,
our own slurred trail.

Like black stones
crows squat, sunning
        among staring sheep
– crow's wing
        brushed on snow,
three strokes
        twice etched
as faint and fine
        as fossil bone.

Evening

            Lilac blossom crests the window sill
mingling whiteness with the good dark of this room.
A bloom of light hangs delicately in white painted angles.
Bluebells heaped in a pot
still hold their blue against the dark;
I see their green stalks glisten.

            Thin as a swan's bone
I wait for the lessons of pain and light.
Grief is a burden, useless.
It must dissolve into the dark.
I see the hills, luminous.
There will be the holly tree
the hawthorn with mistletoe
foxgloves springing in thousands.

The hills also will pass away
                will remain
as this lilac light, these bluebells,
the good dark of this room.

Stephen Dobyns

Selection from: *Cemetery Nights*
(1991) and *Velocities* (1994).

STEPHEN DOBYNS was born in 1941. He is one
of America's leading poets, a spinner of dark,
extravagant fables of a world we live or may
live in. His poems are peopled with devils
and angels, ghostly chickens, distorted myth-
ical figures, God, and the risen dead 'pre-
tending they're still alive'. His is a world
haunted by regret, driven by desire and
need, illuminated by daring make-believe.
In his often frightening and sometimes
strangely funny poems, Dobyns creates a
remarkable bridge between pure entertain-
ment and deep psychological insight. He is
also a cult writer of detective novels. ●

Roughhousing

Tonight I let loose the weasel of my body
across the plantation of your body,
bird eater, mouse eater scampering across
your pale meadows on sandpaper feet.
Tonight I let my snake lips slide over you.
Tonight my domesticated paws have removed
their gloves and as pink as baby rats
they scurry nimble-footed into your dark parts.
You heave yourself – what is this earthquake?
You cry out – in what jungle does that bird fly?
You grunt – let's make these pink things hurry.
Let's take a whip and make them trot faster.
These lips already torn and bleeding –
let's plunder them. These teeth banging together –
prison bars against prison bars. Who really
is ever set free? Belly and breasts –
my snout roots in your dirt like a pig
rooting for scraps. Arm bones, hip bones –
I'll suck their marrow, then carve a whistle.
Woman, what would you be like seen from the sky?
My little plane sputters and coughs. I scramble
onto the wing. The wind whips across the fuselage.
Who needs a parachute? Wheat fields, a river,
your pastures rush toward me to embrace me.

The Gun

Late afternoon light slices through the dormer window
to your place on the floor next to a stack of comics.
Across from you is a boy who at eleven is three years
older. He is telling you to pull down your pants.
You tell him you don't want to. His mother is out
and you are alone in the house. He has given you a Coke,
let you smoke two of his mother's nonfilter Pall Malls,
and years later you can still picture the red packet
on the dark finish of the phonograph. You stand up
and say you have to go home. You live across the street
and only see him in summer when he returns from school.
As you step around the comics toward the stairs,
the boy gives you a shove, sends you stumbling back.
Wait, he says, I want to show you something.
He goes to a drawer and when he turns around
you see he is holding a small gun by the barrel.
You feel you are breathing glass. You ask if it is
loaded and he says, Sure it is, and you say: Show me.
He removes the clip, takes a bullet from his pocket.
See this, he says, then puts the bullet into the clip,
slides the clip into the butt of the gun with a snap.
The boy sits on the bed and pretends to study the gun.
He has a round fat face and black hair. Take off
your pants, he says. Again you say you have to go home.
He stands up and points the gun at your legs. Slowly,
you unhook your cowboy belt, undo the metal buttons
of your jeans. They slide down past your knees.
Pull down your underwear, he tells you. You tell him
you don't want to. He points the gun at your head.
You crouch on the floor, cover your head with your hands.
You don't want him to see you cry. You feel you are
pulling yourself into yourself and soon you will be
no bigger than a pebble. You think back to the time
you saw a friend's cocker spaniel hit by a car and you
remember how its stomach was split open and you imagine
your face split open and blood and gray stuff escaping.
You have hardly ever thought of dying, seriously dying,
and as you grow more scared you have to go to the bathroom
more and more badly. Before you can stop yourself,

you feel yourself pissing into your underwear.
The boy with the gun sees the spreading pool of urine.
You baby, he shouts, you baby, you're disgusting.
You want to apologise, but the words jumble and
choke in your throat. Get out, the boy shouts.
You drag your pants up over your wet underwear and
run down the stairs. As you slam out of his house,
you know you died up there among the comic books
and football pennants, died as sure as your friend's
cocker spaniel, as sure as if the boy had shot your
face off, shot the very piss out of you. Standing
in the street with urine soaking your pants, you watch
your neighbors pursuing the orderly occupations
of a summer afternoon: mowing a lawn, trimming a hedge.
Where is that sense of the world you woke with
this morning? Now it is smaller. Now it has gone away.

Spiritual Chickens

A man eats a chicken every day for lunch,
and each day the ghost of another chicken
joins the crowd in the dining room. If he could
only see them! Hundreds and hundreds of spiritual
chickens, sitting on chairs, tables, covering
the floor, jammed shoulder to shoulder. At last
there is no more space and one of the chickens
is popped back across the spiritual plain to the earthly.
The man is in the process of picking his teeth.
Suddenly there's a chicken at the end of the table,
strutting back and forth, not looking at the man
but knowing he is there, as is the way with chickens.
The man makes a grab for the chicken but his hand
passes right through her. He tries to hit the chicken
with a chair and the chair passes through her.
He calls in his wife but she can see nothing.
This is his own private chicken, even if he
fails to recognise her. How is he to know
this is a chicken he ate seven years ago

on a hot and steamy Wednesday in July,
with a little tarragon, a little sour cream?
The man grows afraid. He runs out of his house
flapping his arms and making peculiar hops
until the authorities take him away for a cure.
Faced with the choice between something odd
in the world or something broken in his head,
he opts for the broken head. Certainly,
this is safer than putting his opinions
in jeopardy. Much better to think he had
imagined it, that he had made it happen.
Meanwhile, the chicken struts back and forth
at the end of the table. Here she was, jammed in
with the ghosts of six thousand dead hens, when
suddenly she has the whole place to herself.
Even the nervous man has disappeared. If she
had a brain, she would think she had caused it.
She would grow vain, egotistical, she would
look for someone to fight, but being a chicken
she can just enjoy it and make little squawks,
silent to all except the man who ate her,
who is far off banging his head against a wall
like someone trying to repair a leaky vessel,
making certain that nothing unpleasant gets in
or nothing of value falls out. How happy
he would have been to be born a chicken,
to be of good use to his fellow creatures
and rich in companionship after death.
As it is he is constantly being squeezed
between the world and his idea of the world.
Better to have a broken head – why surrender
his corner on truth? – better just to go crazy.

Pauline Stainer

Selection from: *The
Honeycomb* (1989), *Sighting the
Slave Ship* (1992), *The Ice-Pilot
Speaks* (1994).

PAULINE STAINER was born in 1941. Her
first two collections were both Poetry Book
Society Recommendations.

'Stainer writes sacred poetry for the scien-
tific 21st century. Her poetry preserves a
surety of vision, insisting that belief can only
increase with knowledge, and that wisdom
and faith are still provinces of careful, crys-
talline language. Her poems are unlike any-
one else's, but they're so strong and clear
they bring to mind that in-her-own-time
ignored, painfully sensitive yet tough-minded
American metaphysical Emily Dickinson.
Stainer, though, is deeply English and draws
from a wealth of sources: medieval lyrics,
Eastern as well as Western art, Christian
liturgy, and an impressive familiarity with
chemistry and optics' – Anne Stevenson. ●

The Honeycomb

They had made love early in the high bed,
Not knowing the honeycomb stretched
Between lath and plaster of the outer wall.

For a century
The bees had wintered there,
Prisoning sugar in the virgin wax.

At times of transition,
Spring and autumn,
Their vibration swelled the room.

Laying his hand against the plaster
In the May sunrise,
He felt the faint frequency of their arousal,

Nor winters later, burning the beeswax candle,
Could he forget his tremulous first loving
Into the humming dawn.

Walking the Water

Feet skirr the membrane –
the child before birth
walking the water.

Siphon from the sac;
amniosis
is ghost on a glass-slide.

X-ray the running-light;
the lit watermark
of the flesh.

Divine
the foetal heartbeat,
the pulse through the caul.

Corpuscles are cautionary magic;
crucifixion
a red suspension in the blood;

visitation
a velvet-runner –
the spirit sexed.

Sighting the Slave Ship

We came to unexpected latitudes –
sighted the slave ship
during divine service
on deck.

In earlier dog-days
we had made landfall
between forests of sandalwood,
taken on salt, falcons and sulphur.

What haunted us later
was not the cool dispensing
of sacrament
in the burnished doldrums

but something more exotic –
that sense
of a slight shift of cargo
while becalmed.

Piranesi's Fever

It could have been malaria –
the ricochet of the pulse
along his outflung arm,
grappling-irons
at each cautery-point on the body.

She lay with him between bouts;
pressed to his temple
the lazy estuary of her wrist;
brought him myrrh
on a burning salver.

How lucid they made him,
the specifics against fever:
the magnified footfall of the physician,
the application of cupping-glasses
above the echoing stairwell,

windlass and shaft,
the apparatus of imaginary prisons;
a catwalk slung across the vault
for those who will never take
the drawbridge to the hanging-garden.

None of this he could tell her –
that those he glimpsed
rigging the scaffold
were not fresco-painters,
but inquisitors giddy from blood-letting;

that when he clung to her
it wasn't delirium
but a fleeting humour of the eye –
unspecified torture,
death as an exact science.

Only after each crisis, could he speak
of the sudden lit elision
as she threw back the shutters
and he felt the weight of sunlight
on her unseen breasts.

Sarcophagus

Today
in that cold yellow pause
before the rape fluoresces,
I saw the blue glow
of plutonium

men in masks and boiler-suits
on the roof
of the sarcophagus
running, running
with divining-rods in their hands

nimble as matadors,
the sun catching
the sellotape at their ankles,
the speech of birds
graphite against the sky

the oracular dove
nesting
in the reactor.

Paragliding over the Spice Routes

It's as if the blood billows
over the parachute-shadow
on the sea

azure sensation
of gossamer-harness
along the skin

white terns diving,
the moving ruffle of shoals
just under the surface

an indigo upsurge
as the wind freshens
to the smoking horizon

and beyond the curving wake
of the speedboat
tensile, shining

vessels drawing their cargoes
into the haze
more whitely than adamant.

Jeni Couzyn

COLIN MARR

Selection from: *Life by
Drowning: Selected Poems*
(1985).

JENI COUZYN was born in 1942 in South
Africa, and grew up in Johannesburg. She
emigrated to Britain in 1965. She edited the
*Bloodaxe Book of Contemporary Women
Poets* (1985). Her Selected Poems, *Life by
Drowning* (1985), draws on four previous
collections, including *Christmas in Africa*
– with its bittersweet evocations of her
African childhood, as in the extract from
the title-sequence below.

Her poem sequences contain her most
imaginative and profound poetry, particul-
arly *A Time To Be Born* and *The Coming
of the Angel* in *Life by Drowning* and the
whole of her new book *In the Skin House*
(1993), which charts a spiritual journey. ●

The Punishment
FROM *Christmas in Africa*

One autumn afternoon when I was nine
feeding the chickens near the grapevine, brooding
in sunshine, my mother asked me to choose

a christmas present that year.
Anything I said, but a doll. Whatever you choose
but not a doll

my faith in her to know
better than I could myself what gift would please me.
And so at the height of summer

we made our pilgrimage
to the earth's greenest riches and the ample ocean.
And christmas eve

was three white daughters
three bright angels singing silent night as my mother
lit the candles

the tree blooming
sea breathing, the beloved son in his cradle sleeping.
Over the hills and skies

on his sleigh the father
the awaited one, made his visitation. Weeks of dreaming
and wondering now

in a box in my hand.
Shoebox size. Not waterwings then or a time machine no
something the size

of a pair of shoes.
Not a pony then or a river canoe. Not a new dress no.
I pulled at the bright bowed ribbons

and little christmas angels
with trembling hands. Underneath the monkey-apple branch
dressed up in baubles and tinsel

and blobs of cotton wool
the sea soaring, stars and the fairy at the treetop
shining

his hand on my shoulder
my mother's eyes on my face two burning suns
piercing my mind and in the box

a doll.
A stupid pretty empty thing. Pink smiling girl. The world
rocked about my head

my face fell into a net
from that moment. My heart in me played possum
and never recovered.

I said I liked the wretched thing
joy broke over my face like a mirror cracking. I said it
so loud, so often

I almost believed it. All that christmas
a shameful secret bound me and the doll and my mother
irrevocably together.

When I knew she was watching
I would grab for the doll in the night, or take it
tenderly with me to the beach

wrapped in a small towel.
At last on the last night of the journey home
staying at a hotel

my mother woke me early
to go out and find the maid. In my pyjamas, half asleep
I staggered out into the dawn

heat rising like mist
from the ground, birds making an uproar, snakes
not yet awake

a sense of something
about to happen under the heavy damp rustle
of the trees.

My feet left footprints
in the dew. When I returned I was clutching that precious
corpse to my chest

like one of the bereaved.
Now I know, said my mother, that although you didn't
want a doll, you really do love her.

I was believed!
Something fell from my face with a clatter –
my punishment was over

and in that moment
fell from my mother's face a particular smile, a kind of
dear and tender curling of the eyes

fell. Two gripped faces
side by side on the floor, smiled at each other
before we grabbed them back

and fitted them with a hollow rattle
to our love. And I laid the doll down in a suitcase
and slammed the lid on its face

and never looked at it again.
And in a sense my mother did the same, and in a sense
my punishment and hers

had always been, and just begun.

Dave Smith

DEE SMITH

Selection from: *Night Pleasures: New & Selected Poems* (1992).

DAVE SMITH was born in 1942. He is the most outstanding American poet of his generation. Robert Penn Warren has called him 'a poet of lavish talents...a splendid and massive achievement'.

'His poetry shows a powerful and driving imagination...He is a regional poet of the American South, and has written memorably of the watermen of Chesapeake Bay, where he grew up, and of the small towns of Virginia. He has not hesitated to touch upon the touchiest subjects – adolescence, race relations, sexuality, poverty, family hostility. At the same time, he has been a tender poet of domestic relations (one of the few decent poets of fatherhood). Smith deserves an English readership, as one of the most interesting and undiluted voices now alive in the United States. He is at the height of his powers' – Helen Vendler. ●

Of Oystermen, Workboats

The wide, white, wing-boned washboards of twenty
footers, sloped, ridged to hold
a man's tongs and stride,
                              the good stance
to scrape deep with a motion like big applause,
plunging the teeth true beyond the known
mounds of the dead, the current carried
cloisters of murk,
                         miracles that bloom
luminous and unseen, sweet things to be
brought up, bejeweled, culled from husks,

as oystermen like odd angels glide far off enough
to keep a wake gentle as shirts on a line,
red baseball caps dipping like bloodied
heads upright, the clawed hands slapped
at the air in salute,
                          those washboards that splinter
the sun on tongs downlaid, on tines humming,

those womb-hulls harbored flank to flank at dusk
until the white-robed priest of the moon
stands tall to the sea's spume-pour
in nostrils
            of the men who sway from heel to heel,

the season come again, the socketed gray
of their eyes rolling outward,
forearms naked past longjohns,
the salted breast-beaters at first light

lined up, ready to fly.

On Looking into Neruda's *Memoirs*

At the end of Elliewood Avenue one black night
the police came whirling batons
to crack heads and leave
the students in the seeping flush
of camellias that Spring.

A woman found me and into the riot we went, me
tugged by the ghost-tendril of her arm,
bolting by the tidy lawns until down
we lay at the serpentine wall,
panting, in new music

beating from an open window – 'The Famous Flames'
maybe, but she was cool, wordless, alert
as a dove to the night noise.

She uncradled her hungers in the dark, then rose
lank as the poet Gabriela Mistral,
whom Neruda saw in his youth.
He called her gray stick,
as if she were the heron
owning the world with icy steps.

Why has she waited to enter this poem, a small
scald at my brain's back?
Whatever she put in my hand
was grim and hard in the heaving.
Go on, show them, she said, *give them a taste.*

She hovered on the corner, a tall shadow.
When they came to beat me she stepped away
through helmeted heads, a saint
with an eye of disdain
for all my earnest words.

It doesn't matter, the dutiful life, the poems.
A man will complain for his first loves,
brick smell, lost village, sexual
odor of swamps, the scarf
of a nightwalker, a single camellia.

Mistral, who worshipped the long-stick God
of the Crusaders, kneeled in the huts
where Neruda grew. He saw her
once, enough,
a stick making poems.

Bitch, you almost hear him hiss,
pressing her hard in the story of his life.

John Hartley Williams

JOHN HARTLEY WILLIAMS was born in 1942 in Cheshire, and grew up in London. A specialist in linguistics, he has taught English Language at universities in France, Cameroun and the former Yugoslavia, and since 1976 at the Free University of Berlin.

His second book, *Bright River Yonder*, a Poetry Book Society Recommendation, is a baroque Wild West poetry adventure. Its centrepiece, the long poem, *Ephraim Destiny's Perfectly Utter Darkness*, won first prize in the Arvon poetry competition. His other Bloodaxe collections are *Cornerless People* (1990) and *Double* (1994).

'He is comic, ironic, satirical and ridiculous but most important of all he is impatient and angry...Writing out of a Europe where the Cold War has been "won" Williams might well be its first true chronicler' – David Kennedy. 'The real McCoy' –Sean O'Brien. ●

Selection from: *Bright River Yonder* (1987) and *Double* (1994).

Jack the Lad

Delivering meat on a butcher's bike
With a square steel holder on the front
For a hamper, I kept my mouth open
To catch the groans that dripped from undersides of bridges.

Corpses in my basket, a sawn-off leg,
A pile of lungs like outdoor Japanese inflatables,
I left a trail of blood behind me,
Cheerfully whistling into the stopped-up drains of ears.

Ladies! I said, Ladies! These are
The dissected cadavers of once-were intellectuals!
Chew on this bright & well-informed gristle,
Feel how moist the education of desire becomes!

Behind me the world was pushing
Its flat tyre & cursing.
I heard my father drive off to work
With a flat cap & a complicated oath.

I was the undertaker's assistant, the newsboy.
I was the Sonny Jim, the curly knob, the *you-there!* of my generation.
If anyone was introduced to me, they went out & bought pliers
      & wire;
They stared with slow-directed longing at my toenails.

A man in the park gave me darkness as deep as a well,
'Keep it under yr pillow,' he said, & went off looking strange.
My mother sliced proverbs out of apple peel,
Left me the white quarters on a plate, their bruising flesh.

I didn't tell anyone about the choicest cuts I had.
I wouldn't let the children see them, it wasn't right.
I used to lick them like lollipops in my imagination.
I put the thighs in the attic for later.

But in the end I had to speak out.
They made me stand up at the party and recite female emancipation
Until I blushed. They said I wouldn't have to look intelligent,
But I did of course, & all the delicious frailty turned to jeers.

I'm still the same old sunshine really, tho,
Pedalling round the suburbs like an axeman,
With an ankle sticking out of my pocket, fingers in my hat,
And a couple of ears for buttons.

I've spring-cleaned nightmares to get this far,
And what's wrong with making yr own stuffing,
Especially if you put Christmas in it, some cognac & some poetry,
And talk in a gentle tone to the geese until they put their necks in
      yr hand?

Script Conference

We gotta make a film of this, Jack.
>   *Where's the story?*
It's got everything. Sex. Magic. Despair.
>   *There's no hero.*
There's a part for you in it, Jack. You ride into town.
>   *And ride straight out.*
Jack! It's romantic. Imagine those couples moving closer
>   to watch you on late-night TV.
>   *It's no love-story.*
Of course it is. A he & a she. It's terrific!
>   *It is about it.*
At the end you take the girl in your arms. You kiss
>   her. A long, shuddering embrace.
>   *She shudders?*
Well, she could die in the end. Or you could meet her
>   at the end of the trail.
>   *Six-guns blazing.*
Hey, what kinda story you want? What
>   excites you, Jack?
>   *I like to waltz young women, Benito.*
I know, Jack. Believe me. I know. But this is
>   a movie! It has emotion!
>   *I like to play no emotion.*
Whaddaya mean, Jack?
>   *I like to make a film about*
>   *a shadow in a street. Just a*
>   *shadow. Then you watch it*
>   *crack like a china plate. Very slowly.*
That's poetic, Jack! You're a poet! Let's get down to
>   details. The old guy is in love with Liza.
>   *Yeah. He's sitting on the bed.*
>   *Then he leans forward & begins*
>   *to clip his toenails. Close-up.*
>   *Fingers working on toes. About*
>   *five minutes.*
We can think about that, Jack. They take
>   the girl away from him.

Or we could show her mouth.
I'm really interested in that mouth.
No tongue in it.
Just that mouth.

Jack! It doesn't exist, the actress with
        no tongue!

We could cut it out ourselves.

O.K. O.K. Jack. Now the marriage. He comes
        into the church

Then we could cut our own
tongues out.
We could just stand around.
Tongueless.

Jack!

And one final shot.

What's that?

A man & a woman on a bed.

Good, Jack. That's adult.

The woman makes weird noises.
Man groans the same thing over and over.
It's dark.
Bed begins to whine.

I don't know if...

The door flies open.
I just stand there & you have to guess who I am.

Who are you, Jack?

Then nothing happens at all.
Absolutely nothing.

It won't sell, Jack. Not in this country.

Annemarie Austin

PETE BROWNETT

Selection from: *On the Border*
(1993).

ANNEMARIE AUSTIN was born in 1943. Her
richly imaginative, unsettling poems are like
paintings in which what is seen is held as it is
about to happen, or as it has just happened.
They evoke thresholds or border states.

'Austin is a fable maker. Hers is a poetry
of parts held together by powerfully imag-
ined dream associations. As her world deli-
quesces and reforms, her imagination breathes
life into other people in other times, weirdly
authenticating the material she draws from
history' – Anne Stevenson. 'She sees the
skull beneath the skin. Her world is dark,
but her sensibility bright as an arc light, and
her writing sharp' – Julian May. ●

Shape-shifting

You see the same face across the generations –
her there, half a shadow and half concrete
in a real coat with mud-flecked facings,
a fraying hem, and lugging a leather suitcase
tied with string. She sings the same thread song

that her mother whispered above her cradle
in the winter dark about a thousand years ago;
the look in her eyes dissolves into a landscape
puddled with mud, far trees against the sky
and a rider going between them – herself maybe.

For she rises up wherever you might be watching
in a different costume, with various coloured hair
or lion's pelt, bird feathers – your glance catches
her even in the fireside cat that licks its paws
then turns its flexing gaze towards your face

before stalking out to the dusk and its dissolving.
And she is there at the gate, unlatching it and entering,
leaving her horse by the fence, feeling the cat's fur cold
against her legs as she advances up the shadowed path
to temporary safety. A woman within a home

for the briefest moment, she boils a kettle at the fire,
hangs her frayed coat on a peg and hunkers down
before the hearth to sing for anything arriving
out of the old winter dark – the gold-leaf lion
hauling a leather suitcase, a peacock trailing string.

Pen and Paper

Before the ladder to the platform closed in by fleering voices,
the tying of the feet, the laying on the tilted board face down
but with no place for cheek or lip to rest on,
before the oblique blade, the bloody basket;
arrived at the foot of the scaffold, Madame Roland asked
that she might have pen and paper to record
'the strange thoughts rising in her'.
                                    Request refused,
as if it were some clever-dick trick of postponement;
the page remaining at the stationers, the quill untrimmed,
the strange thoughts in the skull as in a vase
that spilt them quite illegibly under the guillotine
a moment later.
                    A fate she knew could not be much delayed,
she would not read her own words back to her
at leisure after, what she felt urged to keep
could not be kept by her more than a minute's space;
but nonetheless she wanted pen and paper, meant
to snatch out of the blood-stained air those phrases
that would cage the strangeness lifting through her now.

For only words could net and hold the foreign birds
long enough in her sight for naming, recognition
under the single lightning-flash that time had left her;
only with pen and paper could she possess her death,
the momentary owner of a basket loud with wings
that the imminent blow would knock from her hands and scatter.

On the Border

The revolver, the just-emptied casket of woman's ashes,
the beach at dusk under a squally wind;
the bathroom, a slew of toothpaste-streaked water,
a motorbike starting up at the back of the house:
the first, the distant, overlays the second which is near,
at hand, the tooth-glass insensibly in the fingers;

and the ashes can reassemble, climb up each other's ladder
into bone and flesh and hair, the woman stride
the slope of the dunes from the sea's thump and spillage

if I desire it, stilled momentarily at the white basin
by my open-eyed dream of strewn objects in the sand
and of the man whose hand is on the cold revolver
in November, the pulse that follows the motorbike's kick-start.

He does not grow old in my possession, this man of air
who nonetheless on the beach can upturn the open casket
to show her ashes quite gone away in the squall,
blown to less than himself who is nothing

but stronger than this house, falling apart as if card-built
so his wind can reach my mouth over the roofs of the town
and all the rest that is only real landscape
trying to hold out against the imagined, the dream

minutely articulated, organised fiercely, revised
and polished till it shines out diamond-hard
to write on the glass of my windows and mirrors,
on the tumbler whitened by toothpaste in my hand
(that even now, in the sand, is gathering up the woman).

György Petri

GYÖRGY PETRI was born in 1943. He belongs to the generation of Hungarian poets who grew up after the 1956 Uprising.

Ideas of freedom have always been central to Petri's concerns, from the existentialism of his early work to the broader, political perspective of his more recent poetry. Sexuality is often the glass in which the nature of freedom is disclosed, while death, the ultimate restraint, is evoked with a morbid fascination and black humour that are almost medieval in feeling.

Selection from: *Night Song of the Personal Shadow* (1991), translated by George Gömöri and Clive Wilmer.

'It is a long time since a major verse satirist has emerged in any European language. That is what Petri is, and he combines an almost Juvenalian savagery with a striking range of techniques and genres. His bile is the product of injustice and moral outrage. He is funny, angry, sexy, morbid, disillusioned and wildly intelligent' – Clive Wilmer. ●

Now Only

now only the filthy pattering of rain
now only heavy coats and squelching shoes
now only the din of steamed-up cheap cafés
now only trodden sawdust on the stone

now only mouldy buns in cellophane
now streetlights decomposing in thin fog
the advice given by a friendly cop
the last drink bought with the last of the small change

now only the tram-island's desolation
now only the variable course of the night wind
rushing through a town of alleys to no end

now only the unfinished excavations
the night's prospecting-hole its weeds and thorns
now only shivering now only yawns

Apocryphal

The holy family's grinding away –
Mary lies back, God screws;
Joseph, unable to sleep,
starts groping about for booze.
No luck: he gets up. Grabs his things.
Over pyjamas pulls vest and pants.
Then walks down to the Three Kings
for (at last!) a couple of pints...
'God again?'
                    'Him again.'
                                    He sighs,
knocks back his beer, gets wise,
gesticulates:
                    'Anyway,
I can tell you, the other day
did I make a fuss: before my very eyes,
the two of 'em on the job!
So I told my Mary straight,
at least shut your gob,
it's enough that the damn bed shakes
and rumbles on as if there was an earthquake.
I mean it now: if he's really got to screw yuh,
I can do without all the ha-ha-ha-hallelujah!'

To Be Said Over and Over Again

I glance down at my shoe and – there's the lace!
This can't be gaol then, can it, in that case.

Night Song of the Personal Shadow

The rain is pissing down,
you scum.
And you, you are asleep
in your nice warm room –
that or stuffing the bird.
Me? Till six in the morning
I rot in the slackening rain.
I must wait for my relief, I've got to wait
till you crawl out of your hole,
get up from beside your old woman.
So the dope can be passed on
as to where you've flown.
You are flying, spreading your wings.
Don't you get into my hands –
I'll pluck you while you're in flight.
This sodding rain
is something I won't forget,
my raincoat swelling
double its normal weight
and the soles of my shoes.
While you
were arsing around
in the warm room.

The time will come
when I feed you to fish in the Danube.

Quatrain

George is the name. I know what I was born for,
Idle away my life, let it go hang.
When they hang *me*, I'll profit by my pain.
Losing my life, I'll win it back again.

To Imre Nagy

You were impersonal, too, like the other leaders,
bespectacled, sober-suited; your voice lacked
sonority, for you didn't know quite what to say

on the spur of the moment to the gathered multitude. This urgency
was precisely the thing you found strange. I heard you,
old man in pince-nez, and was disappointed,
not yet to know

of the concrete yard where most likely the prosecutor
rattled off the sentence, or
of the rope's rough bruising, the ultimate shame.

Who can say what you might have said
from that balcony? Butchered opportunities
never return. Neither prison nor death
can resharpen the cutting edge of the moment

once it's been chipped. What we can do, though, is remember
the hurt, reluctant, hesitant man
who nonetheless soaked up
anger, delusion
and a whole nation's blind hope,

when the town woke to gunfire
that blew it apart.

Sisyphus Steps Back

The age of intrepid idiots is upon us.
Fools or knaves? They're both at the same time.
I'm scared of understanding, and yet I laugh at it:
you can't stop a boulder once it's rolling back.

[1988]

Electra

What *they* think is it's the twists and turns of politics
that keep me ticking; they think it's Mycenae's fate.
Take my little sister, cute sensitive Chrysosthemis –
to me the poor thing attributes a surfeit of moral passion,
believing I'm unable to get over
the issue of our father's twisted death.
What do I care for that gross geyser of spunk
who murdered his own daughter! The steps into the bath
were slippery with soap – and the axe's edge too sharp.
But that this Aegisthus, with his trainee-barber's face,
should swagger about and hold sway in this wretched town,
and that our mother, like a venerably double-chinned old whore,
should dally with him simpering – everybody pretending
not to see, not to know anything. Even the Sun
glitters above, like a lie forged of pure gold,
the false coin of the gods!
Well, that's why! That's why! Because of disgust, because it all
          sticks in my craw,
revenge has become my dream and my daily bread.
And this revulsion is stronger than the gods.
I already see how mould is creeping across Mycenae,
which is the mould of madness and destruction.

Eira Stenberg

PERTTI NISONEN / TAMMI

Selection from: *Wings of Hope and Daring: Selected Poems* (1992), translated by Herbert Lomas.

EIRA STENBERG was born in 1943. She is a leading Finnish poet, novelist and children's writer. She lives in Helsinki.

In her poetry she writes mainly about home life, but deals with family relationships like an exorcist casting out demons. She views the conflicts of marriage, divorce, motherhood and childhood with a ruthless eye. The male may meet a hostile, disenchanted eye, a levelled carving knife, but the mother too must see its point, and the rather demotic child. Her poems are full of politics – sexual and family politics, as well as gestures to the larger family. In spite of her tragic view, her poetry can be tender and playful, and she writes with wit, even humour, and a relish of the tongue in her head. Hers is a deadly mind, but the deadliness springs from a lively love of life. 'Whatever the antonym of sentimentality is, she has it' – Herbert Lomas. ●

The Eighth Day of the Week
FROM *Bearded Madonna*

1

It's hotter today than skin, a hundred in the shade.
I'm involved in a crime.
It's my task to find out who the murderer is
that's keeping the family in terror.
He's a way of striking secretly,
kills child after child.
He has a sign
to announce his presence:
a pile of twigs appears on the oven,
and the next one knows
her turn has come.
When all the other children have been killed
and I alone am left,
I suddenly see the sign, the twigs.

Mummy's coming towards me,
feeling affectionate,
wanting to cuddle me in her lap
and promising protection.
I give her a look
and say I know
who the murderer is
and she won't succeed with me.

2

Enough good hidings
to make a birch-broom:
I throw the birch-twigs in the oven –
no love no hatred burns
like the ones you're given
as presents in childhood.
Those souls in the cots,
they're flickering blue flames,
marsh lights in dim fens.
Nothing but the heart
can burn like that, smouldering on
without turning ash.
The world reeks: the concentration camps
are set up at home.
Smutty, those marks on the cheeks.
The barbed wire cuddles round us
and blooms with roses.

3

What a hullabaloo as the whips burn.
The kitchen's full of mothers,
getting tinier and tinier:
it's a Russian doll starting
to hatch out.
They beg rescue from the the stove,
and the stove's gracious:
each gets a flaming ring
as her halo.

4

The heat's getting more and more stifling.
The oven's glowing a bright red!
The mothers' haloes are blazing –
better not touch them.
The porridge is boiling over,
bubbling and simmering the kitchen full,
inching upstairs to the nurseries,
into the cots
where the quilts are imperceptibly mutating
into soil.
Suddenly in the yard the birch-whip tree
bursts into flames
the air boils like water
and the sky rains frenzied birds.
A child pushes out of the fire-grate,
laughing as it's born.
Only prophets laugh as they're born –
they know childhood's the worst betrayal.
He's decided to give it the slip.
Quick as a flash, he's milked his mother dry
and grown up. He can't cry.
For him everyone's heart is a fuse.
He runs out
into the street
and kicks to death
the first old lady.

5

a day when friends are no help
a day when sleet hurls from the phone
a day like riding a fiery horse
a day when deep under the earth's crust
the permafrost rips open
and a bloodthirsty saurian
creeps out

Medusa looks out of the mirror
and I remember my birth

a day when sonny boy smacks his mittens in your face
when mummy's thinking of father's day and her son and daddy
and can't find a single reason why in the cupboard

> The truth's exposed: the child's
> playing in the room
> the floor's covered with hoofmarks
> a horseshoe turns up in father's slipper
> and the skyline's seething:
> ants are piling up a hill.

6

There's a terrible hurry.
The pan's boiling as if it wanted to feed
the entire world.
The porridge is spreading like a dream
or a thicket of thorns
all over Sleeping Beauty's castle.
But father is the eighth day of the week,
a gold trophy.
He comes down through the clouds on a rocket,
dressed in helmet and boilersuit.
He can cope with women, children and porridge.
He has a peacock's tail
and a hundred scintillating tasks.
He's very important.

7

No one can detect if a child's dead
provided it's been filled with porridge.
The cleverer the child,
the more obedient,
so that anyone you like can see
how well-bred she is.
But you mustn't forget the lucky coin and some treacle,
or when she's big she'll claim
there's something missing –
like the stuff of life.
Even though she if anyone
should feel stuffed.

8

The child stares without blinking,
wearing the culprit's crown of thorns.
Verily verily he's learning
that hearts are heavy, and hot
as sizzling saunas.
The sauna-whisk whistles and sheds its leaves:
this is spanking the Finnish way –
hot and naked.
Slowly the tragedy emerges:
the child, the rash person's dream,
is not the philosophers' stone.
The rage of the mothers and fathers is boundless
when they see:
the font is deep as a well,
as a stairwell ringing
with jingling keys.

9

The royal child gazes at a heavenly bosom.
A crown has been thrust on his head.
Promise gazes from the honey in the altarpiece;
a wasp surreptitiously stings
but the candles burn,
the congregation bows in worship, and the monarchs,
coupled together, wait.

Carol Rumens

DAVID HUNTER

Selection from: *Thinking of Skins: New & Selected Poems* (1993).

CAROL RUMENS was born in 1944. Her women's anthology *Making for the Open* (1985) and her novel *Plato Park* (1987) were published by Chatto. Her Bloodaxe selection *Thinking of Skins* (1993) includes work from several collections published during the past 20 years, as well as a large selection of new work.

Rumens confronts the personal with the political in poems which are remarkable for their imaginative daring and their engagement with other lives. Often set against the background of Eastern Europe, Russia or her present home in Northern Ireland, they are filled with a powerful sense of loss and exile. She draws on a wide variety of characters and voices to dramatise the realities of suffering and persecution, or to write direct, honest accounts of love, separation, death and displacement. ●

Unplayed Music

We stand apart in the crowd that slaps its filled glasses
on the green piano, quivering her shut heart.
The tavern, hung with bottles, winks and sways
like a little ship, smuggling its soul through darkness.
There is an arm flung jokily round my shoulders,
and clouds of words and smoke thicken between us.
I watch you watching me. All else is blindness.

Outside the long street glimmers pearl.
Our revellers' heat steams into the cold
as fresh snow, crisping and slithering
underfoot, witches us back to childhood.
Oh night of ice and Schnapps, moonshine and stars,
how lightly two of us have fallen in step
behind the crowd! The shadowy white landscape
gathers our few words into its secret.

All night in the small grey room
I'm listening for you, for the new music
waiting only to be played; all night I hear nothing
but wind over the snow, my own heart beating.

Star Whisper
(for Eugene Dubnov)

If you dare breathe out in Verkhoyansk
You'll get the sound of life turning to frost
As if it were an untuned radio,
    A storm of dust.

It's what the stars confess when all is silence
– Not to the telescopes, but to the snow.
It hangs upon the trees like silver berries
    – Iced human dew.

Imagine how the throat gets thick with it,
How many *versts* there are until the spring,
How close the blood is, just behind the lips
    And tongue, to freezing.

Here, you could breathe a hundred times a minute,
And from the temperate air still fail to draw
Conclusions about whether you're alive
    – If so, what for.

Leningrad Romance

1 *A Window Cut by Jealousy*

Not far from the estuary's grey window
They lit cigarettes and talked. Water kept meeting stone,
Lips kept sticking to paper, time kept burning.
The lilacs were burning down to the colour of stone.
She said, I was born here, I've lived here always.
Stone kept moving in water, time kept burning,
Smoke became palaces, palaces faded and faded.
My home's in Moscow, he said, my wife and children...
Perhaps they are just the white ash-fall of night,
Perhaps they are stone. Stone kept looking at shadows,
Shadows died in the white ash-fall of night.

Water kept playing with windows, time kept burning,
Fingers played with the burning dust of the lilacs,
The palaces faded and faded. I've lived here always,
She said, I've friends in Moscow. Thoughts became palaces,
Time went out, hands became estuaries,
The estuary was the colour of dying lilac.
They talked and lit cigarettes. Shadows flowed over the table.
They fingered them, but they didn't notice mine,
Not far from the estuary's grey window.

2 *Safe Period*

He will unlock the four-hooked gate of her bra,
Not noticing a kremlin of patched cotton,
With darkening scorch-marks where her arms press kisses.
She will pull back her arms, disturbing drifts
Of shallow, babyish hair, and let him drink,
Breathless, the heavy spirit smell, retreating
At length with a shy glance to grasp the chair-back,
And, slightly stooped, tug out the darker bandage.
Her cupped palm will glow as she carries it
Quickly to the sink, like something burning.
He sees the bright beard on each inner thigh,
Carnations curling, ribboning in the bowl.
Her hands make soapy love. The laundered rag
Weeps swift pink tears from the washing-string.
He's stiffened with a shocked assent. She breathes
Against him, damp as a glass. A glass of red vodka.

The Fuchsia Knight
(for Medbh McGuckian)

You gathered his yarn onto unfamiliar looms,
And the vowels you dropped, the soft-signs you appended,
Brindled the cloth and changed it, like the tears
Forged in the hedgerows, bending the thick stems
With weights not even a god deserves to weep.

You bore him flowers which seemed so abundantly
Indigenous, he forgot his planter's rank.
His head grew misty with heather: luminous roses
And the never-heard song of his native nightingale
Brimmed between him and his sword. He learned to drink

Your consonants with childish intensity
As you chased them towards him with a dry-lipped stammer
Less part of the need for love than the search for perfection.
He learned that to open the veins of speech is sometimes
To unzip the fuchsia linings of live skin.

Schoolgirl's Story

The news stayed good until Monday morning
When a taxi-driver was shot in the South of the city,
And his un-named schoolgirl-passenger injured.
Outside the window, clouds made changeable bruises
And spillings. Bad weather, taxi weather.
I picked up my dish, poured everything down the sink,
Unclogged it with bare fingers, ran for my coat,
Played back a dream of how it used to be,
Hearing about these things every day of the week
And not feeling cold and sick and hot: the beauty
    Of being nobody's lover.

I could hardly breathe as I reached the school railings.
The clouds turned heavy again, opened fire
On my face and eyes with stinging rice-grains of hail.
Bad weather, taxi weather. *If it's not there*
I'll run, and my screams run with me, from here to Balmoral.
But the bike was on its stand in the shed as usual.
The square-root of the frame, graceful, ice-blue,
Cut me the old two ways: her nearness, her distance.
The sky paled. I began to look for her
Without seeming to. I stopped feeling sick for her.
    Another sickness took over.

Last of the Lays

Part One

At Ivalo's tyre-crazed cross-roads, snow was the sphinx
And *Murmansk* was what she murmured. One night you got restless.

(The nights were long, alas. We weren't new lovers.
'Follow me. I am your Fate' wouldn't wash any more).

I heard your foot-swords slicing the forest-fleece
With finality. Then from your breast swooped a brilliant birdman.

Choice, choice, choice gasped the wind as you gashed it.
In front of you, ghostly as lilacs, stood your live lungs.

Part Two

In Persil-white Ivalo the enemy was drink.
I had nothing to come to but a Finnish Cosmo

And nothing to read but a radioactive omelette.
My cutlery stuttered, my skis would begin any minute,

So I tacked outside into a mean minus-thirty,
And wound up at the Word, that high-lettered horror.

I turned as it told me. I plummeted and plodged
And became wild-life and expected instant extinction.

I lit on the luminous secret of synchronised movement
Momentarily, but omitted to take it with me.

I slept on my skis, and revolutionary roughnecks
Lobbed snow-lumps like one-off hand-jobs, and roamed the ice

Like spinning-tops wreathed in a frost of eye-water.

Part Three

Bang on the border, they'd opened a Super-Safeways,
Hit by recession, closed for the duration.

Some tanked-up gun-jabber jogged me: 'Nadezhda Krupskaya?'
'Crumbs!' I said. 'Wrong revolution. Julian Clary.'

Part Four

He didn't find that funny, which meant, as I'd feared,
History hadn't happened, it hadn't begun.

And though the ski-tracks still straggled under the *Push* sign
They were being disexisted at serious speed.

This was the hairiest I had ever imagined:
Me, on God's side, just about. You, back on the other:

The border, bristling. Remember those terrible games
– When the sound's switched off, there's got to be someone dancing,

And the grin's de rigeur, because English losers are laughers?
I hope, wherever you're harboured, you look like a natural

– Straight bck, heels tgthr, bm on chr –
I hope when it thaws and the home-thoughts unfreeze our faces,

Whoever I am I'll
                    author an honest tear.

David Constantine

MOIRA CONWAY

Selection from: *Selected Poems* (1991) and *Caspar Hauser* (1994).

DAVID CONSTANTINE was born in 1944 in Salford. He is a lecturer in German at Oxford. His *Selected Poems* (1991) includes poems from three previous collections as well as new work; his latest book, *Caspar Hauser* (1994), is an epic poem about the enigmatic German who was incarcerated for most of his childhood, released and then murdered. His other books include a novel, *Davies* (Bloodaxe, 1985) and translations including Hölderlin's *Selected Poems* (Bloodaxe, 1990).

'He has a generous, self-aware sensuality …His particular gift is for the reworking of classical myth and Biblical narratives so that they are infused with ordinary, accessible emotion and a sense of rich, humane acceptance' – Fleur Adcock & Marina Warner. ●

Eldon Hole

They fastened a poor man here on a rope's end
And through the turbulence of the jackdaws let him down
To where everything lost collects, all the earth's cold,
And the crying of fallen things goes round and round
And where, if anywhere, the worm is coiled.

When he had filled with cold they hauled him up.
The horrors were swarming in his beard and hair.
His teeth had broken chattering and could not stop
Mincing his tongue. He lay in the rope and stared,
Stared at the sky and feared he would live for ever.

Like one of those dreadful fish that are all head
They saw him at his little window beaming out
Bald and whiskerless and squiddy-eyed
He hung in the branches of their nightmares like a swede.
They listened at his door for in his throat

Poor Isaac when the wounds in his mouth had healed
Talked to himself deep down. It was a sound
Like the never-ending yelps of a small stone
Falling to where the worm lives and the cold
And everything hurt goes round and round and round.

'As our bloods separate'

As our bloods separate the clock resumes,
I hear the wind again as our hearts quieten.
We were a ring: the clock ticked round us
For that time and the wind was deflected.

The clock pecks everything to the bone.
The wind enters through the broken eyes
Of houses and through their wide mouths
And scatters the ashes from the hearth.

Sleep. Do not let go my hand.

Birdsong

Most are sleeping, some
Have waited hopelessly for mercy,
Others even by this will not be stayed.
But we who have not slept for quantity
Of happiness have heard
The dawn precipitate in song
Like dewfall.

We think our common road a choir of trees.

A Brightness to Cast Shadows

And now among them these dark mornings yours
Ascendant and of a brightness to cast shadows.
Love the winter, fear
The earlier and earlier coming of the light
When in the mantle blue we turn our dead faces.

Watching for Dolphins

In the summer months on every crossing to Piraeus
One noticed that certain passengers soon rose
From seats in the packed saloon and with serious
Looks and no acknowledgement of a common purpose
Passed forward through the small door into the bows
To watch for dolphins. One saw them lose

Every other wish. Even the lovers
Turned their desires on the sea, and a fat man
Hung with equipment to photograph the occasion
Stared like a saint, through sad bi-focals; others,
Hopeless themselves, looked to the children for they
Would see dolphins if anyone would. Day after day

Or on their last opportunity all gazed
Undecided whether a flat calm were favourable
Or a sea the sun and the wind between them raised
To a likeness of dolphins. Were gulls a sign, that fell
Screeching from the sky or over an unremarkable place
Sat in a silent school? Every face

After its character implored the sea.
All, unaccustomed, wanted epiphany,
Praying the sky would clang and the abused Aegean
Reverberate with cymbal, gong and drum.
We could not imagine more prayer, and had they then
On the waves, on the climax of our longing come

Smiling, snub-nosed, domed like satyrs, oh
We should have laughed and lifted the children up
Stranger to stranger, pointing how with a leap
They left their element, three or four times, centred
On grace, and heavily and warm re-entered,
Looping the keel. We should have felt them go

Further and further into the deep parts. But soon
We were among the great tankers, under their chains
In black water. We had not seen the dolphins
But woke, blinking. Eyes cast down
With no admission of disappointment the company
Dispersed and prepared to land in the city.

Mary Magdalene and the Sun

Hugging her breasts, waiting in a hard garden
For Sun, the climber, to come over the hill,
Disconsolate, the whore Mary Magdalene,
She of the long hair. But Sun meanwhile,

Scaling inch by inch the steep other side,
At last got a grip with his fingers on the rim
And hoisted himself up. She saw the spikes of his head,
His brow, then his brazen face. So after his swim

Leander's fingers appeared on Hero's sill
And he hauled himself inside, naked and salt
And grinning. She closed her eyes and let him feel
Her open face, uncrossed her arms and felt

Him warm her breasts and throat. Thereupon a cock
Crowed once, very red. And something came and stood
Between her and the Sun, something cold, and 'Look,'
It moaned. And there, casting a shadow, naked

And bled white was the nailed man, he whose
Blessing arms they fixed on a beam, and he crouched
There gibbering of love and clutching his
Thin shoulders and begging to be touched.

He was encrusted above the eyes with black,
And maculed in the hands and feet and in his side,
And through clacking teeth he begged her to touch him, and 'Look,'
He moaned, 'at this and this that they did,'

Showing the holes. Sun, the joker, though,
Had leapfrogged him, and more cocks crowed,
And down the green hillside and through
The waking garden the waters of irrigation flowed

And plenteous happy birdsong from the air,
As Sun diminished the ghosts of fruit trees on the grass
And over the nailed man's shoulder stroked the harlot's hair
And fingered open the purple sheaths of crocuses.

Lazarus to Christ

You are forgetting, I was indeed dead
Not comatose, not sleeping, and could no more
Wish for resurrection than what we are before
Can wish for birth. I had already slid

Four days down when you hauled me back into the air.
Now they come to watch me break bread
And drink the wine, even the tactful plead
With dumb faces to be told something, and, dear,

Even you, who wept for me and of whom it is said
You know all things, what I mutter in nightmare
I believe you lie awake to overhear.
You too are curious, you too make me afraid

Of my own cold heart. However I wash
I cannot get the foist out of my flesh.

Christ to Lazarus

They faltered when we came there and I knew very well
They were already leaving me. Not one
Among your mourners had any stomach to go on,
And when they moved the stone and we could smell

Death in his lair they slid off me like cloud
And left me shining cold on the open grave
Crying for you and heaving until Death gave
And you were troubled in your mottled shroud.

They hid their eyes, they begged me let you stay,
But I was adamant, my friend. For soon
By a loving father fiercer than any moon
It will be done to me too, on the third day.

I hauled you out because I wanted to.
I never wept for anyone but you.

'Pity the drunks'

Pity the drunks in this late April snow.
They drank their hats and coats a week ago.
They touched the sun, they tapped the melting ground,
In public parks we saw them sitting round
The merry campfire of a cider jar
Upon a crocus cloth. Alas, some are
Already stiff in mortuaries who were
Seduced by Spring to go from here to there,
Putting their best foot forward on the road
To Walkden, Camberwell or Leeds. It snowed.
It met them waiting at the roundabout.
They had no hats and coats to keep it out.
They did a lap or two, they caught a cough.
They did another lap and shuffled off.

Adam confesses an infidelity to Eve

I dreamed you were stolen from my left side
And woke hugging the pain. There in our room
Lit by the street lamp she appeared to me
Like something pulled from the earth. She is bulb-white;

Her shadowy place as black as wet moss
Or the widow spider. Believe me
She flattened my raised hands. She gripped
The cage of my heart between her knees,

Gluttonous for mandrake, and fed then,
Crammed her nether mouth, so rooting at
My evasive tongue I feared she would swallow it.
Curtained together under her hair

Only when she rose from drinking
And rolled and bucked as though I were reined
Did I see her face, like a slant moon,
Her eyes smudged and cavernous, her mouth bruised.

She cried like a seal. When she bowed down
Her brow on mine as savages pray

Enshrining my head between her forearms
Then, I confess, feeling her cold tears

I lapped them from her cheeks and let her rest.
My seed ran out of her, cold. On the street
Hissing with rain the lamps were extinguished.
You, when I woke, lay hooped on my left arm.

From Caspar Hauser

We never sleep. We have no empty squares.
It would be impossible to deliver him
So he stood out. The wars

Blow children up. Some fall our way.
They know a single sentence. They can say
My father is dead in somewhere in the news,

My mother raped and dead, or thrust it down
In somebody else's capitals
Over our headlines in the underground,

Or howl, just that: a particular girl
Rides the loop, stop by stop,
And holds a stump out and a begging cup

And howls, just that. I have observed her eyes.
They are so absent you would say she hires
Herself as a professional keener in her cause.

And nobody looks at anyone else, we all
Pray there'll be no hold-up for the howl
Cannot be borne beyond its usual

Measure. And much the same
Like wreckage after a catastrophe we have not fathomed yet
Children of our own making squat

Along the concrete walkways and the bridges
We cross to the opera
And hold a cardboard in their laps that says

What their state is.

Selima Hill

SELIMA HILL was born in 1945, and grew up on a farm. She won the Arvon International Poetry Competition in 1988 with part of her book-length poem *An Accumulation of Small Acts of Kindness*. Her poetry is published in two books from Bloodaxe, *A Little Book of Meat* (1993) and *Trembling Hearts in the Bodies of Dogs* (1994).

'She is truly gifted. She invests mundane things with visionary, delirious brilliance' – Graham Swift. 'Her language and imagery is sensual, controlled...Hill's world is strange, dream-like, secretive...delicate, moving and vaguely sinister' – Carol Ann Duffy. 'She evokes, for me, the inner childhood world we're supposed to give up as we become adult yet which artists need to draw upon' – Michèle Roberts. ●

Selection from: *A Little Book of Meat* (1993) and *Trembling Hearts in the Bodies of Dogs: New & Selected Poems* (1994).

Don't Let's Talk About Being in Love

Don't let's talk about being in love, OK?
– about *me* being in love, in fact, OK?
about your bloated face, like a magnolia;
about marsupials,
whose little blunted pouches
I'd like to crawl inside, lips first;
about the crashing of a million waterfalls
– as if LOVE were a dome of glass beneath a lake
entered through a maze of dripping tunnels
I hoped and prayed I'd never be found inside.

At night I dream that your bedroom's crammed with ducks.
You smell of mashed-up meal and scrambled egg.
Some of the ducks are broody, and won't stand up.
And I dream of the fingers of your various wives
reaching into your private parts like beaks.
And you're lying across the bed like a man shouldn't be.
And I'm startled awake by the sound of creaking glass
as if the whole affair's about to collapse
and water come pouring in with a rush of fishes
going *slurpetty-slurpetty-slurp* with their low-slung mouths.

Sleepless Nights

Because you scream like a sluice,
because you scream like someone waking up at night
with raging toothache,
like a cargo of half-wrapped lorries
being unloaded into some remote terminal
with lots of shouting and gesticulation;
like the Mongolian Empire itself,
thundering with obese horesemen;
because the last night I spent longing for you
was like spending the night with no clothes on
in a Daimler full of chows
with the windows closed,
I have decided to calm myself down,
and imagine my head as a tinkly moss-padded cavern
where nothing happens.

A Small Hotel

My nipples tick
like little bombs of blood.

Someone is walking
in the yard outside.

I don't know why
Our Lord was crucified.

A really good fuck
makes me feel like custard.

Cow

I want to be a cow
and not my mother's daughter.
I want to be a cow
and not in love with you.
I want to feel free to feel calm.
I want to be a cow who never knows
the kind of love you 'fall in love with' with;
a queenly cow, with hips as big and sound
as a department store,
a cow the farmer milks on bended knee,
who when she dies will feel dawn
bending over her like lawn to wet her lips.

I want to be a cow,
nothing fancy –
a cargo of grass,
a hammock of soupy milk
whose floating and rocking and dribbling's undisturbed
by the echo of hooves to the city;
of crunching boots;
of suspicious-looking trailers parked on verges;
of unscrupulous restaurant-owners
who stumble, pink-eyed, from stale beds
into a world of lobsters and warm telephones;
of streamlined Japanese freighters
ironing the night,
heavy with sweet desire like bowls of jam.

The Tibetans have 85 words for states of consciousness.
This dozy cow I want to be has none.
She doesn't speak.
She doesn't do housework or worry about her appearance.
She doesn't roam.
Safe in her fleet
of shorn-white-bowl-like friends,
she needs, and loves, and's loved by,
only this –
the farm I want to be a cow on too.

Don't come looking for me.
Don't come walking out into the bright sunlight
looking for me,
black in your gloves and stockings and sleeves
and large hat.
Don't call the tractorman.
Don't call the neighbours.
Don't make a special fruit-cake for when I come home:
I'm not coming home.
I'm going to be a cowman's counted cow.
I'm going to be a cow
and you won't know me.

The Dog-Man
(for Janie)

But something is certainly moving
down at the lair-like, scented, suddenly-occupied
other end of the room –
the dog-man from next door has come to play the piano,
to pour out his horrible notes
like a deluge of ripe, exhausted plums:
they stick in her hair
and mess up her ironed, imported, daisy-spangled cotton dress
that glares out sententiously
like one of those little flower-gardens
harbour-masters and sandwich-bar-owners
dedicate their lives to
with the kind of murderous possessiveness
small seaside towns
obsessed by being the nicest
go over the top with;
she's pressed against by plums as big as radiators,
emperors,
sweating Clydesdales,
suicide
over-heated Japanese 'bath-houses for sexual relief'
she's read about, and puzzled over, and tried not to see herself in –
plums buzzing with bright wasps

that cross and recross the precinct of her chair
like a switched-on electric fence
she can't move through.
Her eyes are glazed,
and her face could be basked on by lizards it's so still.
She's mistress of the art of frozenness,
hiding at the side of herself
like a pilgrim bathing in the Ganges
being cruised past by loudspeaker-toting boats;
like a diseased tomato;
like a brain-damaged child strapped in a van
who's watching, or anyway parked in front of,
an open-air, wrap-around, drive-in,
completely incomprehensible picture-show,
and the van has a sliding door
that might accidentally slither open any minute
and send a whole avalanche of untouchable things
that have no business to be there,
and should never be seen,
tumbling out into the open
like mutes or brains;
and at night,
when I'm nearly asleep,
I sometimes come across her –
vicious, hunched-up and incapacitated,
still hugging her hairless awkward little thighs.

Crocuses

And is her father with her on the lawn?
Absolutely not.
She needs to be quite alone.
And what is she drinking, on the lawn?
Hot tea.
And what is she writing?
Things that have made her angry.
*And has a certain bunch of flowers
made her angry?*
Yes.

He stepped out
into the sunlight,
still in his nightclothes,
and made his way
down the hill
to the orchard.
Her first gold crocuses
were pushing up like fish
(she wanted *no one* to see them)
between striped wasps on plums.

And what sharp implement
was he carrying down with him?
Scissors.
And if he were to cut himself –
remember he's an old man now –
would she come running down the bank with sheets
to stanch the bleeding?
No, she would not.
And will she forgive him?
Never.

My First Bra

A big brown bear
is knocking at the door:

he wants to borrow a dress
and matching knickers.

The smell of lilac
smothers me like wool;

beyond the lawns,
I hear my naked sister

crying in the nettles
where I threw her:

nobody else is having
my first bra.

Peter Didsbury

PAT DIDSBURY

Selection from: *The Butchers of Hull* (1982), *The Classical Farm* (1987) and *That Old-Time Religion* (1994).

PETER DIDSBURY was born in 1946 in Fleetwood, Lancashire, and moved to Hull at the age of six. His two most recent books have both been given Poetry Book Society Recommendations, and yet he remains the least known of the major names on the Bloodaxe list. He is a poet whose powers of invention are staggering, whose flouting of convention and subversive humour can be outrageous.

'Didsbury's is the kind of work which makes you realise what you've been putting up with in the meantime. The product of a large and peculiar imagination, it shows a sense of adventure hardly to be paralleled in contemporary poetry...In Didsbury's work there is glimpsed an alternative history where Catholic Europe and the East are strangely mixed, where matters of faith and damnation are still alive' – Sean O'Brien. ●

The Drainage

When he got out of bed the world had changed.
It was very cold. His breath whitened the room.
Chill December clanked at the panes.
There was freezing fog.
He stepped outside.
Not into his street but a flat wet landscape.
Sluices. Ditches. Drains. Frozen mud and leafcake. Dykes.
He found he knew the names of them all.
Barber's Cut. Cold Track. Lament. Meridian Stream.
He found himself walking.
It was broad cold day but the sky was black.
Instead of the sun it was Orion there.
Seeming to pulse his meaning down.
He was naked. He had to clothe himself.
The heifers stood like statues in the fields.
They didn't moan when he sliced the hides from them.
He looked at the penknife in his hand.
The needle, the thread, the clammy strips.
Now his face mooned out through a white hole.
The cape dripped. He knew he had
the bounds of a large parish to go.

His feet refused to falter.
Birds sat still in the trees.
Fast with cold glue. Passing their clumps
he watched them rise in their species.
The individuals. Sparrow. Starling. Wren.
He brought them down with his finger.
Knife needle and thread again.
It happened with the streams.
Pike barbel roach minnow gudgeon.
Perch dace eel. Grayling lamprey bream.
His feet cracked puddles and were cut on mud. They bled.
There was movement. He pointed. He stitched.
His coat hung reeking on him.
He made cut after cut in the cold.
Coldness and the colours of blood.
Red blue and green. He glistened.
He stitched through white fat.
Weight of pelts and heads. Nodding at the hem.
Feathers. Scales. Beaks and strips of skin.
He had the bounds of a large parish to go.
Oh Christ, he moaned. Sweet Christ.
The Hunter hung stretched in the Sky.
He looked at the creatures of the bankside.
He glistened. He pointed. He stitched.

In Britain

The music, on fat bellied instruments.
The fingers, swarming down ladders
into the bubbling cauldrons of sound.
The mouths, greasy, encouraging the prying fingers
with songs of fecund stomachs.
The hands, transferring to the singing mouths
whatever is lifted through the scum.
The choicest morsels, the collops of dog and the
gobbets of pig. The orchestras and bands,
the minstrelsy arranged in tiers,
dripping on each other. The larded steps.
The treacherous floors in the wooden galleries.

The garlands of offal, plopping on heads
from a height of some feet.
The offal sliding off down the front of the face,
or over the neck and ears. The offal reposing like hats.
The curly grey-white tubes, dangling jauntily
above the left eye of the bagpipe player.
The guests, similarly festooned.
The guests at their conversation,
abundance of dogs and pigs in these islands.
The guests at their serious business, lying in pools.
The stories, farting and belching across the puddled boards.
The gross imaginations, bulging with viscera.
The heads full of stories, the stories thwacked like bladders.
The stories steaming in time to the music.
The stories, chewed like lumps of gristle.
The stories describing extravagant herds.
The stories, reasons for killing each other.

A Priest in the Sabbath Dawn
Addresses His Somnolent Mistress

Wake up, my heart, get out of bed
and put your scarlet shirt back on and leave,
for Sunday is coming down the chimney
with its feet in little socks,
and I need a space in which to write my sermon.
Although the hour's already late
it can still be done, if only you'll depart!
Down the pipe and out across the lawn
would take you to the station yard
in which you left your bicycle last week
and give me time to clothe in flesh the text
I have in mind for the instruction of my flock.
Please hurry dear. The earliest note of the matin bell
has left its tower like an urgent dove
and is beating its way to woods outside the town.
The sun is up, the parish breakfasted,
the ghosts are all returned into the flint
yet still you lie here, shaming me with sleep.

Wake up, I say, for Sabbath legs
are landing in the grate. Go naked if you must
but grant me these few minutes with my pen
to write of how I cut myself while shaving.
Be useful, at least, and fetch my very razor,
for the faithful have set their feet upon the road
and are hurrying here with claims on the kind of story
which I cannot fittingly make from your sudden grin.

Eikon Basilike

(for the soul of William Cowper)

During the late and long continuing cold
I went for a walk in the empty heart of the city.
I stuffed the sun and moon in a deep string bag
and let them hang from my shoulder as I marched.
I noted the resemblance that my home now suddenly bore
to a level Baltic town, its frozen gardens, and its
bright green civic domes. The new white lawns
had frosted to such a depth that they'd lost
the visual texture of grass and begun to make pastiche
of a pavement, a complement to some old and
disgruntled buildings. I cast around for a route,
and chose to follow three hares in winter coats
who hopped across my path. They tempted me away
from that novel plaza which the ice revealed
and I found myself on a track beside a canal,
or rather a drain, which is different,
for it empties into the turbulent German Ocean.
There was dereliction on one side of the stream
and an Arctic kind of Xanadu on the other.
I shivered. My hip-flask was out of action.
I hadn't actually invented it yet
but knew I wouldn't be leaving it very much longer.
If this was what linguistic exercise meant
then I didn't think much of it. The deep structures
I could cope with, but the surface ones
were coming at me in Esperanto, and fragments of horrible Volapük.

I was walking through the urban fields that surrounded
the Stalag or temple or star-ship of the Power Station.
Yellow electricity vans kept cornering on the road
that crossed the bricky and entrenched landscape.
I recognised the faces of the drivers, and later spotted
most of the leading Romantic poets, all of whom were eating
substantial packing-up, in tents pegged out by the kerb.
It was a case of etcetera etcetera. Tiney, Puss and Bess
were proving considerate guides. I found I had plenty of time
to inspect the ceramic formers on their poles.
I noticed many ordinary things, several of which were lying
on the ice, between the high and weedy banks of the drain.
I began to think of the slicks of grey lawn that must exist
between runways on the edge of international airports.
Hot moonlit nights in Athens or Cairo, powdery channels of grass
that might just as well be anywhere, all of them rising in Hades.
The fat and impersonal transports were lifting on either side
and threatening my creatures with their cruel and silvery wings.
I could see the black pylons here and there but the power lines
were all of them lost in the low-level brume. I only heard them hum,
thrupping the atmospheric fridge with over and over again
a Vulgar Latin sentence which my guts were scarcely screwed to.
'It is all up with thee, thou hast already utterly perished.'
The hares bounded on, and finally halted outside the gate
on the bridge that carried the road across the stream
and into the precincts of the Generating Board.
I stood next to them, making the fourth in their row,
and I looked where they looked: below the rusty barbed wire
was an old white notice bearing the four bold letters
that denoted which mesmeric authority
we laboured under the caring aegis of.
Something – Something – G – B.
Like a name of God. But the letters were all wrong.
The three hares looked at me like animals in anthropomorphic films
when they've just led the hero to the scene of his triumph.
I thought I might begin to weep and yet I scarcely knew why.
The enamel plate was now announcing that this was *Eikon Basilike*,
a place whose sub-title I had no problem supplying
from my sad and emotional erudition, justified at last
by a portraicture of his sacred majestie, in his solitude and sufferings.

A Winter's Fancy

To write a Tristram Shandy *or a* Sentimental Journey *there is no way but to be Sterne; and Sternes are not turned out in bakers' batches.*

A winter's fancy.
I look out of my window
and perceive I am Laurence Sterne.
I am sitting in Shandy Hall.
It is raining.
I am inventing a Bag,
which will accommodate everything.
I'd weave it out of air if I could
but the rain slants down like a page of Greek
and the afternoon is a dish of mud,
far removed from gentle opinion.
I am heavy with God.
The weather used
to cloak itself in sentiment
but today it imitates the tongues of men
and wags in curtains at me, along a yard.
I am also John, an elderly bibliophile.
Once, long after I died, I returned to Coxwold
on a literary pilgrimage.
A red-faced lout leaned over my gate
and instructed me curtly to Sodding Sod Off.
He was full of choler.
I sometimes feel I can understand
what's been eluding me ever since Christmas.
I'm exhausting my karma of country parson
in a dozen lives of wit and kidneys,
caritas, the pox, and marbled endpapers.
Looking out from here, this afternoon,
I can just discern the porch of my church
where Nick and Numps are sheltering from
Thucydides, Books Six and Seven.
By the look of that cloud looming up like a skull
there will soon be nothing left to do
but to take to my bed.

The cattle squelch past beneath a sodden sky,
below my windows and before the eyes
of Peter Didsbury, in his 35th year.
I consider other inventions of mine,
which rise before me in the darkening pane.
Light me that candle, oh my clever hand,
for it is late, and I am admirably tired.

A Bee

Become at last a bee
I took myself naked to town,
with plastic sacks of yellow turmeric
taped to my wizened thighs.

I'd been buying it for weeks,
along with foods I no longer had a need for,
in small amounts from every corner grocer,
so as not to arouse their suspicion.

It was hard, running and buzzing,
doing the bee-dance. I ached
at the roots of my wings, and hardly yet discerned
that I flew towards reparation,
that in my beehood my healing had been commenced.

Words they use in this hive. To me it seems still
that clumps of tall blue flowers,
which smiled as they encroached,
had been born of my apian will,
in which to my shame I struggled for a moment,
and stained the air with clouds of my dearly bought gold.

Tua Forsström

LEIF ROSAS

Selection from: *Snow Leopard*
(1990), translated
by David McDuff.

TUA FORSSTRÖM was born in 1947. She is a
much acclaimed Finland-Swedish poet writ-
ing out of the central tradition of European
poetry that includes Hölderlin, Rilke and
Paul Celan. Her poems are remarkable for
their directness and emotional courage, her
deeply musical voice seeming to speak out of
the fabric of existence itself, its utterance
organised and structured through a crystal-
line compactness and density of diction. Each
poem is a subtly yet strongly constructed
image of an inner world that is not merely
hers, but one we all share – that of intimacy
and its denial, of loss and despair, of an un-
recoverable childhood joy shadowed down
the years by a sense of pain and want. ●

From Snow Leopard

There is a certain kind of loss
and September's objectivity

Something is released imperceptibly,
and is displaced: it does not

matter. There is a coolness
that has settled on the surfaces,

it kept me calm. One sits
on a bench that looks like other benches,

trains leave on time, dogs bark,
one is. Close to you

I read books and confused my name
with names of other places: a summer kitchen

with radio news in front of blowing curtains,
the cousin sailing in the bay

I stood on the threshold of my mother's
bedroom, she was not there

Bedrooms smell differently in summer:
a weather of gentle snowfalls

One sees a snake and treads carefully
on the grass for a few days   Still weakened

by revenge: I inform against myself. There was
a magic room called Childhood

and always the same alien particulars
I have kept calm for a long time. And now

the wind takes hold of the sail
and drives my cousin straight across the bay

the small red sail red against the green

*

The Fieldmouse's Prayer

Father, in the blowing greenery of Your summer,
Father, in the endlessly green vault of Your summer:
Help me to get down into the ditch when Your
elect draw near along the road.

*

They come out at dusk, flat
shadows across the fields. They are composed in equal
parts of pig, badger, fox. Helplessness
is their principal distinguishing mark. They root in the snow
for something to eat. We find them unnatural:
their aimless wandering, their hunger, their obscene
lack of protection. At the first sign of danger the he-marten
lies down and pretends to be dead. We find such behaviour
pitiful, we find the pitiful repulsive, we
are outraged by the hungry shadows of
this sugar-beet field, so unlike the snow leopard that silently
pursues its prey six thousand metres
above sea-level.

*

Thank you for Your kind parcel.
I must, however, return everything:
there are plenty of scissors, stones grow
into mountains, and the chains were too heavy
even for Selma, my cow.
That's enough of the Flowers of Evil, and one
thing and another.
Mother said I was a darling child,
but she has stopped crying.
Sometimes it is spring, and sometimes it is winter.
It was brilliant night, and the courtyard plummeted
like a swarm of shooting-stars through space.
Fire burns more quickly than one thinks.
It's like this: there's a house somewhere,
whoops! there's no house anywhere.
I have seen a photograph of the University.
But where are you at nights?
They found charred newspapers in the snow
right up at the Marsh, I miss
Father and Mother, but one has to be somewhere.
Everyone says I shouldn't have done it.
I have bits of fur and snot in my hair,
one shouldn't get oneself in such a mess.
It's a question of being a good pupil!
A Nebula is a mist of incandescent garbage.
Before, I used to mourn both life and death, ought
I all the same to be sorry about Selma?
They bring the food in on green trays
I am terribly hungry, so I
must eat instead
Mother said I fluttered like a butterfly
over the garden path, but she's not crying now.
Mother raked the garden path beautifully.
It's not nice to eat so much.
It's nice not to be sad any more.
I dreamed that someone unbuttoned my blouse
and rusty iron bled and bled from my mouth
onto the floor. Otherwise everything is fine.

Micheal O'Siadhail

Selection from: *Hail! Madam Jazz: New & Selected Poems* (1992).

MICHEAL O'SIADHAIL was born in 1947 in Dublin. His New & Selected Poems *Hail! Madam Jazz* (1992) includes work from six collections, the first three of which were originally written and published in Irish.

'Micheal O'Siadhail is a writer whose rampant love of language is fortunately disciplined by an austere, scholarly intelligence ...His poems convey this vivid sense of a shrewd, meditative observer, a perceptive critic of the life that is about him and within him' – Brendan Kennelly. 'Controlled sensuousness of language...it comes as near as poetry can, without being confessional, to conveying the overtones and textures of actual experience' – Anne Stevenson. ●

Cosmos

'All right?' booms the saxophone man,
'everybody feeling chameleon?' The combo
expands the tune of a well-battered song.
An opulence of sound, clash and flow
as a spotlight tunnels dust in its beam,
glints the trumpet's bell and the hall
turns hot and hybrid, beery listeners
swaying and bobbing the mood of a theme.

From rainbows of timbre a strand of colour
floats into the air: the trumpet solo
burping one phrase of a melody, ripe
and brassy and buttoned down as though
a song is breathing over its origins,
those four hot-blooded notes weeping
their pleasure again on an old civil war
bugle. A sleazy backroom in New Orleans.

Sax and rhythm. The brightness of a reed,
winding tube and crook are working on
another hue of the tune that moves
into its own discourse: *Bud Freeman,
Johnny Hodges, Charlie Parker*. 'All right?'

he drawls, then scats a little as we clap
a tradition of subversions. But he's off again.
I watch swarms of dust in the spotlight,

swirls of galaxies, and imagine he's blowing
a huge balloon of space that's opening
our world of order. In a waft of creation
his being becomes a music's happening.
A red-shirted pianist now leans to seize
a gene of the song which seems to veer
and improvise, somehow catching a moment's
shifts and humours. Hail! Madam Jazz.

Let the theme return, its mutants echoing
as a tune balances against its freedom.
One key – so open-toned and open-stitched.
A beat poised, a crossgrained rhythm,
interplays, imbrications of voice over voice,
mutinies of living are rocking the steady
state of a theme; these riffs and overlappings
a love of deviance, our genesis in noise.

Coastlines

A temperament takes on the world. I chose bleak
slabs of limestone, lone outcrops, promontories
poking their stubborn arms against an Atlantic;
supple elbows of strand seemed like cowardice.
Lines will blur, a seaboard fret and shift,
waves spending and being spent into the silence
of endless sands, rhythms of challenge and drift
husbanding or yielding the jigsaw shore of an island.
It's best the blue-grey rocks know nothing of how
constant water wears, a coiling uncoiling motion
flushing each snag or edge, ebb and flow
scouring the grain, their work being worked by ocean;
clenched fists of will jutted in their prime,
tangs of stone daring a tide or time.

Tradition

A feeling of passivity, of handing over.
All that was received I again deliver

by just being here. Available. No more.
A watch of dependence, complete exposure,

not even trying not to try to achieve.
This work is a waiting, almost as if

a host, his palms held up in supplication
between two guests, begins an introduction:

'For years I've wanted you two to meet.'
The middle voice fading as they greet

in the sweet nothingness of a go-between.

Between

As we fall into step I ask a penny for your thoughts.
'Oh, nothing,' you say, 'well, nothing so easily bought.'

Sliding into the rhythm of your silence, I almost forget
how lonely I'd been until that autumn morning we met.

At bedtime up along my childhood's stairway, tongues
of fire cast shadows. Too earnest, too highstrung.

My desire is endless: others ended when I'd only started.
Then, there was you: so whole-hog, so wholehearted.

Think of the thousands of nights and the shadows fought.
And the mornings of light. I try to read your thought.

In the strange openness of your face, I'm powerless.
Always this love. Always this infinity between us.

Ruth Padel

CHRIS ANDREWES

Selection from: *Angel* (1993).

RUTH PADEL was born in 1947. She is a poet
and writer on Greek tragedy, religion and
psychology. Her scholarly work, 'exquisitely
written word-painting' on madness and self
in ancient Greece, has been prized for the
'gruesome brilliance and richness' with which
she portrays 'an intense and exotic mental
world' (*New York Review of Books*). Her
poetry, plunging into psychologically est-
ranged worlds, does something similar.

Her second collection, *Angel*, is a Poetry
Book Society Recommendation. It highlights
history and control of meaning, and is about
madness and unknowability. Its figures are
opaque to one another, like the sources of
their hurt. *The Starling* mentions trepan-
ning and bloodletting: these were early 17th-
century "cures" for insanity. ●

The Starling

They are talking of trepanning the Indian starling
because the starling thinks she is the Empress of Oslo
and besides, she is very lonely. The Kissagram boy,
off duty, brought her in from the westwoods
under the flyover, her tertiaries dipped in ink:
smaragdine plus a lavender-cum-royal blue.

She looked, then, a bedraggled poisonous orchid.
We bled her at the hip or wherever roughly
you might expect a hip in all that tininess.
She lies alone on puffed flannel and can't sleep.
I've slipped out, nights, against orders
to feed her cinnamon toast, read her *The Golden Bough*.

Her eye is cloudy, suspicious. She voids phlegm
and half-dreams of a childless woman
killed in a bar in backstreet Friedenstadt,
and that nobody, nobody mourned her
as the starling thinks *she* should be mourned.
Bedlem's Managing Director, the one man

who can save our starling, has evaded diagnosis.
He says she was a present from the King.
After the first incision, he kept his scalpel
under the lid of its Royal Society box
in a self-shaped baize hollow like the bed
of a chestnut in its shell. Or a sharp empty egg.

Without

They decided they'd keep just the head.
I heard she was imposing
recession régime on the household
(three little boys

and they were asleep now
anyway, missing things),
because another body,
female, wouldn't do.

I shimmied in early but
the others had got there first
and in she came, all
buttoned-through Jaeger

for the occasion.
I couldn't speak for tears
but she wouldn't see me anyway.
She sailed up smiling,

reeling in the bouquets
like Thatcher after the war
on telly, at the little
top of her steps.

This way, you can have it sent.
It's a service, like any other.
No screams, no mess.
Because it's easier without.

You haven't to bother
over the mysteries and waste.
Nothing to get in the way.
But all I could think of

was a head in a box
arriving later from the hospital.
Mentally female, once female,
all future

in a thermo-nuclear vaccuum,
dreaming of bodies to hold.
Bodies she'd build for
herself, one day.

On the Ice Label

I got there through the battle-zone
leaving a four-year-old
alone with 6 oz puma paté
for the day. Someone had taken
another shot at the Booker winner,
a guy with an electronic voicebox
in a roller-chair. The cops were out.
Rocket-launchers on white vans
down the Strand. Fire in bottles.
Catshouts over health-cuts. Caltrops.
TV crews in khaki. You know the pitch.

We had string quartet that day
with the reggae. His *Dies Irae*
under the griffin-claws
of a de-sanctified cathedral
with a seven-minute decay
on the *re*verb – dead right
for serpent, ophiclide, bassoon.
That's the last I saw of him.
The two of us were double glazing,
two walls of mismatched dust,
glaring at each other. I've learned
the corner the light doesn't reach
is the one the dime rolled to.
But we cut that disc OK.

Elena Shvarts

Selection from: 'Paradise':
Selected Poems (1993),
translated by Michael Molnar
and Catriona Kelly.

ELENA SHVARTS was born in 1948 in Lenin-
grad, but not openly published there until
1989. Bella Akhmadulina has called her 'a
miracle', describing her poetry as 'the pur-
est of creations'. Shvarts draws backwoods
Russian folklore with its cruelty, its relig-
iosity and its quaint humour into her own
image of St Petersburg, a haunted, demonic
city nearer Dostoyevsky's than Akhmatova's
or Brodsky's. She celebrates and reviles her
native city as a crossroads of dimensions, a
reality riddled with mythical monuments
and religious symbols.

'A dark, free, northern spirit...Bulgakov
and Tsvetayeva (and Angela Carter) would
feel at home in her violently imagined town-
scapes and landscapes' – Edwin Morgan. ●

From Cynthia

*(Cynthia is a Roman poetess of the 1st century B.C., the heroine
of the elegies of Propertius and famous not only for her talent
but also for her bad temper. Her poems have not survived,
nevertheless I have attempted to translate them into Russian.)*

II *To Father*

Father butts in again with admonitions:
'You shouldn't be living this way,' he says, 'but that.'
'Very well, daddy,' I say to him,
'I won't do it again, daddikins.'

Meek and mild I look at his grey beard,
His clawlike hands, his red red mouth.
I tell the slaves: 'This very moment
Hurl the halfwit into the fish pool.'

He is dragged across the marble floor,
He tries to cling, there's nothing for him to cling to,
Blood flows down his face and with it tears:
'My own little daughter,' he cries, 'forgive me, please!'

'No! the unfed moray eels shall tear you,
Lecherous bigot, mealymouthed prude.'
Or I picture to myself – a lion
At the circus gobbling up his liver.

'All right,' I say, 'all right – I'll change my ways.
Oh you poor thing, my dear old daddy.'
When a tiger had licked away even the scent of blood
I began to be just a little bit sorry for him.

In spirit I execute him variously – a thousand ways
And yet another thousand ways –
In the end, however, in actual fact,
The hammer raised – I never strike his temple.

III *To a Serving Girl*

How could you dare, slattern, how could you dare!
Too mild a punishment, exile to the country
Married off to an Iberian Celt
Who cleans his teeth with his own urine,
Or, as your soul's shade, to an Ethiop.
O you hussy! I was reciting Catullus,
Softly wandering through the house – and the lantern
Standing in the corner lengthened my shadow –
She came stamping in out of the kitchen
Heaving some mackerel on a gilded salver
And stepped directly onto my very shadow –
Onto my head, and then onto my forearm!
And my shadow is more bruisable and tender –
Well she knows it! – than her padded hide is.
If they were to fry you in a skillet,
In the same one as the noble mackerel,
Even that would be less painful to you
Than it was to me – when your foot trampled
Into the floor – the shadow of my ringlets.

[MM]

Elegy on an X-ray Photo of My Skull

The flautist boasts but God's enraged –
He stripped the living skin from Marsyas –
Such is the destiny of earthly flautists:
Grown jealous, He will say to each in turn: –
'You've licked the honey of music but you're just muck,
You're still a lump of that same dirt
And lodged inside you is the stone of death.'
Apollo was the god of light
But he grew dark
When round his hands, you Marsyas,
Twisted in pain.
And now he is a god of glimmer,
But eternal also are your groans.

And my God, growing dark,
Slipped me this photograph
In which my glowing skull,
Etched from the invisible,
Swam, blocking out the dusk
And the stripped naked park –
It was a mass of fog
Embraced in liquid dark.
In it shadow and cloud were blended
And my hand began to tremble.
This skull was my own
But it didn't know me,
Its intricate pattern
Like a damascene dagger
Is skilfully crafted,
How pure and how strong.
But the mouth is bared,
Still alive its grin.

Bone, you yellowed a long time,
Grew as heavy as sin,
Like a walnut you aged and you ripened,
A present for death.
Grown brazen inside me, this yellow bone
Has lapped itself in a sleigh-rug of skin

And taking my reins sped off headlong
But come to a halt at my brow.
In anguish here before my God I stand
Holding my skull in a trembling hand –
O Lord, what shall I do with it?
Spit in its eyesockets?
Fill it up with wine?
Or put it on my neck and wear it once again?
So I hurl it aside – this light-looking shell
And it flies off thundering among the stars like a pail.
But it returned and landing on my neck, reminded me in consolation:
Way back at someone's house, its fellow stood as a table decoration
And led the deathlife of a dehydrated plant
As if it were a temple or a chalice.
There was a lot to drink but not enough –
And someone took this skull and began to pass it round
To collect the money for a vodka bottle.
Small change was scattered clinking on the dark occiput
But straightaway I confiscated it,
Put it back where it belonged – calm down –
And like a kitten it rubbed against my palm.
For this I shall be granted as reward
That nobody will desecrate my skull –
No worm will crawl inside, no new Hamlet take it in his hands.
When my end comes – I shall walk up the aisle in flames.
But something else strikes me as weird,
That I can't sense my skeleton inside –
Neither skull nor flesh nor bones –
More like a crater after the explosion
Or a memory of missing news,
Mistiness or mist
Or a spirit drunk on its new life.

But you will be my lodgings when
They start to pipe the Resurrection.
You, my spirit's navel, fly
Sooner to the East. And I
All around you as a dusty cloud
Erupting, swirling, setting as the Word.
But what a shame you won't be filled again
With all that soft old curd.

[MM]

Piotr Sommer

DAVID HUNTER

Selection from: *Things to Translate* (1991), translated by Piotr Sommer with John Ashbery, Douglas Dunn, D.J. Enright and others.

PIOTR SOMMER was born in 1948. He is known in Poland both as an important poet and as a leading translator of English poetry into Polish. He has translated Robert Lowell and produced editions of O'Hara and Reznikoff, and has been an editor and translator for the magazine *Literatura na swiecie* since 1976.

'Piotr Sommer's poetry is low-key and terse; to adapt one of his phrases, it wants to say nothing it doesn't need to. Irony there is, but it keeps its head down, while the occasional uncertain joke raises an uncertain smile. Obliquity is the rule. An old dog entertains metaphysical thoughts, and in its own way expresses an opinion. Or a knock on the door announces a milkwoman, not the secret police, but the one caller mirrors the other' – D.J. Enright. ●

Don't sleep, take notes

At four in the morning
the milkwoman was knocking,
in plain clothes, threatening
she wouldn't leave us anything,
at most remove the empties,
if I didn't produce the receipt.

It was somewhere in my jacket,
but in any case I knew
what the outcome would be:
she'd take away yesterday's curds,
she'd take the cheese and eggs,
she'd take our flat away,
she'd take away our child.

If I don't produce the receipt,
if I don't find the receipt,
the milkwoman will cut our throats.

[PS/DJE]

Grammar

What was, one should speak of in the past tense,
what isn't, in some other tongue.

[PS/DJE]

A maple leaf

A maple leaf with the sun shining through it
at the end of summer is beautiful, but
not too much so, and even an ordinary
electric train passing by
nearly three hundred yards away
makes music, light and unobtrusive,
and yet to be remembered, for some sort of
usefulness perhaps, or even
instructiveness (the world somehow
doesn't quite say it knows everything,
has a good memory and, above all,
won't show it off).

[PS/JA]

This is certain

Young provincials have literary hopes.
They will follow their first lyrical impulses,
then they'll grow more bitter, but thanks to that, mature.
Lyric poetry, they believe, leads to an understanding
of themselves and the world, to perfection.
They'll look suspiciously upon the avant-garde,

and with some superiority, which will be reflected
in their modesty, their solid lyrical craft
and aspirations deliberately curtailed
(this much is certain· better a modest yet sound performance).

But they'll be full of enthusiasm.
And optimism.
Serious matters are at stake.
Far from the quarrels of the capital,
they know what to think.
There are always landscapes on their doorstep:
woods, a river, puffy pancakes of cloud,
or even wooden fences nibbled at by time.

There are places perhaps
where only what's good gets printed.
But that's an issue you can bypass and go to the field
through a hole in the fence, best of all on an autumn evening,
and look at the sky, or trees,
just about anything –
for everything reminds you of impermanence!

[PS/DD]

Two gestures

A woman drags herself from bed.
You know, I think I ought to make myself some dinner.
But she doesn't have time
and dies between
two gestures: her mother's
and her child's, never discovering
who, or whose, she was
more.

[PS/DD]

Gillian Allnutt

MOIRA CONWAY

Selection from: *Blackthorn*
(1994).

GILLIAN ALLNUTT was born in 1949. She has published three collections of poetry: *Spitting the Pips Out* (Sheba, 1981), *Beginning the Avocado* (Virago, 1987) and *Blackthorn* (Bloodaxe, 1994). Denise Levertov described her work as 'at once hard and delicate, like wrought iron'.

Much of *Blackthorn* is a post-feminist exploration of the feminine – and, correspondingly, necessarily, of the masculine. It is an affirmation of human androgyny and a plea for the androgyny of God. The poems come out of worlds known and imagined, outer and inner, exploring archetypal and spiritual levels of the psyche, often within the ambivalent framework of Christianity. ●

After The Blaydon Races

Look how the big yellow bus of the sun bowls breakneck into
        Benwell also.

Shall it not, for a while, be still, with its wheel flown off?

Shall the old yellow bus, October, stop and beautifully steep us
in its pennyworth of ale, its picnic

cloth of gold unfolded on the rough grass?

Look how it briskly bowls by the rough sky-grass where houses were
and the forgotten, poor, affectionate people are,

berates us not as does the law in its bald helicopter

but, like that ribald bus on its breakneck way to Blaydon,
braves us, hedging bets

before our houses, waving, wild at heart and unrepentant
as the river, with its staithes and bridges.

In 1945

My father sat down where Belsen had been
and no birds came.

He could not listen any more.

Later the roots and stars would bring him a daughter.

They'd try to hurt him through her
singing.

He'd make her a home, he'd tell her
'Old Macdonald had a farm'

but he'd never hear again.

His ears were clogged wells. Hart's tongue
covered them.

His legs lay dying of typhus and rags.

His heart was a burnt-out chapel.

All the old hymns dried up in him like lentils.

His shoulders bore with him. Because of the farm
before the war

he'd spare his Uncle Tom.

My father sat down where butter and eggs had been
laid out.

It was in a Dutch kitchen.

The stars shone down like bits of shrapnel.

Scrub as he would, his hands would not
come clean.

Preparing the Icon
Andrej Rublev (c.1370 – c.1430) instructs his apprentices

Do not imagine, now, the austere sad face of John.
Before the snow falls, go to the forest.
Bring wood for the board. For days, while the stove remains
unlit in the studio, work that wood with chisel and plane
until it is smooth.
Break the ice on the water-butt then.
Prepare and apply to the board the first thin layer of gypsum
like a skin. Stretch the canvas. Then put on
a second layer of gypsum. When it is hard and dry, like bone,
rub it down till your shoulders are tired.
Draw the outline of John from the book of tracings,
the Authorised Version.
Begin your illumination with the background. Green.
Bring a bowl of eggs from the monastery farm.
Let him come loud and clear as a locust in your listening
to his God, ours. Break the eggs.
Use only the yolk for the dilution of your colours.
In the silence of falling snow and of the imagination's
cold dark halls, you'll know your own
austerity and John's.

George Charlton

NORMAN STAFFORD

Selection from: *Nightshift Workers* (1989) and *City of Dog* (1994).

GEORGE CHARLTON was born in 1950 in Gateshead, and lives in Newcastle. He has two collections from Bloodaxe, *Nightshift Workers* (1989) and *City of Dog* (1994), winner of a Poetry Book Society Recommendation.

'His writing issues from somewhere very close to the warm, affectionate and whole-hearted centre of the Tyneside and Northumberland where he lives. It is a generous poetry, urban in its awareness of lives other than his own, as well as industrisal dynasties, work, imperial foolishness and a manipulative economy. It is an unfussy, clear poetry, but often mysterious in its lyricism. For all its rootedness, it is far from "regional", but a poetry of place and community in which a perceiving self gasps to understand the everyday and its resonances' – Douglas Dunn. ●

Nightshift Workers

They have come from a factory
Where fluorescent strips flared all night

And ears grew numb to machinery;
They are going home to working wives,

To cooling beds at breakfast time,
Undressing fatigue from their skin like clothes;

Later to wake at four and taste teeth
Soft as fur in their mouths.

They live in a dislocation of hours
Inside-out like socks pulled on in darkness

Waking when the day is over.
They are always at an ebb, unlike others

Going out to work in the morning
Where sun and moon shine in the sky together.

Gateshead Grammar

There must be hundreds like us now,
Born since the war, brought up
In terraced streets near factory yards
And on expansive council estates.

We were the ones who stayed on at school
In academic quarantine. Others
Took apprenticeships in the skilled trades,
And left us indoors to finish homework.

And we didn't notice it at first –
All the literature that wasn't written
For us: passing an exam
Was an exercise in its own right.

To live like Spartans, think like monks
Had something heroic about it...
Now we dress carefully, and at
Introductions in expensive restaurants

Suppress the local accent in our voice,
Not to give ourselves away.
And little by little we go home less
To parents who seem to have fostered us:

We are like those bankrupt millionaires
With our own social-success stories
And personal failures. Remaindered
Fashions at give-away prices.

Twocked

(Police slang for 'taken without owner's consent')

It is the morning after the morning
After a Friday night out.

On land that lies waste –
That was once a school field –

There stands the squat wreck
Of a 'C' reg. Metro City,

Its flame-tinctured bodywork
Still tingling with heat.

From heat-fractured tubing
A sigh, a brief sigh,

Is sadder than the saxophones
Of Holland-Dozier-Holland.

The radio-cassette
Has been taken from its slot:

An unlooted tape
Has congealed in smoked plastic:

A dangling talisman no longer tells
Memento Mori or *Carpe Diem* –

While the clicking of the metal as it cools
Is like a telephone about to ring,

A voice, anticipated, about to break
The news – the composed voice

In no way like
The voice transfixed in this burnt-out wreck.

Medbh McGuckian

BILL DOYLE / GALLERY PRESS

Selection from: *Marconi's Cottage* (1991/1992).

MEDBH McGUCKIAN was born in 1950 in Belfast. She is one of Ireland's most important poets. After publishing three books with Oxford University Press, she joined Gallery Press in Ireland and Bloodaxe in Britain with her fourth collection.

In the mysterious and unsettling poems of *Marconi's Cottage*, she grapples with feminine and masculine principles, and tries to reconcile the conflicting claims of motherhood with the artist's freedom to write. A sequence of poems mourning the apparent sacrifice of one fertility to the other is followed by a spate of poems celebrating the physical, culminating in the birth of a child. Romantic and religious, she chronicles the conditions of her life and the loss and recovery of self in poems that are both challenging and mesmerising. ●

The Unplayed Rosalind
(for Anne Devlin)

July presides, light with a boy's hat,
Dressed in black with his feet on a cushion,
His voice-print is too dry for the stage.

The long-stemmed flowers comparatively
Rained, and the tumultuous sea was making me
Sterile, as though a hand from within it
Slowly drove me back, we were small objects
On its edge.

The telegraph pole sang because a horseshoe
Brushed its foot, and a spider's web darkened
On my finger like a kiss that has to be paid
With the veil lowered, a sweet-sour kiss through tight-
Bitten lips that could make me drunk.

I have lived on a war footing and slept
On the blue revolution of my sword;
Given the perfect narrative nature of blue,

I have been the poet of women and consequently
Of the young; if you burned my letters
In the soiled autumn they would form two hearts.

The room which I thought the most beautiful
In the world, and never showed to anyone,
Is a rose-red room, a roseate chamber.
It lacks two windowpanes and has no waterjug.
There is red ink in the inkwell.

Upstairs above my head lives someone
Who repeats my movements with her double
Weeping. My heart beats as though it were
Hers, and sometimes I have her within my clothes
Like a blouse fastened with a strap.

She moved in her dream, she lost her dream,
She stretched her arms and tossed her head
As a river burrows its bed till the bed burns.
Her dress reminded me of curtains torn
Like a page from a bedroom window.

There was a rustle in the lock of the door,
A noise like grasshoppers as though a great
Moth were caught in it. Then the door
Simply waved, and a long white sheet
Of paper came gliding from under it,
Like a coaster shoved beneath everyone's
Wineglass, or glass being cut under water.

In her there was something of me which
He touched, when she lay on his arm like the unknown
Echo of the word I wanted to hear
Only from his mouth; she spoke words to him
I had already heard.

She said, 'This is too bright for me',
Preferring to see the fire-red rip down heaven
As a saucer of iced water where she could
Dip her hands, as in the reciprocal blue
Ashes of his eyes.

She kissed him as if he were her child
Like a gull rubbing its beak against
A jagged window, and my body felt
All its gossip's knots being traced.

She removed the rose from my mouth
Like the taste of fruit or a button left
On the top of a cupboard. Though she swore
That she did not carry
Another man's child under her heart,
My seed is a loose stormcoat
Of gold silk, with wide sleeves, in her uterus.

Turning the Moon into a Verb

A timeless winter
That wants to be now
Will go on taking shape in me.
Now everything can begin.

Everything can reach much
Further up; with this new
Listening, the longing at the window
For the missing season weakens.

When springtime had need of him,
He did not offer me the winter,
He took away each of the seasons
In its visual turn.

Dark does that to you also,
And the headlessness
Of a turning of light that mentions a green
A little darker than all other greens.

A secret year, a secret time,
Its flight is a written image
Of its cry, its capacity for sound
I call spring, the experience

When the sky becomes a womb,
And a vision of rivers slanting
Across the doubly opened page
Of the moon turns her into a verb.

An image I have consciously
Broken like a shoulder on your hearing,
The inconstancy within constancy
That is the price of a month.

Oval of a Girl

The summers of our house peel and rot.
Sunset has begotten them, thinking he could shut
It in with varnish. But one discarnate shadow
Can be worth a whole generation; I am flooded
By no ocean but a second you.

Who might just as well have been water
Breaking and mending with a dark little movement,
A kind of forlorn frenzy leaking over into sound,
For whose unpronounceable blue I am an ear,
Alerted, stretching, not as I had prayed.

I have a hundred ways of turning
This year of the world's redemption
Into an ominous nativity, a face too fast
And fallen, too formed and fresh to seem asleep,
Already soiled by this eye-opening winter.

Near-child, much-needed, present tense,
Your first grown-up spring is under wordless control,
Beyond poetry, like a poem of the deepest calm
Never to be written, or a city re-beguiled
By useless fields that were all but air to me.

Andrew Greig

MOIRA CONWAY

Selection from: *Western Swing: adventures with the Heretical Buddha* (1994).

ANDREW GREIG was born in 1951 in Bannock-burn. He is a mountaineer and freelance writer whose books include two accounts of expeditions to the Himalayas, four poetry collections, a collaboration with poet Kathleen Jamie, *A Flame in Your Heart* (Bloodaxe, 1986), and a novel, *Electric Brae* (Canongate, 1992). *The Order of the Day* (Bloodaxe, 1990) was a Poetry Book Society Choice.

His latest book, *Western Swing*, is a dazzling long poem, an adventure, a game, a riddle, an act of healing: lyrical, reflective, jokey, archetypal. Deeply Scottish yet international, it "samples" at will from contemporary rock music and classic texts from Eliot to MacDiarmid. A wise-cracking Heretical Buddha and his motley crew go in search of a Healing Blade, from Glencoe to Katmundu, via the High Atlas in Morocco – where we meet them in the extract printed here. ●

From Western Swing

Two men rose like quivers of heat
from the dried-up wadi, greeted us
in Allah's name, demanded a light.
We agree: God is good, shook on that.
But the tall man's grip
                    tightened on my wrist
as he bent to light his cigarette
and the short one drew a knife
to pare his nails;
                    in the glittering
I saw the three who stood behind us.

It's that simple: sun overhead,
four blades, the oddly plastic
barrel of a semi-automatic
stroked idly against the ribs.

I wondered how this was going to feel,
hoped it brief, especially for her
whose fair hair shivered in the heat
while the youngest plucked her necklace,
swung it gently in his hand...

'Well,' she said, 'no point
giving up smoking now. Can I
mooch one too, please?'

    '*Hal anta mai?*'

     'Whit's he sayin?'

    ' "Whose side are you on?" '

'Ooh la la,' Stell murmured. 'Such ancient questions.'

     '*Hal anta American?*'

'Je ne suis pas americain, nous sommes
des écossais. (Hold on tight, babe.)
Je n'ai pas fait cette guerre. (Christ,
we should've stayed at your cousin's,
the Archduke's.)'

    ' *You speak very bad French. So,
    you are English, I think?*'

'Pas du tout!'

   '*Alors, British.*'

'Pas tellement. Scottish. Wee place up North.'

The youngest man looked up.
'*Scotland!*
   '*Scottishers?*
        Kenny Dalgleish!'

  'Oui, oui. Kent his faither. Uh,
  j'ai connu son père...'

'Ours too is a small country,
our football team also loses.
One day we shall win, Inshallah.'

'We are travellers, innocent travellers.'

'There are no innocent tourists.
You must know this.'
The blade lay on my cheek, scraped:
'You need a shave, mon cher,
you look like a terrorist.'

– He laughed, flipped the blade
high into the blue, where it spun
whittling the breeze to nothing,
    and when it clattered at our feet

        all men had gone

and we were alone in the wadi,
        sweat running from our boots.

        'Think ah've wet masel.'

'Nice knife,' Ken noted, 'but not the one.'

'These bad dreams
should not be in poetry
but some days insert themselves
like a shiv between the ribs.'

We walked on, but from then
the world was hotter, focused,
as if those men had been
                        guardians
waiting at the arc of an invisible lens.

Up ahead, distance and almond trees.
We drank a little wine and came quickly to the village,
pausing only every so often to be sick.

Tony Flynn

TONY FLYNN was born in 1951. He read Philosophical Theology at Hull University, and is now a social worker in Birmingham. When his first book appeared, Peter Porter called his poems 'gaunt and lit by guilt'. That guilt has been heightened into an acutely felt sense of pain and loss, a shared unease, in poems of love and sorrow, personal estrangement and political terror. Always honest and unflinching, Flynn celebrates the human, in all its fragility, at the same time as he confronts the horror which constantly threatens.

Selection from: *A Strange Routine* (1980) and *Body Politic* (1992).

'The delicacy and restraint with which Tony Flynn approaches his material of a working-class Catholic background in no way inhibit an extremely individual voice' – Christopher Hope. ●

TONY HILL

Jessica Drew's Married Son

Where streetlamps burn
their orange glare
through windows into rooms –
into a room;

by the bed a tattered
Roman missal, above it a bleeding Sacred Heart;

and Jessica Drew, five-days-dead,
is staring from her cold grey sheets
over dark roofs
and rain-drenched fields,

through centrally heated
air and through
his wife's blue chiffon evening-dress,

down the long curve
of his sleeping spine.

After Mass

Sweet candle-smoke wreathed
the Virgin's

blue smile, and incense
sickened the air.

Behind the old mill? Theresa hissed,
as we dipped our fingers together into

the cold stone font
and blessed ourselves.

Girl on a Swing 10.00pm

A cold wind streamed her hair,
unravelling the braid she wears for school;

and her forehead shone
in the distant glow from the motorway.

A deserted park, an empty swing,
and I remember how
as she walked past me towards the gates
I caught sight of her small school badge:

a heart, a wreath of thorns, Latin
circling her breast.

The Bride
(for Piotr M.)

They made their way,
his family and her family,
towards the grave –

Past the lamp-post
they strung him from
once he was dead,

and the shipyard that
troops now patrol
night and day

where workers shuffle
behind the gates
like lifers who trudge

the exercise yard.
At Easter she was
to have married the boy.

All down the street
each frozen patch
of blood under ice

looked like a map
of their little country.
By the graveside she let

her wedding-dress fall
like a long night of snow
on the coffin lid.

Later, alone
in her narrow bed, she wept
her wedding vows to the wall.

No comfort came –
only this, at last –
her body a ridge

of gentle peaks,
her groom
a slow cloud descending.

Gerald Mangan

FANNY DUBES

Selection from: *Waiting for the Storm* (1990).

GERALD MANGAN was born in 1951 in Glasgow. He has worked mainly as an artist and journalist in various parts of Scotland, Ireland and France. He now lives in Paris.

'Quite simply he is one of the best Scottish poets of his generation. At times his energy reminds me of MacNeice's – it is pointed up by *Scotland the Ghost*, his version of *Bagpipe Music*...His best work is meditative, probing, imaginative, and original. He has a sharp eye for Glasgow, but his imagination embraces Scotland as a whole place, which is what I like best about him – his patient response to a breadth of nation, his refusal to be hemmed in by the finite and local, his unwillingness to compromise intelligence and imagination' – Douglas Dunn. ●

Waiting for the Storm

It's the sweeper with the torpid broom
wading through swamp-air, mopping his nape;
the mounds of crayfish waving feelers,
clawing space, and craving sea.

The dogs announce it, and the tingling comb.
It's the flash on the overhead metro,
the beaded cleavage advertising
fan-cooled booths, for quick relief.

It oozes out from a bed of glaur,
till crooked fissures open in the cloud –
a jagged hand, on airmail blue.
It's the welling up that blurs the page,

and the deluge wipes it clean:
the window slamming suddenly inward,
and the clatter of running heels,
like a burst of automatic-fire.

Glasgow 1956

There's always a headscarf stooped
into a pram, nodding in time
with a plastic rattle, outside a shop
advertising a sale of wallpaper.

There's a queue facing another queue
like chessmen across the street;
a hearse standing at a petrol-pump
as the chauffeur tests the tyres,

the undertaker brushes ash off
his morning paper, and my mother,
looking down at me looking up,
is telling me not to point.

The background is a level site
where we recreate the war.
Calder Street is Calder Street,
level as far as the Clyde.

Without a tree to denote it,
the season is moot. That faint
thunder is the Cathcart tram,
and the sky is white as a trousseau

posed against blackened bricks.
A grey posy in her hands,
the bride stands smiling there
for decades, waiting for the click.

Scotland the Ghost
(Tune: any bagpipe music)

It's no deid, the auld land, it's no deid in spirit:
All it wants is a stirrup-cup, and a coronach to stir it.
Drinking up at closing-time, it's girning in its chains:
O when, O floo'er o Scotland, will we see your like again?

It's no deid in spirit, no, it's never done with haunting;
But it never makes its mind up, to tell us what it's wanting.
The spirit's weak without the flesh, but still it lifts the hackles –
With its head below its arm-pit, and its ankle still in shackles.

It drags the sword of Wallace, it's lugging Bruce's helmet;
But spiders make their webs in it, and a draught would overwhelm it.
The heart inside the armour's like the queen inside her cell:
The breath of Knox has chilled it, and blasted it to hell.

The crown fell off with Jamie, when he took the English tiller;
The head fell off with Saltoun, who sold the tongue for siller.
When Bonnie Charlie dreamed his dream, to stick it back together,
He met a butcher's cleaver, and it ended up in slivers.

The heart grew black as Glasgow, then, and rumbled underground;
The disembodied head was known as Edinburgh town.
When Burns sprang up to sing of flesh, and earth, and barley-grain,
He sang too low, too late to touch the Socratean brain.

Sheriff Walter found the body stripped to bare essentials,
And shivering in the heather; but he saw its true potential.
He dressed it up in tartan plaid and kilt, for exhibition,
Installed it in his stately home, and charged them all admission.

Victoria had it dance a fling, and played it for a puppet –
A gillie on a string, without a *sgian dubh* to cut it.
Mass-produced in clockwork, it made the perfect vassal
To paint the atlas red for her, or dandle in her castle.

Burke and Hare worked double-time, supplying all the clients
Who analysed the body in the interests of science.
Doctor Jekyll knew the head was severed from the heart,
And drank a heady potion to explore the private parts.

MacDiarmid woke in a whisky haze, and saw a headless thistle –
Stuck his own on the prickly stalk, and sharpened up the bristles.
He kept the spirit neat and drank it deeply through a chanter,
Till the skull swelled beneath the skin, and stretched his Tam
        o'Shanter.

It's no deid, the auld land, it's no deid in spirit:
All it wants is a drunk man, and a World Cup to stir it.
In Gallowgate, in Canongate, it's girning in its pain.
It's watering the stones to make the floo'er bloom again.

Ann Sansom

Selection from: *Romance* (1994).

ANN SANSOM was born in 1951, and lives in Huddersfield. Three small press pamphlets – published as Ann Dancy – enhanced her growing reputation. *Romance* (Bloodaxe, 1994) is her first full-length collection.

'Her poetry will stay news,' according to John Lucas. Stanley Cook admired her 'authentic Northern mix of realism and imagination' and 'her eye for detail, the pure phrasing of a largely unfigurative language and the range of her imagination'. Mark Robinson was impressed by 'very intense' poems which 'use clear detail and firmly, though quietly expressed emotion to tell elliptical but heartfelt stories, mainly from a female perspective'. ●

Base Linguistics

A morning of received pronunciation:
subtle differences between the *ah* and *oh*
fricatives, bi-labials and a diagram
of how the teeth may work together with the tongue.

Midday we adjourn/retire/repair to the pub. Wordy
but if we speak now, if we ever open up again
it will be too much, too wide, too soon.

We are not girls. We weigh the things we're told
and there is little that we swallow whole
but sometimes there's a joke that makes you smile
in the dark. It may be weeks before it makes you sick.

Have you heard the one, he said, About the graduate
who couldn't count to twenty-eight? She had.
She's smart, she's numerate and anyone can calculate

four women divided by two elbows on a table divided by
an ashtray, a full round of dead glasses united by
five kids, a series of old debts, divided by one man
and multiplied again. Anyone. It's a simple equation.

But for all our command of semantics, lexis,
the clear physiology of speech, women fresh from lectures
women awash with nausea and beer are seldom articulate.

She slurs it. Alive to the fact that words
are often mouth and air and her answers lie
in neat subtraction, she states it. *He'll blame me.*
And she can place it. It dates back months,

it dates back years, it dates back to the apple.
Between us we have the plosives, the stops,
the hard core that sticks in the throat

and makes us dumb. Together we discover
that there are no synonyms, no common tongue
to cover every case and gender
but there is safety of a kind in numbers.

Confinement

That winter the stairs were always unlit.
Home late from work, I'd feel my way,
unlock the door by touch
and before I pressed the switch look up, wait
to see my lamp put out a saucer to the dark.

The skylight was almost clear then,
night came down to it at once,
a movement quick and weighty as water.

At first I'd count you by the moon, by my own fingers,
half believing I could feel you in my skin.
Then it snowed for weeks, accumulating on the glass,
filtering a tracing paper air. A diffuse frost
charged the constant underwater I crossed and crossed
mindless as a swimmer, keeping time for you.

At night, in the cold sheets, unable to sleep
I began to count you in days and hours,
I named you, held your head, your feet,
felt you turn in my own body heat.

Tonight, you've slept for twenty years.
I leave an overheated house, go out
Into the cold backyard for air.
A neighbour calls me to the fence to watch.
He's opening the ice on his pond. The fish come up
preserved by their cold blood, their trust.

I close a frozen room on you, your placid drowning face,
and listen to my neighbour, who has learned to wait,
obedient to the rules that govern living things.
We share a cigarette and then discuss
the nature of confinement and release.

Is This Business?

Is this one hell of a night for a girl to be out;
vulgar as a boozy duchess, loud kissy as sleet on slabs,
chatty as maiden's water in the gutter? You tell me.
Your game, your taste, your price. You name it.
I'll turn it over on my tongue, spit like a connoisseur.

but you're welcome, welcome
now the rain's let up, left the pavement glamorous,
a film; neon off the jewellers frayed in it,
these shiny shoes, a backing track
        I pass the freezer shop, the bank,
and stop at *Next*. He's barred and lit. He's nice.
My type. One big hard man
and cool and smart and what a suit...

Take care. I always say it after.
Turns me over, men who never speak,
men who say, You too, lover
I look at them gone out. I'm lucky
I'm smart as stilettos...Something special, love?
Just ask. Come on, don't fret. I'm tender
like the bag held flat inside my coat.
You're warm. I'll breathe in your hands,
thaw my face. My feet are mottled red and numb.
I pass. And you're just browsing, are you?
Maybe? And you want history, do you?
Same as yours, sweetheart.

Got to my feet and unlicked cold, barefoot
as a baby, naïve as a new wife,
anything you like. We'll spin a tale,
turn a trick, feed a line. Who's hooked?
Who reels it in? Take care, my love.
Come back again. You're the best. Best I ever.
You, love. You can. You can tell me.
I'm soft, clean as a vicar's hand,
dirty as you want. The truth?
You want the one about my kids,
my debts, my dad? Want one of your own?
Come on. I'm safe as a mother.
Open my coat and see. Patent, plastic, empty.
Come on my dear my love my pet,
Is this business or what?

Helen Dunmore

STEPHEN MOLLETT

Selection from: *Short Days,*
Long Nights: New & Selected
Poems (1991) and *Recovering*
a Body (1994).

HELEN DUNMORE was born in 1952. She is a
poet, novelist and children's writer, and lives
in Bristol. She has published five collections,
all with Bloodaxe, one given a Poetry Book
Society Choice, another the Alice Bartlett
Award; her other books include a novel,
Zennor in Darkness (Viking, 1993).

Iain Crichton Smith has called her 'a poet
whose words can be savoured on the tongue'.
Lachlan Mackinnon admired her 'gentle,
humane poems which do not ignore the
darknesses daily life is prone to overlook'.
Bill Turner found her 'haunting' poems
'sensitive to all changes in weather...able
to poach subliminal forebodings at will,
and suddenly we are in that hallucinatory
other-world, sharing her viewpoint.' ●

The marshalling yard

In the goods yard the tracks are unmarked.
Snow lies, the sky is full of it.
Its hush swells in the dark.

Grasped by black ice on black
a massive noise of breathing
fills the tracks;

cold women, ready for departure
smooth their worn skirts
and ice steals through their hands like children
from whose touch they have already been parted.

Now like a summer
the train comes
beating the platform
with its blue wings.

The women stir. They sigh.
Feet slide
warm on a wooden stairway
then a voice calls and
milk drenched with aniseed
drawls on the walk to school.

At last they leave.
Their breathless neighbours
steal from the woods, the barns,
and tender straw
sticks to their palms.

The bride's nights in a strange village

At three in the morning
while mist limps between houses
while cloaks and blankets
dampen with dew

the bride sleeps with her husband
bundled in a red blanket,
her mouth parts and a bubble
of sour breathing goes free.
She humps wool up to her ears
while her husband tightens his arms
and rocks her, mumbling. Neither awakes.

In the second month of the marriage
the bride wakes after midnight.
Damp-bodied
she lunges from sleep
hair pricking with sweat
breath knocking her sides.
She eels from her husband's grip
and crouches, listening.

The night is enlarged by sounds.
The rain has started.
It threshes leaves secretively
and there in the blackness
of whining dogs it finds out the house.
Its hiss enfolds her, blots up
her skin, then sifts off, whispering
in her like mirrors
the length of the rainy village.

The parachute packers

The parachute packers with white faces
swathed over with sleep
and the stale bodily smell of sheets

make haste to tin huts where a twelve-hour
shift starts in ten minutes.
Their bare legs pump bicycle pedals,
they clatter on wooden-soled sandals
into the dazzling light over the work benches.

They rub in today's issue of hand-cream.
Their fingers skim on the silk
as the unwieldy billows of parachute flatten
like sea-waves, oiled, folded in sevens.

The only silk to be had
comes in a military packaging:
dull-green, printed, discreet,
gone into fashioning parachutes
to be wondered at like the flowers'
down-spinning, seed-bearing canopies
lodged in the silt of village memory.

A girl pulling swedes in a field
senses the shadow of parachutes
and gapes up, knees braced
and hair tangling. She must be riddled,
her warm juices all spilled
for looking upwards too early
into the dawn, leafy with parachutes.

Heavenly wide canopies
bring down stolid chaps with their rifle butts
ready to crack, with papers
to govern the upturned land,
with boots, barbed wire and lists on fine paper
thousands of names long.

I look up now at two seagulls,
at cloud drifts and a lamp-post
bent like a feeding swan,

and at the sound of needles
seaming up parachutes in Nissen huts
with a hiss and pull through the stuff
of these celestial ball-dresses

for nuns, agents, snow-on-the-boots men
sewn into a flower's corolla
to the music of Workers' Playtime.

At dusk the parachute packers
release their hair from its nets
and ride down lanes whitened by cow-parsley
to village halls, where the dances
and beer and the first cigarettes
expunge the clouds of parachute silk
and rules touching their hair and flesh.

In the bar they're the girls who pack parachutes
for our boys. They can forget
the coughs of the guard on duty,
the boredom and long hours
and half-heard cries of caught parachutists.

The horse landscape

Today in a horse landscape
horses steam in the lee of thorn hedges
on soaking fields. Horses waltz
on iron poles in dank fairgrounds.

A girl in jodhpurs on Sand Bay
leads her pony over and over
jumps made of driftwood and traffic cones.

A TV blares the gabble of photofinishes.
The bookie's plastic curtain releases
punters onto the hot street
littered with King Cone papers.

In a landscape with clouds and chalk downs
and cream houses, a horse rigid as bone
glares up at kites and hang-gliders.

One eye's cut from the flowered turf:
a horse skull, whispering secrets
with wind-sighs like tapping on phone wires.

The group leader in beautiful boots
always on horseback,
the mounted lady squinnying
down at the hunt intruders,
draw blood for their own horse landscape
and scorn horse-trading, letting the beasts mate
on scrubby fields, amongst catkins
and watery ditches.

Here's a rearing bronze horse
welded to man, letting his hands
stay free for banner and weapon –
mild shadow of Pushkin's nightmare.

Trained police horses sway on great hooves.
Riders avoid our faces, and gaze
down on our skull crowns
where the bone jigsaw cleaves.

Grooms whistle and urge
the sweaty beasts to endure battle.
We're always the poor infantry
backing off Mars field,
out of frame for the heroic riders
preserved in their horse landscape.

The sea skater

A skater comes to this blue pond,
his worn Canadian skates
held by the straps.

He sits on the grass
lacing stiff boots
into a wreath of effort and breath.

He tugs at the straps and they sound
as ice does when weight troubles it
and cracks bloom around stones

creaking in quiet mid-winter
mid-afternoons: a fine time for a skater.
He knows it and gauges the sun
to see how long it will be safe to skate.

Now he hisses and spins in jumps
while powder ice clings to the air
but by trade he's a long-haul skater.

Little villages, stick-like in the cold,
offer a child or a farm-worker
going his round. These watch him
go beating onward between iced alders
seawards, and so they picture him
always smoothly facing forward, foodless and waterless,
mounting the crusted waves on his skates.

Three Ways of Recovering a Body

By chance I was alone in my bed the morning
I woke to find my body had gone.
It had been coming. I'd cut off my hair in sections
so each of you would have something to remember,
then my nails worked loose from their beds
of oystery flesh. Who was it got them?

One night I slipped out of my skin. It lolloped
hooked to my heels, hurting. I had to spray on
more scent so you could find me in the dark,
I was going so fast. One of you begged for my ears
because you could hear the sea in them.

First I planned to steal myself back. I was a mist
on thighs, belly and hips. I'd slept with so many men.
I was with you in the ash-haunted stations of Poland,
I was with you on that grey plaza in Berlin
while you wolfed three doughnuts without stopping,
thinking yourself alone. Soon I recovered my lips
by waiting behind the mirror while you shaved.
You pouted. I peeled away kisses like wax
no longer warm to the touch. Then I flew off.

Next I decided to become a virgin. Without a body
it was easy to make up a new story. In seven years
every invisible cell would be renewed
and none of them would have touched any of you.
I went to a cold lake, to a grey-lichened island,
I was gold in the wallet of the water.
I was known to the inhabitants, who were in love
with the coveted whisper of my virginity:
all too soon they were bringing me coffee and perfume,
cash under stones. I could really do something for them.

Thirdly I tried marriage to a good husband
who knew my past but forgave it. I believed in the power
of his penis to smoke out all those men
so that bit by bit my body service would resume,
although for a while I'd be the one woman in the world
who was only present in the smile of her vagina.
He stroked the air where I might have been.
I turned to the mirror and saw mist gather
as if someone lived in the glass. Recovering
I breathed to myself, '*Hold on! I'm coming.*'

Steve Ellis

JIM DAVIES

Selection from: *Home and Away* (1986) and *West Pathway* (1993).

STEVE ELLIS was born in 1952. When he was a youthful Gregory award-winning poet, *The Literary Review* hailed him as 'a wonderfully no-nonsense writer...a sardonic Yorkshireman monitoring scenes rooted in directly accessible experience'. Life may have frayed him a bit since then, but his deadpan humour is as wicked as ever, and he's still able to chronicle the rituals of family and the sad or absurd nuances of ordinary lives with warmth, affection, and just a little grumpiness. He's moved to Birmingham, is something of an authority on Dante and Eliot, but still writes his wry, often hilarious poems, on matters of great and small importance.

'Ellis is very much a Bloodaxe poet: toughly comic, anti-metropolitan, often verbally exuberant' – John Lucas. ●

The Age of Innocence

At school, we all had to pick a plague
out of Exodus; round the table,
elbowing each other in innocent enthusiasm,
the girls drew mostly feverish first-borns, the boys
boils and frogs; while I fancied the river of blood.
Except some little s-d had pinched all the reds.
So I did locusts: houses, palm trees, pyramids
carefully laid in; arabs arranged unsuspecting,
a sudden camel; stood back, aimed, and

FURIOUS blitzings with the pencil,
God's green pepper milling down,
marvellously missing Moses,
tucked with his rifle in the margin.
Our work went up round the walls, whereon
the headmistress appeared
in a clap of lavender,
benign and gratified,
and scattered gold stars like benedictions.

To Ted Hughes

While I was cooking dinner
(some friends were coming round)
I thought I'd try your new cassette.

But you know how it is –
pans and peeling to synchronise,
recipes, and then the phone ringing:

you faded into far-off noise,
a low drumming
seeping from the lounge.

So going in there was a shock –
like opening the door of an oven
on your simmering concerns,

the rolling prophetic growl
that preached its elementals
to our carpets and chairs

unheard, unattended. To resume
butchering the chicken
seemed an act of homage;

but to eat it afterwards
with cutlery, wine and conversation
an act of sneaking treachery.

We should have daubed each other
all over with it
and danced among the bones.

On the visible ageing of Steve Davis

It must be all of seven summers
since I first saw your immaculate head
bulging into the quiet of our living room,
served on a platter of green baize.
Fixed frigid icon of our era,
Marilyn Monroe of the Thatcher years.
I suppose it's because you always won,
expressionless efficiency,
a colourless triumph over colours;
the Grecian Urn in a dickie-bow
only your balls always reached their goal.

But tonight I caught you again by chance
after a long interval, marked on your face.
And I see Time, the unsnookerable,
rising one day in a hushed house
to pot the final black.

The death of Joe Loss

Didn't know you hadn't died
until you died, and the paper
gave you a small quiet corner,
restoring you in your absence,
reminding me of all the rest
ahead in the queue before me,
with luck. So it's good to know
you were with us until today,
a long reassuring retrospect
just gone away.

Linton Kwesi Johnson

JAMES C. MARSHALL

Selection from: *Tings an Times: Selected Poems* (1991).

LINTON KWESI JOHNSON was born in 1952 in Jamaica, and came to London in 1963. He has been a pioneering figure in black poetry and music. He coined the phrase 'dub poetry', and went on to develop it into a gutsy musical idiom along with fellow poets such as Oku Onuora, Muta and Mikey Smith.

His Bloodaxe Selected Poems *Tings an Times* includes work from his three previous collections, *Voices of the Living and the Dead* (1974), *Dread Beat An' Blood* (1975) and *Inglan Is a Bitch* (1980). It charts the progress of our times with poems about racism, race riots, radical politics, police oppression, black youth and black Britain. ●

Sonny's Lettah
(Anti-Sus Poem)

> Brixtan Prison
> Jebb Avenue
> Landan south-west two
> Inglan

Dear Mama,
Good Day.
I hope dat wen
deze few lines reach y'u,
they may find y'u in di bes' af helt.

Mama,
I really doan know how fi tell y'u dis,
cause I did mek a salim pramis
fi tek care a lickle Jim
an' try mi bes' fi look out fi him.

Mama,
Ah really did try mi bes',
but none-di-les'
mi sarry fi tell y'u seh
poor lickle Jim get arres'.

It woz di miggle a di rush howah
wen everybady jus' a hus'le an' a bus'le
fi goh home fi dem evenin' showah;
mi an' Jim stan-up
waitin' pan a bus,
nat causin' no fus',
wen all an a sudden
a police van pull-up.

Out jump t'ree policeman,
di' hole a dem carryin batan.
Dem waak straight up to mi an' Jim.
One a dem hol' aan to Jim
seh him tekin him in;
Jim tell him fi let goh a him
far him noh dhu not'n
an him naw t'ief,
nat even a but'n.
Jim start to wriggle
Di police start to giggle.

Mama,
mek Ah tell y'u whey dem dhu to Jim
Mama,
mek Ah tell y'u whey dem dhu to him:

dem t'ump him in him belly
an' it turn to jelly
dem lick him pan him back
an' him rib get pap
dem lick him pan him he'd
but it tuff like le'd
dem kick him in him seed
an' it started to bleed

Mama,
Ah jus' could'n' stan-up deh
an' noh dhu not'n:

soh mi jook one in him cyc
an' him started to cry
mi t'ump one in him mout'
an' him started to shout

mi kick one pan him shin
an' him started to spin
mi tump him pan him chin
an' him drap pan a bin

an' crash
an de'd.

Mama,
more policeman come dung
an' beat mi to di grung;
dem charge Jim fi sus,
dem charge mi fi murdah.

Mama,
doan fret,
doan get depres'
an' doun-hearted.
Be af good courage
till I hear fram you.

I remain
your son,
Sonny.

Di Great Insohreckshan

it woz in april nineteen eighty wan
doun inna di ghetto af Brixtan
dat di babylan dem cauz such a frickshan
dat it bring about a great insohreckshan
an it spread all ovah di naeshan
it woz truly an histarical occayshan

it woz event af di year
an I wish I ad been dere
wen wi run riat all ovah Brixtan
wen wi mash-up plenty police van
wen wi mash-up di wicked wan plan
wen wi mash-up di Swamp Eighty Wan

fi wha?
fi mek di rulah dem andahstan
dat wi naw tek noh more a dem oppreshan

an wen mi check out di ghetto grape vine
fi fine out all I coulda fine
evry rebel jussa revel in dem story
dem a taak bout di powah an di glory
dem a taak bout di burnin an di lootin
dem a taak bout di smashin an di grabin
dem a tell mi bout di vanquish an di victri

dem seh di babylan dem went too far
soh wi ad woz fi bun two cyar
an wan an two innocent get mar
but wha
noh soh it goh sometime inna war ein star
noh soh it goh sometime inna war?

dem seh wi bun dung di George
wi coulda bun di lanlaad
wi bun dung di George
wi nevvah bun di lanlaad
wen wi run riat all ovah Brixtan
wen wi mash-up plenty police van
wen wi mash-up di wicked wan plan
wen wi mash-up di swamp eighty wan

dem seh wi comandeer cyar
an wi ghaddah ammunishan
wi bill wi baricade
an di wicked ketch afraid
wi sen out wi scout
fi goh fine dem whereabout
den wi faam-up wi passi
an wi mek wi raid

well now dem run gaan goh plan countah-ackshan
but di plastic bullit an di waatah cannan
will bring a blam-blam
will bring a blam-blam
nevvah mine Scarman
will bring a blam-blam

Fred Voss

JANE THOMAS

Selection from: *Goodstone*
(1991).

FRED VOSS was born in 1952. He is poetry's
answer to American fiction's Dirty Realism,
but he really does gets his hands dirty: he
doesn't just write about factory life, he
lives it. The really big as well as the really
petty issues of today are acted out by his
fellow workers, with Voss looking on from
his cutting machine, missing nothing in the
drama of boss, foreman and worker.

'Fred Voss has driven up and down the
California coast for 15 years, with a toolbox
in his back seat, getting fired and hired by
various machine shops. One result is a body
of poetry whose directness of address to
factory experience is without parallel in
Anglo-American verse' – John Osborne. ●

Rough Job

The machinist who tried to kill himself
because he couldn't stop crying like a girl
when he was on PCP;
the machinist holding up the pussy magazine
in front of his face
to be sure everyone knows he's staring at it;
the machinist in a constant rage
because his wife won't give him a blowjob;
the machinist telling everyone how much he hates
the queers on the 2nd tier of the L.A. County Jail;
the machinist who walks around with a tape measure
pulled out to 12 to 15 inches
and held in front of his fly;
the machinist who wears a hat saying 'U.S. Male'
and smokes big cigars
and weightlifts steel bars and arbors
while his machine runs:

being a man in a machine shop
is not easy.

Cutting Corners

To position the half-ton wing carry-through sections
on our machine tables,
our Lead Man
was always grabbing the 50 lb lead hammer
we refused to pick up
and holding it like a baseball bat swinging it
extra far back
digging his toes in throwing his entire body into it
and driving the head of the lead hammer
SMACK into the side of the titanium carry-through section
that would join wings
and fuselage of a K-20 bomber,
as we remembered what we had been told
about never touching the sections
with lead hammers at all
because the lead contaminated the titanium
and caused cracks and imperfections
up to an inch beneath the surface
of the titanium.

Of course,
that was before
they'd found a big pile of fucked-up wing carry-through
sections hidden in back of building 75
that had to be finished and delivered to the Air Force
right away.

Sometimes you can't afford
to be too picky.

It's Okay

For years they'd seen
the KKKs drawn and carved in the bathroom stalls
and heard the nigger jokes,
but when they began to see hangman's nooses

hanging from the beams
above their machines,
the black machinists
began to get excited and angry demanding
an end as they screamed in white machinists' faces
things like 'Some of my relatives have died that way!' –
but Verl the old 39 year veteran
of the shop
didn't twitch a muscle or blink an eye
as he stayed stone-faced as ever
in the face of their screaming
and with utmost calm and reassurance
shrugged and said it was nothing it was just
that maybe the guys' sense of humor
went a little too far
sometimes.

The Stud

He had worked out at Gold's Gym
until he could bench-press 450 pounds.

He walked around the machine shop
waving a 50-pound lead hammer above his head
with one hand,
and his hammer blows
echoed off the machine shop walls
like gunshots.

Then he started talking
about how much he liked to fuck
his boyfriend.

For the first time in the machine-shop's 20-year history,
no one was telling any faggot jokes.

Killarney Clary

KATHLEEN DELANO

Selection from: *Who Whispered Near Me* (1989/1993).

KILLARNEY CLARY was born in 1953 in Los Angeles, of Irish descent, and lives in Pasadena. Her first book *Who Whispered Near Me* was much acclaimed in the States. In Clary's poems, everything is illuminated by her intense, utterly genuine way of seeing. Written in short, dense, allusive, prose paragraphs, they evoke with haunting power the artefacts, characters and mysteries of a life.

'At first it feels as though an amazingly precise but alien eye were observing us…the severity of her look is constantly nuanced by tenderness and doubt. Hers is a stunning new voice in American poetry' – John Ashbery. ●

From Who Whispered Near Me

Sacrificed so that I could be uncertain, the dead were not me. It was the end of the suburbs, Vietnam. Sprinklers on the lawn, sunlight in large rooms with wooden floors, the anxiety of having things 'just so' – that sweet package was finally opened. But my dreams will not punish me enough, nor can I blame Calley, who thought if he could kill them all, he could go home. I think it's good to want to go home.

The scare leaks now into little, patient countries where the U.S. chases ghosts, where heroes fight and heroes refuse. I can't imagine the pain; I cannot feel the United States of America. I know I lost the war, but to what does knowledge bring me? An open field with no trail and cries for help from all directions? If bad is only sickness and the wrong are just misunderstood, it was a war to sap the Big Fear and there will be no answer. Like being awake all the time.

*

Because the ones I work for do not love me, because I have said too much and I haven't been sure of what is right and I've hated the people I've trusted, because I work in an office and we are lost and when I come home I say their lives are theirs and they don't know what they apologise for and none of it mended, because I let them beat me and I remember something of mine which not everyone has, and because I lie to keep my self and my hands my voice on the phone what I swallow what hurts me, because I hurt them –

I give them the hours I spend away from them and carry them, even in my sleep, at least as the nag of a misplaced shoe, for years after I have quit and gone on to another job where I hesitate in telling and I remember and I resent having had to spend more time with them than with the ones I love.

*

My whispered song, the tune replaced by breath, weakens, loses its place in a thin, icy draft. The cold lowers, by the rules. What turns a whisper to full sound pulls the colors from gray. Shaky, it skips like a stylus until time hints there is hope. But there is no more logic in this power to persevere than there is to the placement of Los Angeles or the ease on the faces of men and women who finish their long ride in. What clicks on or off after months of indecision? Did I choose to give in?

As I drive deeper into the corridor of downtown where the wind is crooked and fast between the office towers, as I try again the brightest song, I know the dead sailor who changed his mind in last night's dream will stay with me for days; I won't be afraid. And yet the friend who says good night on the phone is gone. I own nothing; I don't know my spirit. In sleep where the counting can't survive, I hear songs I've never heard, though there are no premonitions, only the teases of anxiety and fantasy. If I could turn my eyes from the experiment, it would run on smoothly with pure, unstudied results. Instead, I send off questionnaires, and wait.

*

Sleep was streams of red and white lights curving through the passes. I saw them from a melancholy, silent and weary. I want to fall in love every moment. The ache is fine and selfish, so huge and sad. If someone were here tonight, he would know what I should do with my arms which are so heavy and the numbness spreading from my spine. I might talk with him and learn how to find places for the gifts. If there were skin other than my own or a certain need. Time wears the dazzle of the small lights. I am chilled. I begin to smell the trees. Sleep was all that was left. A small and comfortable boat on the whole ocean.

*

You're bent in the reeds and behind you feathers alight on the lake, tremble to the shadow of a cloud. Water, brush, then hills darken. Your restless hands in the rough lawn turn grass blades into whistles. Sun again now on the colored boats, but you cannot see that brighter clutter. Ducks bobbing and knocking near the pilings. Funny, the burden of their weightlessness. A flag, sail, shirt, a ribbon of crêpe paper caught on wire. Your eyes follow the sound of a crow in back of me.

In the closet of your dark body, I forget what were, for you, the icy flowers of your own need; I leave their translucence – what we cannot help. And leaving is different from something learned or comfort or afternoon, less brave than understanding how the place behind me widens and deepens in your life. How it is good as it fits me here, between.

Marion Lomax

MOIRA CONWAY

Selection from: *The Peepshow Girl* (1989) and new poems.

MARION LOMAX was born in 1953 in Newcastle, grew up in Northumberland, and now lives in Berkshire. In 1981 she received a Gregory Award and won first prize in the Cheltenham Festival Poetry Competition with her poem *The Forked Tree*. Her first collection *The Peepshow Girl* was published by Bloodaxe in 1989; her second is forthcoming. Peter Porter admired the 'assurance and singularity' of her 'abiding and spiritual' poetry.

'There are passionate emotions in these poems, sometimes guarded and obliquely expressed. But Marion Lomax has access to a wide range of voices as well as her own' – Ruth Fainlight. ●

Compass

From the back yard look across the valley:
the Tyne winds east past castle and factory,
imperceptibly tidal. If you live
here long enough you learn to sense changes
as surreptitious as the river's ebb.

Once it was easier to keep your bearings –
the West Road to Hexham, the old East School;
though I lived in South Road the view was north,
child and woman before me would look up,
eyes drawn over fields to the Cheviots.

We were rivers who flowed from west to east,
to work and school, who faced north when we stopped
because it was known. Yet at our backs there was
always the south, enjoying the most sun,
making the needle quiver, faces turn.

The Forked Tree

I killed two hares last night in the heart of the garden.
Long ears in moonlight, mimicking the shape of the tree.
I crept round the side of the house before they sensed me
And when they heard the gun clear its throat it was too late.
I hit the buck first, then the doe – stupidly standing
To stare at me. Her powerful hind-quarters refusing
To kick and run, though I knew she could have bounded up
The lane in an instant, back to her young. I can cope
With hares: they are easy to cook. I feel no remorse.
Now I'll wait for the vixen who raids the chicken house.

I feed my chickens. Gather and sort the eggs. I wipe
The dirt and straw collage from the shells of those I sell.
I have the dogs too. My husband trained them, but I was
Surprised how quickly they obeyed me. I talked to them –
More easily than I talked to the children. Could share
The shadow with its dark gun lurking by our house wall
And the silent bullet lodged inside before we knew
That it was growing. His coming out of hospital,
Then the sniper's second strike when he was off his guard.
In the end I could only stand stupidly and stare –

Even with warning, could not believe such treachery.
The children were swinging from the tree in the garden
With no one to catch them. Darkness made the ground tremble
With hooves which left the grass trampled and the roses spoiled.
I guard this warren – small rooms and scattered outbuildings.
Not even chickens shall live in fear of predators.
My children shall feed better than before. Lonely nights
Are not without fear, but I cope with darkness now that
I have seen it bring young deer down from the wood to play.
Jumping in and out in the moonlight, through the forked tree.

Gruoch

I have a name of my own. Gruoch –
a low growl of desire. He'd say it
and crush me against his throat. Gruoch –
his huge hands stroking my hip-length hair,
grasping it in his fists, drawing it taut
either side of my arms in ropes,
staked like a tent. He'd gasp when
folds slipped open, succulent
as split stems, to welcome him in.
How I held him squeezed the sorrow
of no son out of him – for Lulach
was only mine, fruit of first union –
of Gillecomgain, forgotten by time.

He brought me Duncan as a trophy,
sweet revenge for my father's slaughter.
Upstarts never prosper: I was the true
King's daughter, Gruoch – uttered in wonder.
Seventeen years we reigned together through
keen seasons of hunger, feasting one to other.
War nor wantons wrenched him from me:
Gruoch – a whisper, sustaining fire.

He died before the battle with Malcolm:
obsequies cradled in a dry bed.
My mouth meandered down his body –
but it was winter, no bud stirring.
Gruoch – despairing: our death rattle.

Irina Ratushinskaya

JANE BOWN

Selection from: *No, I'm Not Afraid* (1986), translated by David McDuff.

IRINA RATUSHINSKAYA was born in 1954 in Odessa. In 1982 she was arrested by the KGB and charged with 'anti-Soviet propaganda', and in 1983 was sent to a labour camp and held there for three years in the Small Zone, a special unit for women prisoners of conscience. Her crime: writing poetry.

Her poems were smuggled out of the camp, and in 1986 Bloodaxe published *No, I'm Not Afraid*. An international campaign was mounted on her behalf, spearheaded by the book. Mikhail Gorbachev was given a copy, and on the eve of the Reykjavik summit, Irina Ratushinskaya was released from prison. She has since published two other collections of poetry with Bloodaxe, *Pencil Letter* (1988) and *Dance with a Shadow* (1992), and two volumes of autobiography with Hodder. ●

No, I'm not afraid

No, I'm not afraid: after a year
Of breathing these prison nights
I will survive into the sadness
To name which is escape.

The cockerel will weep freedom for me
And here – knee-deep in mire –
My gardens shed their water
And the northern air blows in draughts.

And how am I to carry to an alien planet
What are almost tears, as though towards home...
It isn't true, I *am* afraid, my darling!
But make it look as though you haven't noticed.

I had a dream

I had a dream: steeds and horse-cloths,
A hand with a prickly ring on my shoulder,
And the bitter face of a brown icon,
And the solid murmur of a thousand swords.
After that I don't remember. The grasses grew tired
Of lamenting injuries, the wolves of howling,
And someone sang over the corpses at the transit camp,
And our wounds dried up, and we were thirsty.
It was August. The stars grew ripe
And fell into the campfires of the soldiers,
And it was still not too late to save the Motherland,
So it seemed to us. We waited for the hour,
We rose – and in saving for the umpteenth time,
We walked into the grass and ceased to be.
A crazy girl ran barefoot
Among us with a cry. Not to kill –
It's so simple! Just when I think
My motherland is going to absorb the guileless lesson...
No! The waters rust, the women wail.
And we shall rise up when the moment comes.

Some people's dreams pay all their bills

Some people's dreams pay all their bills,
While others' gild an empty shell...
But mine go whimpering about a velvet dress,
Cherry-red and sumptuous as sin.
O, inaccessible! Not of our world!
Nowhere to get you, or to put you on...
But how I want you!
Against all reason's reproaches –
There, in the very narrows of the heart's
Recesses – flourishes the poison
Of heavy folds, and obscure embroidery...

The childish, flouted right
To beauty! Not bread, not domicile –
But unbleached, royal lace,
Enspiralled rings, sly ribbons – but no!
My day is like a donkey, bridled, laden,
My night deserted, like the prison light.
But in my soul – it's no good! I am guilty! –
I keep on sewing it, and in my mind I make
The thousandth stitch, as I do up my anorak
And try on my tarpaulin boots.

The white-hot blizzard

We are branded with Russia
By a white-hot blizzard,
By the mad labyrinth of dark craters,
Cavities under the snow:
Go away, eyeless woman, go away!
Only how are we to leave each other,
In our infinite whirling,
In our kinship and conflict with her?

And when at last you break loose
From the oppressive tenderness
Of her despotic embraces,
In which to fall asleep is to do so forever:
Your head swims,
As from the first childish drag at a cigarette,
And your lungs are torn to shreds
Like a cheap envelope.

And then, as you wait for everything that
Has emerged alive from her unpeopled cold
To recover from the narcosis –
To know that the angels of Russia
Freeze to death towards morning
Like sparrows in the frost
Falling from their wires into the snow.

'I will live and survive'

I will live and survive and be asked:
How they slammed my head against a trestle,
How I had to freeze at nights,
How my hair started to turn grey...
But I'll smile. And will crack some joke
And brush away the encroaching shadow.
And I will render homage to the dry September
That became my second birth.
And I'll be asked: 'Doesn't it hurt you to remember?'
Not being deceived by my outward flippancy.
But the former names will detonate my memory –
Magnificent as old cannon.
And I will tell of the best people in all the earth,
The most tender, but also the most invincible,
How they said farewell, how they went to be tortured,
How they waited for letters from their loved ones.
And I'll be asked: what helped us to live
When there were neither letters nor any news – only walls,
And the cold of the cell, and the blather of official lies,
And the sickening promises made in exchange for betrayal.
And I will tell of the first beauty
I saw in captivity.
A frost-covered window! No spyholes, nor walls,
Nor cell-bars, nor the long-endured pain –
Only a blue radiance on a tiny pane of glass,
A cast pattern – none more beautiful could be dreamt!
The more clearly you looked, the more powerfully blossomed
Those brigand forests, campfires and birds!
And how many times there was bitter cold weather
And how many windows sparkled after that one –
But never was it repeated,
That upheaval of rainbow ice!
And anyway, what good would it be to me now,
And what would be the pretext for that festival?
Such a gift can only be received once,
And perhaps is only needed once.

Ian Duhig

IAN DUHIG was born in 1954 in London of Irish Catholic parents, and lives in Leeds. In 1987 he won first prize in the National Poetry Competition with his poem *Nineteen Hundred and Nineteen*. His first collection *The Bradford Count* was shortlisted for the Whitbread Prize in 1991.

Brendan Kennelly called his poetry 'an exciting blend of the old and new, the tragic and comic, the grave and the light-hearted ...Ian Duhig sets out to create his own proverbial world'. Sean O'Brien thought his book 'essential reading for anyone who wants to know what is going on in poetry written in England today'. ●

Selection from: *The Bradford Count* (1991).

MOIRA CONWAY

Fundamentals

Brethren, I know that many of you have come here today
because your Chief has promised any non-attender
that he will stake him out, drive tent-pegs through his anus
and sell his wives and children to the Portuguese.
As far as possible, I want you to put that from your minds.
Today, I want to talk to you about the Christian God.

In many respects, our Christian God is not like your God.
His name, for example, is not also our word for rain.
Neither does it have for us the connotation 'sexual intercourse'.
And although I call Him 'holy' (we call Him 'Him', not 'It',
even though we know He is not a man and certainly not a woman)
I do not mean, as you do, that He is fat like a healthy cow.

Let me make this clear. When I say 'God is good, God is everywhere',
it is not because He is exceptionally fat. 'God loves you'
does not mean what warriors do to spear-carriers on campaign.
It means He feels for you like your mother or your father –
yes I know Chuma loved a son he bought like warriors
love spear-carriers on campaign – that's *Sin* and it comes later.

From today, I want you to remember just three simple things:
our God is different from your God, our God is better than your God
and my wife doesn't like it when you watch her go to the toilet.
Grasp them and you have grasped the fundamentals of salvation.
Baptisms start at sundown but before then, as arranged,
how to strip, clean and re-sight a bolt-action Martini-Henry.

Sundry Receipts of Vatsyayana called Mrillana written in the form of Sutra

The black pigment produced by grinding the burned bone
of a hawk or kite with antimony and brushed
under the eyelashes gives power over men.

Lac wetted seven times in sweat from the testicles
of a white horse will brighten the lip.
The lip may be darkened by chewing madayontikas.

Juice of cassia, jambolana and veronia,
thickened with powdered lohopa-jihirka,
destroys love when smeared on a woman's yoni.

Congress with a woman bathed in the stale milk
of buffaloes, garlic and hog-plum
dried with thorn-apple works to like effect.

A paste of milk-hedge, myrabolons, kuili
and monkey-excrement thrown over a woman
against a golden moon will keep her faithful.

A woman who comes near a man playing bagpipes
dressed with juice of vajra, the urine of hyena
and goat-butter will be disgusted by him.

A man garlanded with asparagus, jasmine,
blue lotus and the sloughed skins of cobras
will be the source of endless conversation.

Shlakshnaparni, worn while hunting tiger
alone, unarmed, on foot, by moonlight,
is a certain cure for constipation.

Seeds of pomegranate and cucumber
ground to an ointment with ghee and arabicus
are, to my knowledge, completely useless.

Margin Prayer from an Ancient Psalter

Lord I know, and I know you know I know
this is a drudge's penance. Only dull scholars
or cowherds maddened with cow-watching
will ever read *The Grey Psalter of Antrim*.
I have copied it these thirteen years
waiting for the good bits – High King of the Roads,
are there any good bits in *The Grey Psalter of Antrim*?

(Text illegible here because of teeth-marks.)

It has the magic realism of an argumentum:
it has the narrative subtlety of the Calendar of Oengus;
it has the oblique wit of the Battle-Cathach of the O'Donnells;
it grips like the colophon to The Book of Durrow;
it deconstructs like a canon-table;
it makes St Jerome's Defence of his Vulgate look racy.
I would make a gift of it to Halfdane the Sacker
that he might use it to wipe his wide Danish arse.
Better its volumes intincted our cattle-trough
and cured poor Luke, my three-legged calf,
than sour my wit and spoil my calligraphy.
Luke! White Luke! Truer beast than Ciarán's Dun Cow!
You would rattle the abbot with your soft off-beats
butting his churns and licking salt from his armpits.
Luke, they flayed you, pumiced your skin to a wafer –
such a hide as King Tadhg might die under –
for pages I colour with ox-gall yellow...

(Text illegible here because of tear-stains.)

Oh Forgiving Christ of scribes and sinners
intercede for me with the jobbing abbot!
Get me re-assigned to something pagan
with sex and perhaps gratuitous violence
which I might deplore with insular majuscule
and illustrate with Mozarabic complexity
Ad maioram gloriam Dei et Hiberniae,
and lest you think I judge the book too harshly
from pride or a precious sensibility
I have arranged for a second opinion.
Tomorrow our surveyor, Ronan the Barbarian,
will read out loud as only he can read out loud
selected passages from this which I have scored
while marking out his new church in Killaney
in earshot of that well-versed man, King Suibhne...

(Text completely illegible from this point
because of lake-water damage and otter dung.)

From the Irish

According to Dineen, a Gael unsurpassed
in lexicographical enterprise, the Irish
for moon means 'the white circle in a slice
of half-boiled potato or turnip'. A star
is the mark on the forehead of a beast
and the sun is the bottom of a lake, or well.

Well, if I say to you your face
is like a slice of half-boiled turnip,
your hair is the colour of a lake's bottom
and at the centre of each of your eyes
is the mark of the beast, it is because
I want to love you properly, according to Dineen.

Julie O'Callaghan

JULIE O'CALLAGHAN was born in 1954 in Chicago, and moved to Dublin in 1974. Her first collection, *Edible Anecdotes* (Dolmen, 1983), was a Poetry Book Society Recommendation; her second, *What's What* (Bloodaxe, 1991), a Poetry Book Society Choice.

She observes life with a sharp wit and a wicked gift for mimicry. Her characters vent strong feelings and betray revealing weaknesses in their own colourful words. 'The variety of voices at her command is displayed most impressively...Her poems have broken new ground in the American quest for the apparently artless and natural' – *TLS*. 'She is as sharp as Muriel Spark, nosey as Alan Bennett' – Michael Gorman. ●

Selection from: *What's What* (1991).

Pep-Talk to Poets from Their Sales Manager
(for Gerald Dawe)

Alright, you Irish guys –
first off – I love ya – got it?
Hey – where's the blarney?
Quit looking like you were just included
in a 'Contemporary British Poetry' anthology
or something; we got books to sell!
Now, what abouta few Volkswagens in bogs
or grey streets with graffiti on the walls –
scenes like that;
you haven't been turning it out lately.
How come? I need stuff with slogans, guys.
Folksy stuff – know what I mean?
I'm doin my best but it's all lookin
a little like a yawner at this stage.
That's all, lads – keep at it.

I wanna see all a you extra-terrestrials
gravitating over here double quick, fellas.
'Take me to yer reader' – right, guys?
Now let's get serious – huh?
Here's your sales chart – up, up, up!

Kinda like a flying saucer discovering
new universes of humanoids who wanna book of poetry.
We're gonna capture new markets, aren't we,
and no more traitors writing
transvestite translations or we'll zap them
with our lazer gun – right?

Goils! Move yer feminist little butts over here.
Yer doin terrific. Lots of sarcasm
about what termites we guys are, lots of PMT,
lots of mothers acting square – magnificent!
My god, you're going great guns, ladies.
OOPS! I mean WOMEN don't I?
We want a lot of hype comin up to Christmas
so those cash registers keep singing.

Just one word of advice: see if you can
Virginia Woolf-up your images a bit
and who knows what we can do?
Sisterhood is powerful!

All miscellaneous misfits, up front please.
Lookit pals, *you* want an easy life,
I wanta easy life and *we all* want super-sales,
so why not give up this poetic individuality baloney
and get yourselves an angle, join a group.
My job is tough enough
without you weirdos
lousing it up even more!

Opening Lines

Welcome to Potawotamee Summer Camp.
We ain't interested in any wise-crackers,
smart-alecs, spoil-sports or louses.
Any of the above a-ree-va-dare-chee.
You guys'll be comin wid me for some warm-ups
around the track before we get down to
a few wunnerful games a baseball.

The ladies'll be in da parkhouse for crafts:
keychains, beads and macramé, right Miss Chwingyard?
After lunch we'll all go out to the
volleyball courts for a battle between the sexes.
Losers'll do latrine duty for a week.
Lunch'll consist of
hot dogs with relish, mustard and ketchup, Doritos,
chocolate milk and a piece of cake.
Like it or lump it.

Auschwitz

I says to him, 'Cutie-pie, come out of that.'
I says, 'You're asking for it, Brad.
These people don't care a damn
if you saved-up for three years
to travel over here – they wouldn't care
if it was ten years and they seem
awful nasty – so I think you'd better
get the hell outta there real soon.'
He kept saying, 'Check the focus;
have you included the whole scene?;
is there enough light?; check it again,
I can't afford another trip if you don't do it right;
can you see my face?'
I took a few snapshots and said,
'You're gonna be murdered if you don't get out
of that rotten old gas oven.'

Anne Rouse

MARY ROOT

Selection from: *Sunset Grill*
(1993).

ANNE ROUSE was born in 1954 in Washington,
DC, grew up in Virginia, and later moved to
London where she has been a nurse and a
shop steward, and now works for a mental
health charity. Her book *Sunset Grill* (1993)
is a Poetry Book Society Recommendation.

Rouse's ability to 'use the resources of
poetry in an unexpected way' was admired
by Neil Powell; describing her sonnet *Eng-
land Nil*, he wrote: 'The risks are triumph-
antly taken: how much more devastatingly
effective this is as a result of its Shakespear-
ian sympathy with a thoroughly unlovely
speaker'. Sarah Maguire: 'Her curt, ironic
poems display a wonderful degree of con-
trol and dry understatement.' ●

England Nil

The advance to Hamburg broke with all the plans.
Doug spelled them out in Luton Friday night.
Someone had ballsed it up. A dozen vans
Waited in convoy, ringside. Blue and white
We stumbled through. The beer
When we found it in that piss-hole of jerries
Was all we needed. Who won the war,
Anyway? Who nuked Dresden? Two fairies
Skittered behind the bar, talking Kraut
Or maybe Arabic. We clocked the poison
Smiles and chanted till the SS threw us out.
Stuttgart was a tea-party to this. One
By one they've nicked us, berserk with fear.
You've been Englished but you won't forget it, never.

M3

Mean as a length of flex, it snubs the B road,
Disliking breakdown and hiker, impedimenta;
Droning the highway code
At shuddering lorries, and the reps for shampoo,
Blurring southward to the postcard rack
And coffee on the lido.

As time stripped down to mere emergency,
It tarmacs older memories of sense,
Of littering picnic; of plum tree,
Rooks, and manure,
Nerves like a harp in the blown high grass.
Inland, it simply hands over.

Springfield, Virginia

Colonels live there, commuters to the Pentagon
In sweetly-named estates: King's Park, Orange Wood.
Springfield proper is a set of asphalt lots,
A catch-all town for realtors and mail.

At *Peoples Drug*, and the fast-food joints,
The hands popping open the cylinders of change
Hail from Vietnam or Nicaragua, arrivistes
Wondering at the sourness of God's people.

The high schoool kids who used to do the jobs
Were white, immune to history:
Andy Sulick, sheepish in a Big Ranch Stetson hat,
A row of enforced dim smiles at *Burger Chef.*

Eight hundred graduated in '71. That night,
Crawling the backroads, jumping in and out
Of unfamiliar cars, I found a party at a shack.
A boy mashed me against the lean-to floor.

Along the wooded road lightning bugs flared
Like drunks with matches, seeing their way home,
And whipperwills nagged the sleeper
Until a dawn as pink and blue as litmus paper.

Daytrip

We'd left the cameras in the Hertz
But made St. P's for the tourist Passion.
I knew one of the trio:
This is what he did on his vacations.
The bearded heads bled from the corbels.
We walked by the pleated steps of a temple
In whose maw the usual type was being tried with flame.

We took in the long galleria before lunch.
Sloan made some remark about art being *vox populi*.
I sent him back to the Excelsior with a flea in his ear.
The roofs stretched out, pale in the heat and peaceable.
Your shoulder touched mine. I could tell you were moved.
The wine and the drowse of pigeons dismissed
Any rancour between us. Rested we'd be as good as gold.

Geoff Hattersley

MOIRA CONWAY

Selection from: *Don't Worry*
(1994).

GEOFF HATTERSLEY was born in 1956 in South
Yorkshire, and lives in Barnsley, where he
edits the magazine *The Wide Skirt* and its
press. The best poems from several small
press titles are published with new work in
his Bloodaxe collection *Don't Worry* (1994).

His poems are accessible and entertaining,
but their apparent simplicity belies a shrewd
intelligence as much in tune with larger
events as with the daily happenings which
seem to form their subject. His reading of
many other poets, especially Americans like
Frank O'Hara, has produced not show-off
quoting, but tonal balance and sly humour,
and a subtle, streetwise style in which New
York meets New Yorkshire. ●

In Phil's Butchers

They're sure they know me from somewhere:
'Aren't tha t' bloke that rode naked
on a bike through Jump for charity?
Thi picture wa' in t' Chronicle.'
The previous customer leaves, coughing
something red and green onto the pavement.
'That's a poorly mister, dead on 'is feet 'e is.'
One of them decides he worked
with my brother at Johnson's
though I've no brother who worked there.
'Are tha sure?' he wonders.
An older man (is it Phil?)
pops his head in from the back room:
'Leave t' lad alone 'n' gi' 'im 'is pies.'
I hold them in my hand as I say 'Ta-ra'
and leave, taking off my dark glasses.
There's a patch of blue sky
where my eyes should be, which startles
an old woman crossing the road.
'By' I say, to reassure her,
'it's cold enough for a walking stick.'
'All laughter is despair' she replies,
'it's t' human condition, like.'

Theology

A good friend of mine
one day; the next,
someone who just happened
to look like her.

'God tapped me on the shoulder'
she said
and handed me the leaflet.

Returning home on the bus
I heard one schoolgirl
telling another
'Simon Bletsoe put his hand
on my fanny last night.'

Later, the same one
tapped me on the shoulder
to ask for a light.

Forever Changed

You're tired, running a temperature, carrying
your empty medicine bottles to the dustbin.
The man you used to call dad hides behind it,
leaps out, boots you in the balls and face,
tips a bucket of piss over your head.
This happens every day, you're never ready.

Then you lose your job and all your savings
on a stupid bet. Your wife packs her bags,
takes the kids, moves to another country.
She's drilled holes in the radiators,
trampled avocados into the carpets
and warped your entire record collection.

The next thing you know you're beat up
and arrested in a dawn raid, charged with
possession of narcotics and firearms
and assaulting a police officer.
You're innocent but no one believes you.
Your lawyer washes his hands of you,

someone nails your cat to the door. Suddenly
you're getting letters of abuse, death-threats,
gift-wrapped substances that sting your fingers.
The postman tells you he hates you,
the milkman refuses to leave you milk,
people turn up to laugh and jeer at you

in the hairdresser's and supermarket,
follow you down the street throwing bottles
and rocks, dogs snapping at your heels.
The man you used to call dad kills himself,
leaves a note blaming you. Your novel
is dismissed as the ravings of a sick man.

Then every lover you've had publishes memoirs
in the Sunday papers, the details are awful.
Tuesday, you're photographed in a night-club
with two fourteen-year-old girls and described
as a kinky pervert, a corrupter of youth,
a collector of soiled knickers.

Then your house is destroyed by fire.
Everything's gone, you don't even have one
photo of your kids' birthday parties left.
Your terrapins were boiled alive.
Your mother was asleep in the spare room.
Your wife hadn't renewed the insurance.

You wake in the night in a cheap hotel
to find you're deaf in your left ear,
have gone bald and have an ache
in the only two teeth you still bite with.
Then you're sitting at a bar looking scared.
A good Samaritan moves in to finish it.

Maura Dooley

DAVID HUNTER

Selection from: *Explaining Magnetism* (1991) and new poems.

MAURA DOOLEY was born in 1957 in Truro, grew up in Bristol, and has since lived in Yorkshire, London and Swansea. Her first full-length book, *Explaining Magnetism* (1991), was a Poetry Book Society Recommendation, and confirmed her growing reputation as one of Britain's finest new poets.

Her poetry is remarkable for embracing both lyricism and political consciousness, for its fusion of head and heart. Helen Dunmore admired her 'sharp and forceful' intelligence. Adam Thorpe praised her ability 'to enact and find images for complex feelings...Her poems have both great delicacy and an undeniable toughness...she manages to combine detailed domesticity with lyrical beauty, most perfectly in the metaphor of memory.' ●

Mind the Gap

We have settled on either side of a bridge, under arches,
medieval, Dickensian or twentieth-century. Over the bridge
a flutter of commuters, under the bridge the Thames,
beside the bridge a nest of survivors in cardboard.
Heading North, at night, with a suitcase and new coat
you hear rats in the Underground scratching over what's left,
a recorded voice   calling   Mind the Gap   Mind the Gap.

That swift, sad jump is replayed second by second
in the corner of your eye. But why today when sunlight
made the river almost lovely? Perhaps because it put him
beyond stomach pump or reason and when the sun
came out he was blinded by sorrow, hung up like sheets
for the wind to fill, billowing out over London, gathering dirt.
O take him down, bring him in, bundle him up in time,

before the clouds gather, before the rain comes.

Letters from Yorkshire

In February, digging his garden, planting potatoes,
he saw the first lapwings return and came
indoors to write to me, his knuckles singing

as they reddened in the warmth.
It's not romance, simply how things are.
You out there, in the cold, seeing the seasons

turning, me with my heartful of headlines
feeding words onto a blank screen.
Is your life more real because you dig and sow?

You wouldn't say so, breaking ice on a waterbutt,
clearing a path through snow. Still, it's you
who sends me word of that other world

pouring air and light into an envelope. So that
at night, watching the same news in different houses,
our souls tap out messages across the icy miles.

Six Filled the Woodshed with Soft Cries

From grass-stained eggs we bred eight;
two hens, six fine white cockerels,
they scrambled, fluffing feathers,
for a summer and an autumn month.

Now, hands pinked by the wind,
I watch their maned necks nervously.
Yesterday the tiniest learnt to crow,
latched a strange voice to crisp air,
his blood red comb fluting the wind,
feathers creaming, frothing at his throat.

One month till Christmas, the clouds thicken,
he turns on me an icy, swivel eye,
Do you dare deny me?

My neighbour helps me chase them,
snorting snuff, which rests on his sleeve
in a fine white scatter. A wicker basket
gapes wide as he dives for them.

Six filled the woodshed with soft cries.
Their feathers cover stony ground
like a lick of frost.

Mansize

Now you aren't here I find
myself ironing linen squares,
three by three, the way
my mother's always done,
the steel tip steaming over your
blue initial. I, who resent
the very thought of this back-breaking
ritual, preferring radiator-dried
cottons, stiff as boards, any amount
of crease and crumple to this
soothing, time-snatching, chore.

I never understood my father's trick,
his spare for emergencies, but was glad
of its airing-cupboard comforts often enough:
burying my nose in it, drying my eyes
with it, staunching my blood with it,
stuffing my mouth with it. His expedience,
my mother's weekly art, leaves me
forever flawed: rushing into newsagents
for Kleenex, rifling your pockets in the cinema,
falling on those cheap printed florals,

when what I really want is Irish linen,
shaken out for me to sink my face in,
the shape and scent of you still warm
in it, your monogram in chainstitch
at the corner. Comforter, seducer, key witness
to it all, my neatly folded talisman,
my sweet flag of surrender.

Explaining Magnetism

Isolated here in the South, fiddling with British Rail
network charts, inhabiting the Underground plan, I learn
again how West means left and East means right.
I used to know that North was always straight ahead,
every map showed that cardinal point, a long feathered
arrow, a capital N. Whichever way I walked the land
restored itself to my own order: true North.

A compass only confused, school got in the way,
pointing at things you couldn't see,
explaining magnetism. In order to find out
I just went straight ahead and up there,
out of sight, was never isolated but isolate.
Down here, we move as one and jump like hamsters,
onto the Circle line. The names don't help much,
recalling that dull board game and me,

broke again, moving a top hat listlessly,
back and forth, left to right, round and round.

History

It's only a week but already you are slipping
down the cold black chute of history. Postcards.
Phonecalls. It's like never having seen the Wall,
except in pieces on the dusty shelves of friends.

Once I queued for hours to see the moon in a box
inside a museum, so wild it should have been kept
in a zoo at least but there it was, unremarkable,
a pile of dirt some god had shaken down.

I wait for your letters now: a fleet of strange cargo
with news of changing borders, a heart's small
journeys. They're like the relics of a saint.
Opening the dry white papers is kissing a bone.

Going the Distance

He fills her glass. She raises it.
The nearest he comes to telling her
is here in this silence. With the weight
of his life backed up behind him like a truck,
in the time it takes her heart to skip a beat,
he travels the length of that old road again.

She thinks of leaving then, nipping out for fags,
a box of matches, never looking back.
Returning to the island after years away
only the coinage would feel strange to her,
crenulations beaten smooth by distance,
shifting in her hand like the sea, whose dazed
blue space is calm and flat beneath her:
the Atlantic's slow unfurling of its flag.

She drains her glass and lowers it.
The waiter clearing dishes from the table
is tender and efficient as a priest.
They settle up. She opens a door on London.
He closes it. They move into the crowd.

Night Driving

Across the Pennines maybe, at first frost,
when your headlamps make milky the way ahead,

or approaching Toronto at 4.00 a.m.
when stars lie scattered on the still lake,

driving fast, the windows pulled down,
to let the night winds steady your hands

you're tuned into strange stations
playing old hits you wish you didn't know.

Turning a dial fills the air with static:
oceans, the blueness of night

and you own the road, the country.
The radio speaks only to you.

Deborah Randall

IAN GROUND

Selection from: *The Sin Eater*
(1989) and *White Eyes, Dark
Ages* (1993).

DEBORAH RANDALL was born in 1957, and
lives in Ullapool in Scotland. Her first col-
lection *The Sin Eater* (1989) was a Poetry
Book Society Recommendation, and won
her a Scottish Arts Council Book Award.
Her second, *White Eyes, Dark Ages* (1993), is
a portrait by many hands of that eminent
Victorian, John Ruskin, painted by a poet
writing a century after his death – pictured
through the eyes of his women.

'Deborah Randall has a distinctive, sexy
bravado which gladdens the heart' – Carol
Ann Duffy. 'Her work is earthed, gutsy, fiery
and sensual in its dealings with the basics
of life and death...a deft and womanly art'
– Sylvia Kantaris. ●

Finney's Bar

Ah, you rare old devil, you fine fellow Finney,
Ravishing your fiddle so the tendons won't sing
Of virginity's meaning, Finney, you dog
With your dead-born tunes,
Elbows to the big bugger moon, in Dublin,
Your backside afire as you saw at the throat,
And Irishman's Fancy is spilled.

Finney, you swore on your fathers, you'd kissed
The hem of her sky-blue dress,
Emulsion-skinned holy mother whose waters
Are breaking with sin and piss; and she unbandaged
Her bleeding heart, she reeled
As you cut your fiddle,
And the boys in the backroom reeled with her.

Finney, I'll never forget you, a bless and a curse
On your head and the murder you did,
To music, the black and amber we passed together,
Your white confessional walls,
They fell like snow on my head, Finney, you rogue,
I've looked up your trouser leg.
I'd die to drink with you again.

Nightwatchman

Brother nightwatchman I have shared your way,
Black upon black footfall upon the crazily paved street
And eyes and hands full of each other so drunk
The wine to vinegar as we walk without talk on my tongue
And hands feeling for ourselves as only strangers can,

The lock and the alien roof and the fumble for them
Unseemly unhomely things that we build about ourselves
After marriages have broken I still dream of eggs bitter
And raw such as my father slid down his throat at dawn,
Falling from my fingers so much rage still to come,

I don't remember a time in two years when alcohol
Wasn't wailing in my veins, a substitute for tears
Like the grab and grind with a new nightwatchman,
The surprising angle of the apple in your throat
The lotion in your skin, you don't smell like him,

Stairs are unholy alliances, every one and many
Sneaking under the soles of our feet the squeak
Of female philandering as I size the nightwatchman's shoulders
Estimate the blades in there and how they shall
Rub for pleasure under my hands two wishbones wondering,

The door is the single hymen I have to admit you
And you ahead owning me and my womb without name
Flicking your beautiful hair gold and white and shampoo
And I live alone, lone as the furthest star that cannot
Be seen, little girl frantically signalling,

Nightwatchman on my carpet you are so naked, and proud
As a pose, I have watched this maleness, I see in the dark
And I know, and I'm tired, tired of the drumskin belly
The random muscle below, a perilous house of cards
Is building in me, my history frail and impersonal,

The neon snakes of your arms nightwatchman
Wind and wind about me and the carpet rolls us up
And the solitary bed is empty our flesh on the floor
In choreography, and a neighbour rapping his fifty-year-old
Indignation, an accompaniment to my game,

I open my four lips for your fingertips and my cunt weeps
As my face won't, and like an angry sponge absorbs you,
All, and when you are sleeping I watch the night,
Small boys sleep off their pleasure, I watch
The night, and wonder at such perfect death.

Ballygrand Widow

So, you have gone my erstwhile glad boy,
Whose body, I remember, stained my big cream bed,
And didn't we mix the day and the night in our play,
We never got up for a week.

If I must set my alarm again,
And feed the hungry hens in the yard,
And draw the milk from my cow on time,
And skulk my shame down Ballygrand Street
To get a drink,
It'll not be for you I think,
But my next husband,
A fine cock he shall be.

So, you are no more in this town
My lovely schoolboy, and how the floss
Of your chin tickled me.
And you swam your hands all over,
You shouted for joy, the first time.
Ah, my darling!

I wear your mother's spit on my shoes,
The black crow priest has been to beat me.
But you gave me a belly full, the best,
And they shan't take it.
The days are unkind after you, they are empty.
I lie in the sheets, the very same sheets;
You smelled sweeter than meadow hay.
My beautiful boy you have killed me.

The Custodial Woman

She eclipses all flowers,
Her butcher's arms ready to hack
A meal into being,
Swill a putrid bowl in an aside,
Collect the cuckoo-spit from a sickman's mouth
As if it were pearls.

Her decent ugliness
Checks all beauty,
Even her strong wild hair
Is trussed,
Her head, a walking bust.

She turns duty into an art form,
Her love the rolled sleeve school,
No-nonsense artefacts surround her
And surrender.

Children pass through her,
She wears them awhile on her hip and breast
Maternal medals.
Her husband becomes her son
And she takes her son for a husband.
But her daughters.
Her daughters litter the house and sicken
Like jailed gypsies.

Brendan Cleary

MOIRA CONWAY

Selection from: *The Irish Card* (1993).

BRENDAN CLEARY was born in 1958 in Co. Antrim, and lives in Newcastle where he edits *The Echo Room*. His book *The Irish Card* deals out poems from the double life of an exiled Irish poet: going off his head in his performance pieces, going back inside in the title-sequence of deeply personal poems on rootlessness, inner exile and estrangement.

'These new poems are sad movies of Irish soul...Cleary's given up his joker for the ace of hearts. He's left the pub for the confessional, blabbering his tale of woe like a late night wag who's high on the muse and the music, tearful and brilliant like a kind of Hank Williams on acid' – Harry Novak. ●

Crack

It was a piece of piss then
I'd cracked it

& when the foamy coffees came
we showed off old photographs
from our old bus passes

her freckles, my black rings

& as the woman wiped the floor
we raised our feet in unison
& I knew then that I'd cracked it
when she twiddled her ringlet
dipped her wide saucer eyes
& spoke those magic words

'So what star sign are you then?'

Rose
FROM *The Irish Card*

There was my ideal girl even way back then
at Carrick Grammar & I knew I'd find her 'across the water'.

You see, that's seen as a logical step & entirely natural
to go via Liverpool or Stranraer to colleges & careers

over on the mainland & that was where I knew she was.
For the want of a better name let's call her Rose,

I thought she might live somewhere like Hampshire
& she would have horses & speak with marlies in her bake,

but I wouldn't mind because of her beauty & lustre,
no way, not after growing up with a stack of wee Millies,

girls in Skinners & Crombies always shouting over
'Hey mister, my mate fancies ye' or 'mister, gotta feg?'

Rose would be refined & schooled, we'd discuss all the books
I longed to read, those I've never quite got round to

& one day I would have to go to her house like Bertie Wooster,
to her luxurious country estate where her pompous father

would want to know about my people & she'd be the pride
of all Hampshire but I'd charm her. I do it all the time,

lower my voice an octave & use loads of quaint slang
& they love it & if I was a bastard it would get me laid & has done.

The Home Counties can't ever comprehend me, I'm an outsider,
it's a privilege to watch their class system in action

& I'm never thought of as pig ignorant, a bogman, but clever,
not like Macalpine's men or pissheads from Kilburn.

So Rose would be bowled over by my crack & lilting;
it would all be unreal to her, but enchanting. 'Talk about home,

it must be *so* romantic, is it really beautiful?' she'd ask me
& if I burped or let off a stinker after dinner, she'd tap me,

pretend to be disgusted, but I'd come off with some quip,
some cliché like 'Aye, sure ye can take the man out of the bog

but not the bog out of the man' & she'd be hooked again.
Needless to say this never happened & I never met her

no matter where I am nothing happens & I never meet her...

Slouch
FROM *The Irish Card*

Their bar-stools have slouched them too early
though later half-cut they start to sidle up

'Hey Pat, why not fuck off where you came,
back to the bogs, shouldn't you be picking spuds?'

They have eyes with no causes, their smug voices
in drunken unison jeer & mock my voice.

Perhaps when the hangover hits I'll take them up,
return meekly, submerge myself in landscape,

more like submerge myself in Black Bush –
bury myself in selfish small-town intrigue,

or if I had any passion left for bland slogans
I could even do my bit for the 'armed struggle'.

But the echo of Lambegs burst my skull,
I've spent too long licking up to England.

I've been the brunt of their stunted comedians
I've lived in comfort but amid canned laughter

& this latest encounter could come to fisticuffs
although till now I've played the Irish card with charm.

They probe me: 'Mick, do you even belong in this country?'
I won't slouch too early so I gleefully reply

'just as much as you belong in mine'...

Linda France

MOIRA CONWAY

Selection from: *Red* (1992)
and *The Gentleness of the
Very Tall* (1994).

LINDA FRANCE was born in 1958 in Newcastle.
After some years away, she returned to the
North-East in 1981, and now lives in Hexham. She has two Bloodaxe collections, and
edited *Sixty Women Poets* (1993).

Her poetry is both sensuous and sensitive,
peeling back layers in pursuit of honesty. It
is also highly visual – almost painterly – using startlingly contemporary imagery. Carol
Rumens has called her 'a clever, accessible
new voice. Energetic, ranging, witty, candid, informal and excitingly individualistic,
Linda France's work makes use of many
available styles...*Red* opens up important
new territory for poetry.' ●

If Love Was Jazz

If love was jazz,
I'd be dazzled
By its razzmatazz.

If love was a sax
I'd melt in its brassy flame
Like wax.

If love was a guitar,
I'd pluck its six strings,
Eight to the bar.

If love was a trombone,
I'd feel its slow
Slide, right down my backbone.

If love was a drum,
I'd be caught in its snare,
Kept under its thumb.

If love was a trumpet,
I'd blow it.

If love was jazz,
I'd sing its praises,
Like Larkin has.

But love isn't jazz.
It's an organ recital.
Eminently worthy,
Not nearly as vital.

If love was jazz,
I'd always want more.
I'd be a regular
On that smoky dance-floor.

Weighing the Heart

*Officially the heart
is oblong, muscular
and filled with longing.*
MIROSLAV HOLUB

*The way you love me is a house you've built
of thick stone with fires in every hearth
to warm me. The flames grow like orange flowers
out of black coal and so you sow your seed*

*in me. My lap is a patchwork apron
of photographs of our children, locked
together, like shiny mirrors, in a house
of thick stone, a place called home where the heart is.*

Every year is dangerous. There's always
no knowing. But the time is now that you
must weigh your heart to find out how much
it's worth. The time you find you love him

like a brother, like he's family, just because
he's there, a mountain you're too scared
to climb, where the air's too thin to breathe,
just enough to keep you alive, just enough

to hurt. The foothills on your map are riddled
with history, bullet holes and shifting
borders, traces of blood and little graves
with photographs and fading flowers:

a country of old campaigns. But the heart
is a history lesson you never learn
from. Try it as science instead: weigh it,
dissect it, list its various components.

Discover the truth. Record it. And find
the only heart you can measure is your own.
And once you start dividing it up, it gets
smaller and smaller till there's nothing left

to transplant. This part's for you and this part's
for you. *He loves me. He loves me not. He loves me...*
not. And her. And her. And her.
You're trying your best to walk straight ahead

but every day is another sharp corner
you catch yourself on, the limits of your body
defined by each new scratch and bruise.
You've lost your sense of direction. You're lost.

The map. Your heart. Discover the truth.
He loves you because he knows you so well.
He loves her because he hardly knows her
at all. Is that what the heart is? A mollusc

that doesn't know? An act of the imagination?
Beware the heart that commits a sexual
act. Beware the heart that knows nothing
but penetration, gets under your skin.

The body is a gift you can choose
to give. Or not. In equal measure.
Like your heart, tucked inside, its changing lights.
You are its brother, its keeper. You can not weigh

another's. You are not the keeper of your brother's
heart. But, like mirrors, the heart reflects and,
like rabbits, breeds. So before you know it, or
your heart, you have at least six to try not

to keep. Look at them all red and bloody
in the butcher's shop window. Balance them
on a silver scale. Your stomach will pay
the bill. Discover the truth. Record it.

The way you hurt me is a sitting-room
mirror smashed into fragments of silver.
You stick the shiny pieces onto the mantel
with strong glue. The edges cut your fingers.

You dip a brush in a pot of black paint
and write me a message. It doesn't say
'Welcome Home'. You're telling me the truth.
You love me. You promise. The lulling mantra

of the greedy, the desperate, cowards
who can't face the truth. *If I knew the truth*
I'd tell it you. I'd write it in big black
letters on the orange of the mantelpiece

and decorate it with glittering mirrors,
repeating it over and over.
I love you. I love you. I love you.
The heart like the camera never lies.

Here is a knife, sharp and cruel as the taunt of truth.
Use it to cut out your heart. Check it's still your own,
Kodachrome crimson and complete. *Don't lie*
to me. Ever. Tell me the truth. I don't want

to know what you did in bed. Don't tell me
that. Just tell me the truth. Record it.
The heart, like the camera, often lies,
tells its own version of many different truths.

He kisses my breasts and I see a picture
of hers. My heart's in there somewhere.
Like hers. Double bloom. Double exposure.
This bed's not big enough for all of us:

the telephones, letters, bunches of flowers,
the small, touching gifts, the stains on the sheets.
The bed's a fucking mess. And all I want
is clean linen, crisp, white, a good night's sleep.

He's had another letter. You know
by the way he tells you he loves you
over and over. He's written back. You know
because he buys you chocolate. You know

the rules of the game. Truth, dare or promise.
But now you're playing against the wind
and you can't see for tears. Your feet are cold
and wet. The sharp corners are tumbled bricks

of thick stone, broken promises. Your heart.
You're climbing the mountain whether you like it
or not. You have to see what's on the other side,
to find out if it's a better country,

greener grass. If you can manage without a map.
Your heart. The trek up is bog and rock.
Lichens grow like orange flowers, fragile, strong.
The light changes. Your feet are wet. You feel

the draught blowing through the space where your heart
should be. Weigh the air. Tell me. *The truth is,*
I have the heart of a hungry child
who's been given the key to a ruined house.

Zoology Is Destiny

You won't let me be ostrich, armadillo,
invertebrate. Although for you I'm zoo,
a new creature, prowling behind bars, howling
at the moon, the way you can stroke the hairs
riding the roaring switchback of my spine –
a terrible gesture of tenderness.

If I can't come out, you'll come in – pick
the lock on the door of my cage with your teeth.
We dine on watermelon and figs, milk
and almonds, our tongues cunning as Eden snakes.
Our hands build an ark, two by two, for fur,
feathers flying, hoof, breastbone, muzzle, wing.

This is not a parable wishing itself
would happen, like weather in a fable
by Aesop, a date in *The Fox and Grapes.*
It's simply the vatic utterance
of a white rhinoceros who knows
the difference between rocks and crocodiles.

Elizabeth Garrett

ALISON RICHARDS

Selection from: *The Rule of Three* (1991).

ELIZABETH GARRETT was born in 1958, grew up in the Channel Islands, and lives in Oxford.

'Shapely, measured and measuring, Elizabeth Garrett's poems make no concessions to fashion or facileness. Her subjects are the eternal themes of poetry – love and its transience, time, truth, certainty, childhood and memory – but this is really too naked a summary…The great strength of these poems lies in the poet's ability to establish and maintain a whole network of tensions (spinning and spiders aptly recur) – between philosophical gravitas and sensuous immediacy, between passion and wariness, measured doubt and formal confidence, toughness and vulnerability, between lyrical intensity and riddling playfulness' – Lawrence Sail. ●

Lost Property

Kneel, and let us pray for the departed:
A sulphurous incense chokes the station vaults,
A pigeon coughs; the platform is deserted.
Guilty-eyed, while others slept in prayer
I scoured the hassock's cross-stitch for some fault
As though it were my soul; and found none there.

A labour of devotion: pious kisses
Smothering the cushion where my knees
Grew numb and bore the imprint of those stitches.
Burden of the Cross. A priest intones,
Feet shuffle for Communion to ease
The weight, and catch the last train home.

The rails are silent, empty as the aisle
When rush-hour's past. A platform sweeper brushes
Up confetti into piles.
It's growing dark. A thin girl stands and watches
As he sweeps the crumbs that drowsy birds
Have missed. I wake. And there are words
For this; but none so fittingly expressed
As by my own hand cupped around my breast.

History Goes to Work

The soft-boiled egg is emptied
But makes a humpty-dumpty head
Reversed. Numbskull! Bald pate!
You know the spoon's importunate
Knock knock will wake the dead.

The silver spoon lies on its back
And spoons the room all up-
Side-down but never spills a drop:
The ovoid walls adapt their laws
And never show a crack.

The egg lies in the silver spoon
And yolkless words lie on the tongue
And all that's in the spoon-shaped room
Swears it is square; no books
Were cooked. The egg is done.

Remorse rests in its velvet drawer
Lapped in the sleep of metaphor,
The soul rests in the open palm
And will not put its shell back on,
And calmly waits for more.

Oak Bride

Let earth be my pillow, and the bridal
Sheet be spread beneath this window
Where the moon rocks in its oak cradle.
And I shall sleepwalk down
The centuries until my dream grows
Rootwise; by morning I will know
How many miles four hundred years
Of water must be drawn.

All night the prodigal moon shook florins
On my bedspread. I knew then
I was a well of wishing, and all
Of me was water to be hauled.
The pull of a tree drinking is a kiss
Where darkness marries silence: by osmosis
I entered my dream. What is
Desire but reciprocal thirst?

Down centuries of drought, like a river
I softened the bed of my oak-dark lover
Till dawn broke where the great delta
Cast its branches to the sky.
Arms wide, mouth quick with desire,
Drinking my own reflection, I
Rooted there, palms cupping
The first drops like acorns falling.

Foxglove

Who taught the cunning little vixen
Manicure? – Sure, she's fixing
To make a kill, a half moon waxing

Nacreous on each fingernail.
Two bees jostle the same bell,
Fumbling the purple fingerstall.

Nonchalant, she slips a glove
On either slender paw, as if
Murder were mere elegance of love.

Martin Stokes

HARRY NOVAK

Selection from: *The First Death of Venice* (1987).

MARTIN STOKES was born in 1958 in Mansfield, and lives in Chester. He won a Gregory Award in 1983, and his first collection, *The First Death of Venice*, was a Poetry Book Society Recommendation in 1987.

'The quality of Martin Stokes's poetry is in its strangeness, and in the way seemingly straightforward pieces fail to add up' – Simon Armitage. 'A confident, substantial and wide-ranging collection, with an air of exhilaration in the indulgence of impressive formal gifts. Appropriately for a poet, Stokes is drunk on words, a stylist and an experimenter. He is definitely one to watch' – Robert Johnstone. ●

Hubris, off the White Cliffs

Our bomber flying home
drops eight remaining bombs.
To see the water plume
she circles round the bombs.

For spectacle and noise –
REVERBERATING BOMBS –
she circles in the noise
and passes round the bombs.

A flight of Messerschmitt,
remembering the bombs,
fires at the plane and it,
in smithereens, like bombs

drops and makes another pass
across the pluming bombs.
The Messerschmitt then pass,
then leave the pluming bombs.

The Moehne Dam

'...another and intriguing way thought
Wallis whimsically, of attacking the enemy
at the source of power.
PAUL BRICKHILL, The Dam Busters

I.

A dam

defended by a heavy flak

emplacement, by searchlights,

and beautified

by ornamental pine trees.

A device designed high

and very thick, wide to withstand

stress, the pressure of its lake,   C

and pierced to let out part   O   R

of its catchment. Several pipes   N   A

diverted water for the Ruhr foundrymen   C   M

to drink and wash in. The volume of its depths   R   P

rewarded summer mornings, afternoons,   E   A

light evenings of quiet fishing, and maintained   T   R

high levels for the long, slow, heavy barges   E   T

heaving coal and iron through a network

of canals, delivering to foundries

for the manufacture of more tanks,

more locomotives, aircraft, guns,

more badges for distinguished service

and medals for acts of bravery,

such as bombing.

II.

Gone to flood the coal mines,

cover aerodromes, shut factories,

fuse the valley's hydro-electricity.

Water, pouring out, just gone

One   C O N   R to damage forty-seven bridges

hundred   A and re-align the railways.

and thirty-four   M The whole reservoir gone

million tons   to put its hands over bells and lights

of water   E T E   A and drown a thousand people

gone.   R (half of them were allied troops

T in a prison camp). Leaving behind

a smell of mudbanks, boats, inverted fish,

a pair of ring-necked whooper swans

and other nesting rare birds.

Benjamin Zephaniah

Selection from: *City Psalms* (1992).

BENJAMIN ZEPHANIAH was born in 1958 in Birmingham, grew up in Jamaica and in Handsworth, where he was sent to an approved school for being uncontrollable, rebellious and 'a born failure', ending up in jail for burglary. After prison, he turned from crime to music and poetry: 'I started writing poetry because I didn't like poetry'. As a reggae DJ in Handsworth, he refused to mimic other toasters with their chants about Jamaican life, instead turning to Britain for his own native patter, comic stories and rhymes. He has since become a master of oral and performance art, with many appearances in films, on TV and radio. His plays have been widely performed; he has released several records, and published four books of poetry. ●

Dis Poetry

Dis poetry is like a riddim dat drops
De tongue fires a riddim dat shoots like shots
Dis poetry is designed fe rantin
Dance hall style, Big mouth chanting,
Dis poetry nar put yu to sleep
Preaching follow me
Like yu is blind sheep,
Dis poetry is not Party Political
Not designed fe dose who are critical.

Dis poetry is wid me when I gu to me bed
It gets into me Dreadlocks
It lingers around me head
Dis poetry goes wid me as I pedal me bike
I've tried Shakespeare, Respect due dere
But dis is de stuff I like.

Dis poetry is not afraid of going ina book
Still dis poetry need ears fe hear an eyes fe hav a look
Dis poetry is Verbal Riddim, no big words involved
An if I hav a problem de riddim gets it solved,

I've tried to be more Romantic, it does nu good for me
So I tek a Reggae Riddim an build me poetry,
I could try be more personal
But you've heard it all before,
Pages of written words not needed
Brain has many words in store,
Yu could call dis poetry Dub Ranting
De tongue plays a beat
De body starts skanking,
Dis poetry is quick an childish
Dis poetry is fe de wise an foolish,
Anybody can do it fe free,
Dis poetry is fe yu an me,
Don't stretch yu imagination
Dis poetry is fe de good of de Nation,
Chant,
In de morning
I chant
In de night
I chant
In de darkness
An under de spotlight,
I pass thru University
I pass thru Sociology
An den I got a Dread degree
In Dreadfull Ghettology.

Dis poetry stays wid me when I run or walk
An when I am talking to meself in poetry I talk,
Dis poetry is wid me,
Below me an above,
Dis poetry's from inside me
It goes to yu
WID LUV.

No rights red an half dead

Dem drag him to de police van
An it was broad daylight,
Dem kick him down de street to it,
I knew it was not right,
His nose had moved, bloody head,
It was a ugly sight.
Dem beat him, tried fe mek him still
But him put up a fight.

De press were dere fe pictures
Cameras roll an click.
While dem get dem money's worth
I started fe feel sick.
No rights red an half dead
An losing breath real quick.
I was sure dat it was caused by
Some bad politrick.

Down de road dem speed away
All traffic pulls aside,
Next to me a high class girl said
'Hope they whip his hide.'
Under me a young man's blood
Caused me fe slip an slide,
He pissed his well-pressed pants,
A man like me jus cried.

All de time it happens
Yes, it happens all de time
But 'Helping with Enquiries'
Says newspaper headlines.
If yu don't help wid enquiries
Yu mus be doing fine,
An if yu tink yu seeing justice
Yu mus be bloody blind.

Fred D'Aguiar

NORTHERN ECHO

Selection from: *British Subjects* (1993).

FRED D'AGUIAR was born in 1960. Home is 'always elsewhere' for him: born in Britain, brought up in Guyana, and now living in London and America, he caught up with his past in his two Chatto collections *Mama Dot* (1985) and *Airy Hall* (1989) by writing about his upbringing in Guyana. The focus of his latest book, *British Subjects* (Bloodaxe, 1993), is Britain: being and feeling British, feeling at home but not being made to feel at home.

D'Aguiar maps out new poetic territory in *British Subjects*, re-discovering a sense of belonging in poems charting landmarks in his life, as in this poem about finding the grave of an African slave in Bristol. ●

At the Grave of the Unknown African

1

Two round, cocoa faces, carved on whitewashed headstone
protect your grave against hellfire and brimstone.

Those cherubs with puffed cheeks, as if chewing gum,
signal how you got here and where you came from.

More than two and a half centuries after your death,
the barefaced fact that you're unnamed feels like defeat.

I got here via White Ladies Road and Black Boy's Hill,
clues lost in these lopsided stones that Henbury's vandal

helps to the ground and Henbury's conservationist
tries to rectify, cleaning the vandal's pissy love-nest.

African slave without a name, I'd call this home
by now. Would you? Your unknown soldier's tomb

stands for shipload after shipload that docked,
unloaded, watered, scrubbed, exercised and restocked

thousands more souls for sale in Bristol's port;
cab drivers speak of it all with yesterday's hurt.

The good conservationist calls it her three hundred year war;
those raids, deals, deceit and capture (a sore still raw).

St Paul's, Toxteth, Brixton, Tiger Bay and Handsworth:
petrol bombs flower in the middle of roads, a sudden growth

at the feet of police lines longer than any cricket pitch.
African slave, your namelessness is the wick and petrol mix.

Each generation catches the one fever love can't appease;
nor Molotov cocktails, nor when they embrace in a peace

far from that three-named, two-bit vandal and conservationist
binning beer cans, condoms and headstones in big puzzle-pieces.

2

Stop there black Englishman before you tell a bigger lie.
You mean me well by what you say but I can't stand idly by.

The vandal who keeps coming and does what he calls fucks
on the cool gravestones, also pillages and wrecks.

If he knew not so much my name but what happened to Africans,
he'd maybe put in an hour or two collecting his Heinekens;

like the good old conservationist, who's earned her column
inch, who you knock, who I love without knowing her name.

The dead can't write, nor can we sing (nor can most living).
Our ears (if you can call them ears) make no good listening.

Say what happened to me and countless like me, all anon.
Say it urgently. Mean times may bring back the water cannon.

I died young, but to age as a slave would have been worse.
What can you call me? Mohammed. Homer. Hannibal. Jesus.

Would it be too much to have them all? What are couples up to
when one reclines on the stones and is ridden by the other?

Will our talk excite the vandal? He woz ere, *like you are now,*
armed with a knife, I could see trouble on his creased brow,

love-trouble, not for some girl but for this village.
I share his love and would have let him spoil my image,

if it wasn't for his blade in the shadow of the church wall
taking me back to my capture and long sail to Bristol,

then my sale on Black Boy's Hill and disease ending my days:
I sent a rumble up to his sole; he scooted, shocked and dazed.

Here the sentence is the wait and the weight is the sentence.
I've had enough of a parish where the congregation can't sing.

Take me where the hymns sound like a fountain-washed canary,
and the beer-swilling, condom wielding vandal of Henbury,

reclines on the stones and the conservationist mounts him,
and in my crumbly ears there's only the sound of them sinning.

Stephen Knight

STEPHEN KNIGHT was born in 1960 in Swansea. He received a Gregory Award in 1987 and won the National Poetry Competition in 1992. His book *Flowering Limbs* is a Poetry Book Society Choice. His is a distinctive, youthful voice, always looking at things strangely, revealing surreal truths in external and internal worlds. Nothing is quite what it seems in his bristling poems as he switches his gaze from the egocentric habits of adolescence to a broader view of a contemporary no man's land. 'Here is a level, heart-breaking voice from the outskirts of Larkin country, grown shabbier, quirkier, more garish and desolate, but for all that, indestructible. Perhaps there is no other England' – Joseph Brodsky. ●

Selection from: *Flowering Limbs* (1993).

The Eyeball Works

Ad-men bandy slogans, like *PUPILS GUARANTEED...*
The would-be donors queue all afternoon
while tinted windows of The Eyeball Works run cloud
and passer-by at half their normal speed.
Into the evening, noises draw a crowd –
footsteps on a flight of marble stairs;
murmurs from an unlit foyer and the slow,
self-satisfied give of drapery and armchairs
laundered to the colour of the moon.
Noses flatten on the glass like dough.

Inside, the Eyeball Brochures packed in crates
whiff, unmistakably, of Money and Success;
they leave from the dock doors every night
with details of bargains and sell-by dates.
The workers, clothed in dust-revealing white,
wear gloves that cling and oblong paper hats,
each stamped with a Happy Eyebrows trademark.
For safety's sake, they stand on rubber mats –
before their lightly-greased machines – to press,
drill, gouge and slice until it's dark.

The marble benches are cobbled with eyes
arranged in rows then opened like books;
eyes jostle in dishes, eyes bob in jars
labelled according to status and size.
Eyes for Librarians and *Eyes of the Stars*
anticipate one of those numerous tinges
(from Palimpsest Azure to Paul Newman Blue)
stored in carboys, doled out through syringes.
Every jar is packed with long, blank looks
and the needles are true.

Tonight, Security is a humming sound
and the smell of disinfectant damp on floors.
Tonight, the door knobs are electrified
and the ugly dog let loose in the compound
pads down corridors like a bride...
Small cameras on the ceilings wink and weave
while, tapping the walls with his complimentary stick,
the last of the donors to leave
is 'leaving' through the NO ADMITTANCE doors.
He waves Goodbye. The doors go tick, tick, tick.

The Gift

My parcel was delivered to the college
thoroughly packaged, like an only child.
I tear my father's beautifully-written note
(Please acknowledge receipt, Love Mam & Dad)
then fold the wrapping for possible re-use.
A breeze laps the posters crusting the wall;
like lily pads, they compete to face the light.

I bump into Philip inside the Lodge.
He asks to see the gift – another four-sleeved
pullover! Raising it shoulder-high,
he teases me about the additional arms
till I make my excuses and leave him
at the pigeonholes to scurry to my room.

I lay the jumper on my coverlet
and step back to survey the lively design –
summery shades of green and blue in bars
a centimetre wide around the middle;
and seagulls, too. Trying it on
before my full-length mirror, I turn in circles
like a weather-vane. The sleeves rotate with me!

Dizzier than Lewis Carroll's Alice,
I finish instead an essay due at six...
My sides itch as I write. Just below the ribs,
above my pelvis, carpal bones, knuckles
and ten fingernails push through the flesh like roots.
Should I telephone home, or should I wait?

Dream Kitchen

Envelopes wait by the door like sunsets.
Uncollected in a fortnight,
they shout through their cellophane windows

Congratulations, Miss Collister
you've been specially chosen
Before the landlord sends them back

they swim among the leaflets
and the telephone directories, in the hall,
where the timer turns the light off prematurely.

Three Tenancy Agreements later, the room
where Miss Collister lived is white again
and The Occupant is pregnant.

Pushing fingers through her wavy hair
like dolphins, she watches crumpled paper
open in the corner of that room:

In fifteen words or less – Living in London
without a Kenwood Chef is bearable because
IN MY REVERIES, WE ALL RECEIVE THE LETTERS WE WANT

The Body-Parts Launderette
(for Sacha Brooks)

Four legs go in: the headboard's next: it's grey,
it's cold where a birdcage and a bed in sections
furnish the space outside The Last Chance antique shop.
At sundown, in the launderette, every day
long, neon striplights twitch into life –
light spills across the pavement like a knife.
Windows mist. Shapes move inside and the evenings drag.
The sounds of agitation never stop.
Stuffed with handbills or copies of the local rag,
the letterbox is down at ankle-height.
Footprints lead away in all directions.
The Body-Parts Launderette is open through the night.

In the window, cards and leaflets face the street
like ghosts: the Car Boot Sale that came and went; masseurs
without surnames; *RADIOS FOR SALE*; School Fêtes.
When the ancient machinery shivers and purrs,
puddles appear from cracks in the concrete floor
then seep towards strategically-placed, steel grates.
There's a pay-phone; a bin; a woman's calf
and the patron saint of The Body-Parts Launderette,
Dennis Nilsen, watching from a photograph
nailed to the Supervisor's padlocked, metal door.
One laundry basket's filled with odd feet
customers have left behind. It's dripping wet.

The Supervisor, for her sins, wears
fluffy mules and a quilted dressing-gown.
She burnishes the hacksaws, chains and knives
hung from the yellowing walls; or gathers up
the ticked and folded questionnaires
that quiz the customers about their empty lives.
Have you used 1) *An acid bought in town*
2) *Soap, or* 3) *Detergent in a paper cup?*
Somewhere between a coma and a dream,
alone, on plastic seats, they pass whole days
in front of tedious machines; watching the steam,
the suds, those churning reds and greys.

Eva Salzman

CLAUDIA RICHARDSON

Selection from: *The English Earthquake* (1992).

EVA SALZMAN was born in 1960 in New York where, from the age of 10 until 22, she was a dancer and choreographer. She moved to Britain in 1985, and lives in Brighton. Her first book *The English Earthquake* was a Poetry Book Society Recommendation.

'Eva Salzman is no slouch. She has a satirist's eye and ear alert to the emotional and verbal cliché, the easy lie, and she can be gracefully ruthless. She can shift register from the formal and elegiac to an astringent New York sarcasm. She can shuffle the vocabularies of love and landscape, turn the grotesque poignant, the funny terrifying – a facility rare on either side of the Atlantic' – Michael Donaghy. ●

The English Earthquake

Somewhere, a cup tinkles in its saucer.
A meek 'oh my' passes down the miles
of manicured gardens, as armies rumble

the monuments of cities continents away.
The budgie chirps 'goodness' to thin air
while Bach quivers slightly and the fat roast

sways in the oven, brain-dead, but chuckling
in its oil. Such a surprise: the settling ground,
innocent with rape and mustard, groaning

under its weight of roses. The premier
sees stars, plumps her pillows for photographs.
Alas, *Watchtower* faces are falling as life goes on

and the Ex-Major winds back years to the war –
its incendiary thrill – his wife flushed
with disbelief as the earth moves unexpectedly,

the giant baby at the core of the planet
rocking its apocalyptic cradle
gently, wailing: 'Hungry, hungry, hungry.'

Sin

A flash pool-game, some freak hormonal wiring,
the cab-ride where he gets my drunken yes
and I'm rooked in that dump of a hotel on Forty-Eighth,
that naked room – no secrets but the big one –
with blunt razors studded round a scummy bath,
a dusty portable, no printed matter anywhere,
just a few chairs knifed with the dead initials
of those who went too far, or never far enough.

Forcing Flowers

We are naming hybrids. The next one's
Bastard. It's still possible to make
these new strains up. All the fun's
gone however. You too would like to break me
into what I'm not. We're learning zero
but that things are getting worse, from this
astounding failure to another. Love's missed
because we knew it once. We lie to retrieve it,
hopelessly, with letters and with photos,
pain outweighing pleasure, and still believe,
sure it's not the memory that pinks
it into flower. Leaning over, the erstwhile hero
delicately sniffs: memory *is* a rose.
Now, we keep hothouses. In them everything stinks.

Belial

My neighbours have given birth to a monster
I regret to say. His moon-like pate
glows in the dark like a diabolical nite-lite.
He cuts his milk-teeth on steel, and shrieks
the kind of shrieks which can stop your heart, literally.
He shits mountains wherever he can, moves them too.

Isn't he adorable, croon the harpies from down the block,
cootchie-coo; he sucks their wrinkled fingers dry.

His parents sleep with him in his Alien-papered room
because they are under his thumb
which is as big as the Goodyear blimp.
But when mummy and daddy *have* to go out,
sorrowfully and lovingly, they fasten his furry handcuffs
and wrap him in his terry-cloth straitjacket
which is blue for boys. He bites his mother good-bye.

Then he chews his play-plax, builds Trump towers
and Hefner swimming pools, or DNA with a frightful twist.

Getting home too late that night,
his parents hear him bawl the theme of *Neighbours*
from a block away. They hurry up.
The sitter should have been home hours ago.

W.N. Herbert

Selection from: *Forked Tongue* (1994).

W.N. HERBERT was born in 1961 in Dundee, and divides his time between Oxford and Scotland. He established his reputation as a versatile poet writing both in English and Scots with several small press booklets. His first full-length book, *Forked Tongue*, is a Poetry Book Society Recommendation.

Sean O'Brien has called him 'outstanding …a poet whom nothing – including what he terms "the Anchises of the Scots Style Sheet" – will intimidate'. For Douglas Dunn, his was 'the best writing in Scots – thoughtful, studied, clever – I've seen in years'. Jamie McKendrick admired his 'vibrant' poetry, his 'ear for the sensuous music of Scots' and his 'ability to effect sudden shifts of scale that bring the human and the cosmic face to face. ●

From A Three Year Ode

III *To Rutskoi* (1993)

> *Our concern is human wholeness – the child-like spirit*
> *Newborn every day –*
>> HUGH MacDIARMID
>> Third Hymn to Lenin

As Eh exhaled, trehin tae relax,
Eh heard thi saulter i thi field ootside
whinny, and Eh thocht o thon

puir cuddie in Kutznetsky Street
that Mayakovsky waatcht faa doon,
be whuppit as ut pechd uts life awa.

That wiz whit yi ettlet tae dae
tae thon sair forfochen nag
caad 'Communism' thi ither dey.

Did you no ken tho histry micht
repeat, lyk a wean that huztae eat
naethin but the rehet kail o

slaistery theory, ut nivir can
repeal utsel? Eh luke oot meh windie at
thae horsis that, like me, nivir hud

tae pu as muckle's Orwell's Boxer,
an think we hae medd fictions here
o yir followers' rarest hopes;

fur whit wiz Timex but a tale telt
tae richtless warkirs by thir
virrless union, tae keep thum aa

fae kennan o thir knackirt faa
intae fause timelessness, thi pasture
o a militatin posture.

Aa you did wiz add some killin,
tae mak ut mair Leniny, tae gee ye mair
1917-esque a feelin.

An sae thi tincan cavalry came at last
but no tae sain ye by thi pooer
o thi haimmer an Rab Sorbie,

but, fur twa an a plack o promises
fae Yeltsin, tae mak thi nicht
a dingle-dousie o tracer fire,

a swack an dinnil o rinny daith
in oaffices and oan stairwells. Still
Eh'm vainein at thon gripy bairn,

ridan oan thi back o a bear,
bringan thi Apocalypse o statelessness,
thi furst lowsan-time

o thi reins an bridle o thi harns.

trehin: trying; *saulter:* a horse that jumps in events; *cuddie:* a horse; *pechd:* panted; *ettlet:* attempted; *sair forfochen:* very bewildered, exhausted; *rehet:* reheated; *slaistery:* slimy, unpalatable; *as muckle's:* as much as; *virrless:* impotent; *fause:* false; *sain:* protect from harm by a ritual sign; *Rab Sorbie:* sickle; *twa and a plack:* a considerable amount; *dingle-dousie:* a lighted stick waved rapidly in the dark to form an arc of light; *swack:* a sudden heavy blow; *dinnil:* vibration; *vanein:* calling a horse in harness to turn to the left; *lowsan-time:* the time for unyoking horses and stopping farm-work; *harns:* brains.

Mappamundi

Eh've wurkt oot a poetic map o thi warld.

Vass tracts o land ur penntit reid tae shaw
Englan kens naethin aboot um. Ireland's
bin shuftit tae London, whaur
oafficis o thi Poetry Sock occupeh fehv
squerr mile. Seamus Heaney occupehs three
o thon. Th'anerly ithir bits in Britain
ur Oaxfurd an Hull. Thi Pool, Scoatlan,
an Bisley, Stroud, ur cut ti cuttilbanes in
America, which issa grecht big burdcage wi
a tartan rug owre ut, tae shaw
Roabirt Lowell. Chile disnae exist.
Argentina's bin beat. Hungary and Russia
haena visas. Africa's editid doon ti
a column in *Poetry Verruca*,
whaur Okigbo's gote thi ghaist
o Roy Campbill hingin owre um. Thi Faur East's
faan aff – aa but China: thon's renemmed
Ezra Poond an pit in thi croncit cage.
France disnae get a luke-in:
accoardin tae Geoffrey Hill, plucky wee
Charles Péguy is wrasslin wi
this big deid parrot caad 'Surrealism' fur
thi throne o Absinthe Sorbet.

In this scenario Eh'm a bittern stoarm aff Ulm.

Jackie Kay

INGRID POLLARD

Selection from: *The Adoption Papers* (1991) and *Other Lovers* (1993).

JACKIE KAY was born in 1961 in Scotland. She is a poet, playwright and children's writer. Her poems are, by turns, poignant, bittersweet, joyous and funny.

Alastair Niven described her first book *The Adoption Papers* (1991) as 'a key work of feminism in action...a wonderfully spirited, tender and crafted contribution to Scottish writing, to black writing, and to the poetry of our time...a work of the utmost generosity and truth.' In *Other Lovers* (1993), she achieves an even greater range, exploring the qualities of love in a variety of relationships, rooted in the past or present. In doing so, she looks afresh at the way we now live.

'Warm, tough, painful and often very funny poems' – Fleur Adcock. ●

From The Adoption Papers
Chapter 3: *The Waiting Lists*

The first agency we went to
didn't want us on their lists,
we didn't live close enough to a church
nor were we church-goers
(though we kept quiet about being communists).
The second told us
we weren't high enough earners.
The third liked us
but they had a five-year waiting list.
I spent six months trying not to look
at swings nor the front of supermarket trolleys,
not to think this kid I've wanted could be five.
The fourth agency was full up.
The fifth said yes but again no babies.
Just as we were going out the door
I said oh you know we don't mind the colour.
Just like that, the waiting was over.

This morning a slim manilla envelope arrives
postmarked Edinburgh: one piece of paper
I have now been able to look up your microfiche
(as this is all the records kept nowadays).
From your mother's letters, the following information:
Your mother was nineteen when she had you.
You weighed eight pounds four ounces.
She liked hockey. She worked in Aberdeen
as a waitress. She was five foot eight inches.

I thought I'd hid everything
that there wasnie wan
giveaway sign left

I put Marx Engels Lenin (no Trotsky)
in the airing cupboard – she'll no be
checking out the towels surely

All the copies of the *Daily Worker*
I shoved under the sofa
the dove of peace I took down from the loo

A poster of Paul Robeson
saying give him his passport
I took down from the kitchen

I left a bust of Burns
my detective stories
and the Complete Works of Shelley

She comes at 11.30 exactly.
I pour her coffee
from my new Hungarian set

And foolishly pray she willnae
ask its origins – honestly
this baby is going to my head.

She crosses her legs on the sofa
I fancy I hear the *Daily Workers*
rustle underneath her

Well she says, you have an interesting home
She sees my eyebrows rise.
It's different she qualifies.

Hell and I've spent all morning
trying to look ordinary
– a lovely home for the baby.

She buttons her coat all smiles
I'm thinking
I'm on the home run

But just as we get to the last post
her eye catches at the same times as mine
a red ribbon with twenty world peace badges

Clear as a hammer and sickle
on the wall.
Oh, she says are you against nuclear weapons?

To Hell with this. Baby or no baby.
Yes I says. Yes yes yes.
I'd like this baby to live in a nuclear free world.

Oh. Her eyes light up.
I'm all for peace myself she says,
and sits down for another cup of coffee.

In Jackie Kay's *The Adoption Papers* sequence, the voices of
the three speakers are distinguished typographically:

DAUGHTER:	Palatino typeface
ADOPTIVE MOTHER:	Gill typeface
BIRTH MOTHER:	Bodoni typeface (not included in this extract)

Fridge

In the cold room there is tomorrow:
the red floor to clean,
and a brand new broom.

Your father's body is lying flat out –
the white ledge inside the clean fridge.
Rigid. Serene.

Imagining always starts with death, then
dances the world. A second in a window,
that man, that's him!

It's been done before:
names, letters, photographs.
An ice cube inside your neck.

The fear of turning back.
In the fridge he is the colour of negatives;
he is not in the ballroom, dancing.

You clean the mortuary.
In and out the pail of disinfectant.
The strange smell behind your eyes.

Footsteps vanish. Red tiles shine.
Only the cold breath of the dead in this room.
What was it he might have said?

Nigeria was hot red dust; did he go back?
Then this black man is a stranger.
You are not his.

Somebody else's then. You should not look.
Pull open the fridge panel, frightened.
Kiss the cold lips.

Katie Donovan

MARTIN ROPER

Selection from: *Watermelon Man* (1993).

KATIE DONOVAN was born in 1962, grew up in Co. Wexford, and lives in Dublin. She has published four books, including *Dublines* (1993), co-edited with Brendan Kennelly, and her first collection *Watermelon Man* (1993).

'In the best of these poems, adventures of place meet and mingle with adventures of the body. This is by no means a reliable or frequent encounter in contemporary poetry. Katie Donovan's poems move easily – and with a distinguished and open language – from fuchsia on Achill, or the Börzony Hills in Hungary, to explorations of sexuality and bold statements of identity. The tension in these poems is also their intent: they are discovering and making a private world which also manages, with real grace, to be inclusive and engaging' – Eavan Boland. ●

Underneath Our Skirts

Although a temple
to honour one man's voluntary death,
his ceaseless weep of blood,
the women cannot enter
if they bleed –
an old law.

As the bridal couple glides
down the aisle,
her white veil twitching,
I feel my pains.
A woman
bleeding in church,
I pray for time,
for slow motion.
Unprotected, I bleed,
I have no bandage,
my ache finds no relief.

My thorns
are high heels
and itchy stockings.
He, the imitator, bleeds on
in numb eternal effigy,
his lugubrious journey of martyrdom
rewarded with worship.

Tonight custom demands more blood:
sheets must be stained
with the crimson flowers
of a bride's ruptured garden.
Her martyrdom
will be silent knowledge
suffered in solitude.

As we leave the house
of the male bleeder,
I feel myself wet and seeping,
a shameful besmircher of this ceremony
of white linen
and creamy-petalled roses;
yet underneath our skirts
we are all bleeding,
silent and in pain,
we, the original
shedders of ourselves,
leak the guilt of knowledge
of the surfeit
of our embarrassing fertility
and power.

The Glove

Rain on the black window
like fingernails tapping the silence –
I'm here alone with my charm.
It lies beside me,
a temporarily abandoned glove,
ready to put on.

'Women are too charming,'
you said tonight. 'They aren't honest.'
Wearing my glove I say:
How would you like it without the charm?
You'd hate it.

My glove drops it all far away,
out into the long currents of rain.
gleaming down the street.

These Last Days

I cartwheel like a knife
into the sagging canvas of now –
it's a strange underwater dance,
all weed and drift –
my arrow nose shafts through
hunting you.

Like a whirlwind
coning down,
I'm peeling the brittle skin
of these last days
without you;

only in your arms
will I slowly open
the moist, seeded centre.

Maggie Hannan

MOIRA CONWAY

Selection from forthcoming
first collection (1995).

MAGGIE HANNAN was born in 1962 in Wiltshire,
and lived in Derbyshire and Cumbria before
moving to Hull. She won a Gregory Award in
1990, and is now working on her first book.

Her poems have appeared in several anth-
ologies, including *No Holds Barred*, *The
Gregory Anthology*, and Bloodaxe's *The
New Lake Poets* (1991) and *The New Poetry*
(1993). She was for many critics a surprise
inclusion in *The New Poetry*: for Roger
Garfitt, she was 'a welcome discovery'; for
Gerald Dawe, she was 'a real find', and her
poems were 'the business'. Alan Brownjohn
called her work 'ingenious...highly original,
beautifully funny'; Peter Porter liked her
'welcome sense of fantasy'. ●

The Bone Die

Even the wrist's fast jack
is funked by a thumb's rub,

chances and freaked odds
of plane, pit, dot and dot

are pocketed or scuttled:
a weathered die contrives

its craft of luck from years –
edges all unwhet, or honed

in captivities of palm. Thrown
down for a free run (an ack-ack

clatter after gulling) it's pulling
up dead on a rising surface,

and jinxes still by a worn slant:
two up, two up, where fractures web

the sockets of its eyes – askance –
laugh lines – a probability of chaos.

Drive

1 *Simply Said*

His simple is
in how a spider does

in air, work, but
leaving no stickier

trace – that is,
not even to catch

the metaphorical
fly – will *will*

the uprush of
his hourly idea,

(the one he's certain
of and dreaming),

until his tongue
clucks *You...*,

the work of it
delight and luck,

for this is Billy
talking with his heart,

saying
You. Blue car. Drive.

2 *Said So*

It was under him then, the tar lick
with its slip of miles. Too, the looped
hour, the only map he knew. To this

becoming light was where, as morning
greased it all, he went, followed
the coast road to a pebbled stop

and water, the butt of cool air
shining in his lungs. What colour is
it? *Peacock.* The day it is? *Tomorrow.*

3 Says Who?

Let's say I'm in the quiet bar as usual,
thinking the usual nothing, and the beer,

if you like, is amber. The light is, too.
Well. What happens is, I want to do

what he does: want to play the monkey
with the eye I've caught, mirror that

sad/ stupid/ happy face – show I've learnt
the language for it: body language for cabbage.

4 Sooth

If ever
this unrolling,
reeling, handsprung
wave

or man
did go, *did*
or could leave
mark – you

might say
it was in that
hard black
pebble,

the eye
of anemone, or
fingerprints
of starfish;

in the way
you thought
a man had somehow
touched

and claimed
the dark rock
at the bottom of
the pool.

John Hughes

GALLERY PRESS

Selection from: *Negotiations with the Chill Wind* (1991).

JOHN HUGHES was born in 1962 in Belfast. He established himself as one of Ireland's most exciting young writers with his first collection, *The Something in Particular* (1986). His second book, *Negotiations with the Chill Wind* (1991), is published by Gallery in Ireland and by Bloodaxe in Britain.

'The poems gather into themselves a terrifying mood. They have accordingly a kind of belligerence about them...Their enigmas, sexual tones and imaginative forcefulness call to mind the *surrealistes* as much as the *films noirs* that shadow much of this exciting book...Hughes's poetry is one of the most definite artistic achievements to have come out of the North in recent years' – Gerald Dawe. 'Hughes examines how fiction becomes history. Most of these poems, in fact, are lies, especially in the sense that lies are used in some parts of rural Ireland: entertaining fictions, stories, yarns which bear a side-long, sly reference to the real world; lies told as if they are the truth' – Ciaran Carson. ●

The Story-Teller

In a weather-stripped house behind tall gates
we danced in circles and triangles
to scratched 78s of Bessie Smith,
before going for a swim in the canal –
closed a century before by a Lord Lieutenant
with a morbid fear of barges.

On our second dive we discovered
an Anglepoise, an Armalite,
and an execrable sonnet of uncertain age –
whose discovery together, according to her,
was an omen I wouldn't return to the house.
And because I am the story-teller
it was she, not I, who dived a third time
and never came up again.

Pyewackett

He claimed he could transmute all metals into gold;
that he could make himself invisible,
cure all diseases, and administer an elixir
against old age and the common cold.

He was accused of being an onomancer,
a sternomancer, a gastromancer,
an omphalomancer, an onchyomancer,
and an agent of the police.

You slept with him for three nights.
On the first night he bruised your breasts.
On the second night he scratched your belly.
On the third night he called out my name.

Nagasaki

I arrive in the city
to sell the skull
of Saint Thomas Aquinas
to a retired policeman.

A passer-by tells me to panic.

I prise open the nearest door,
climb to the third floor,
and walk in on a geisha
listening to herself on the radio
describe how she navigated by the stars
out of her dead mother's womb.

She asks why she sweats blood
when I touch her where I shouldn't.

I wake up clinging onto
the second horseman of the Apocalypse
in his disguise as the tail-fin
of a high-altitude American bomber.

Where the Light Begins

Some nights I can still remember
How I tracked down by scent alone
The last she-wolf in Ireland
To the last forest. For nine years

We talked about the future behind us.
And when her fangs at last began to show
I fired into her heart a silver bullet,
And headed west to where the light begins.

Alchemy: A Tale

Un mystère d'amour dans le métal repose – GÉRARD DE NERVAL

A certain man flew from Chicago to his native Golden Vale
To resurrect a recurring dream from his childhood.
The dream: A Frenchman called Lavoisier
Being cooked in a bath till he revealed
The whereabouts of the long-lost philosopher's stone –
The stone which is not a stone.

But his dream brought him to the attention
Of the Angel of Desolation Island
Who took him to Max Brod's city of evil
To stand trial for an unspecified mortal sin
Before Cardinals, Silver, Iron, Tin, and Lead.
They called his sentence of death *Transmutation*,
Washed their hands of him in sulfur water,
Processed into Wenceslaus Square,
And corroded into the nothingness of Mercurial Lore
Screaming, 'One nature rejoices in another nature,
One nature masters another nature.'

A certain man was burnt to death on Desolation Island
By an unflickering, non-luminous tongue of fire.

Kathleen Jamie

Selection from: *A Flame in Your Heart* (1986), *The Way We Live* (1987), *The Autonomous Region* (1993), and *The Queen of Sheba* (1994).

KATHLEEN JAMIE was born in 1962 in Renfrewshire. She won a Gregory Award at 19, which enabled her to travel in the Near East and later to the Himalayas. Her Bloodaxe titles are: a collaboration with poet Andrew Greig, *A Flame in Your Heart* (1986); her first full-length collection, *The Way We Live* (1987); a book of poems from Tibet with photographs by Sean Mayne Smith, *The Autonomous Region* (1993); and her latest collection, *The Queen of Sheba* (1994).

'She can make unrhetorical language glow with mystery' – Peter Porter. 'An almost faultless sense of rhythm' – *Morning Star*. 'Jamie's gusto for life is colossal, but it is the more infectious for being so unconditionally expressed' – *Times Literary Supplement*. ●

November

He can touch me with a look
as thoughtless as afternoon
and think as much of hindering me
as he would of sailing away.

In November, when the storms come
he drums his fingers on his books and turns
them into a fist that crashes. On the shore
where he insists we walk, he holds me like a man
at a deck-rail in a gale. I suspect his eyes
are open, red and gazing over my head
in the direction of abroad.

I am left to tell him in a voice that
seems as casual as his talk of travel:
I think as much of leaving as
of forcing him to stay.

War Widow

You know I keep the photograph
beside my bed. It gathers glances
like I could
when I swayed my way amongst airmen.

The trees behind you are still
fresh, your face never changes.

My stocking seams aren't quite so straight.
My uniform's returned. You wear yours
somewhere,
caught in a snapshot while you slept.

Duet

I am the music of the string duet
in the Métro, and my circumstances,
nowadays, are music too: travelling
the underground like women's scent, or happiness.
Again and again I discover that I love you
as we navigate round Châtelet
and hear once more the music. It's found its way
through passages to where I least expect,
and when you kiss me, floods me.
The trains come in, whine out again,
the platforms fill and empty:
a movement regular as your heart's
beat, mine as lively as the melody.

The way we live

Pass the tambourine, let me bash out praises
to the Lord God of movement, to Absolute
non-friction, flight, and the scarey side:
death by avalanche, birth by failed contraception.
Of chicken tandoori and reggae, loud, from tenements,
commitment, driving fast and unswerving
friendship. Of tee-shirts on pulleys, giros and Bombay,
barmen, dreaming waitresses with many fake-gold
bangles. Of airports, impulse, and waking to uncertainty,
to strip-lights, motorways, or that pantheon –
the mountains. To overdrafts and grafting

and the fit slow pulse of wipers as you're
creeping over Rannoch, while the God of moorland
walks abroad with his entourage of freezing fog,
his bodyguard of snow.
Of endless gloaming in the North, of Asiatic swelter,
to launderettes, anecdotes, passions and exhaustion,
Final Demands and dead men, the skeletal grip
of government. To misery and elation; mixed,
the sod and caprice of landlords.
To the way it fits, the way it is, the way it seems
to be: let me bash out praises – pass the tambourine.

The Panchen Lama rides from Lhasa to Kumbum
(A thousand miles in a single night)

Now the sky is saddled with stars,
a saddle of stars thrown over the hills' back;
night is a horse leaping the mountains,
night is a nomad shifted by morning,
the Panchen Lama rides hard out of Lhasa
low and clung to the horse's mane,
clings to the mane strung like a comet,
and clear of the darkened back-streets chants

to the ready ear, pale as a conch shell
the thousandth tantra's thousandth cycle,
and horse and Lama quit their earthly forms.

That night a wind crossed snow and pasture:
ruffled the feathers of sleeping rivers,
whirled like a cloak round the shoulders of mountains.
The plateau of Tibet
stretched away like an oil-dark painting
to the grass-land, where in tethered yurts
families wrapped in yaks-wool, slept;
and warm-flanked yaks shifted in their dreaming,
and certain dogs
who opened their jaws to the flying hoof-beat
with an invisible gesture of the Lama's hand
were silenced and charmed.

So for a thousand miles:
till the sun coaxed the world to open like a daisy;
splashed gold on the roofs on the gold-rooved monastery,
of the far side of the precious and protecting hill
at will assumed their mortal shape,
and the youngest boy-monk who rushed from the temple,
his face as round as a gong of wonder
to touch the robe, grab the reins, receive a blessing
and though that boy lived to be a hundred
he always swore
the Panchen Lama
winked.

(This is no story, desperate and apocryphal,
the horse is rumoured to be divine.)

Den of the old men

C'mon ye auld buggers, one by one
this first spring day, slowly down
the back braes with your walking sticks
and wee brown dugs, saying: *Aye, lass
a snell wind yet but braw.* Ye
half dozen relics of strong men
sat in kitchen chairs
behind the green gingham curtain
of yer den, where a wee dog grins
on last year's calendar – we hear ye
clacking dominoes the afternoon for pennies.
And if some wee tyke
puts a chuckie through the window
ye stuff yesterday's Courier
in the broken pane, saying
jail's too guid fur them, tellies in cells!
                We can see your bunnets nod
and jaws move: what're ye up to
now you've your hut built,
now green hame-hammered benches
appear in the parish's secret soft-spots
like old men's spoor?
Is it carties? A tree-hoose?
Or will ye drag up driftwood;
and when she's busy with the bairns
remove your daughters' washing-lines
to lash a raft? Which,
if ye don't all fall out and argue
you can name the *Pride o' Tay* and launch
some bright blue morning on the ebb-tide
and sail away, the lot of yez,
staring straight ahead
                like captains
as you grow tiny
out on the wide Firth, tiny
as you drift past Ballinbriech, Balmurnie, Flisk
with your raincoats and bunnets,
                wee dugs and sticks.

Child with pillar-box and bin bags

But it was the shadowed street-side she chose
while Victor Gold the bookies basked
in conquered sunlight, and though
Dalry Road Licensed Grocer gloried and cast
fascinating shadows she chose
the side dark in the shade of tenements;
that corner where Universal Stores' (closed
for modernisation) blank hoarding blocked
her view as if that process were illegal;
she chose to photograph her baby here,
the corner with the pillar box.
In his buggy, which she swung to face her.
She took four steps back, but
the baby in his buggy rolled toward the kerb.
She crossed the ground in no time
it was fearful as Niagara,
she ran to put the brake on, and returned
to lift the camera, a cheap one.
The tenements of Caledonian Place neither
watched nor looked away, they are friendly buildings.
The traffic ground, the buildings shook, the baby breathed
and maybe gurgled at his mother as she
smiled to make him smile in his picture;
which she took on the kerb in the shadowed corner,
beside the post-box, under tenements, before
the bin-bags hot in the sun that shone
on them, on dogs, on people, on the other side,
the other side of the street to that she'd chosen,
if she'd chosen or thought it possible to choose.

Peter McDonald

PETER McDONALD was born in 1962 in Belfast,
and lectures at the University of Bristol.
He won the Newdigate Prize in 1983 and
an Eric Gregory Award in 1987.

'The very composure of the poems – their
surface calm, their unostentatious style –
sharpens the ominous and menacing atmo-
sphere which pervades so many of them...
the angle of vision is often beguilingly oblique,
although riveting eye-to-eye contact is estab-
lished in *Silent Night*' – Dennis O'Driscoll.
Silent Night is based on the true story of the
imprisonment of Harold Le Druillenec, of
Jersey, in Wilhelmshaven (and afterwards,
Belsen) in 1944-45. ●

Selection from: *Biting the
Wax* (1989).

Silent Night
(St Aubin's Bay, Jersey, 1946)

It's summer now, or nearly. Out at the back door, my sister
shows the children how to feed the birds, scattering pieces
of crust into the garden: some sparrows, a couple of starlings
come down and squabble, fly off at the children's applause.
In the bathroom, I'm weighing myself – another stone – smiling,
hearing my name called, catching the smells from the kitchen.

Those weeks when they came to take my story for the wireless
I had to be coaxed at first; they seemed to be after
more than names, or names and facts; they wanted to know
how it felt then, and sounded, what it tasted and smelt like,
though really it was like nothing, nothing before or since,
which I told them, and they understood, they said. But even so.

But even so, as they added, there was a story to be told,
and I was the man to tell it. First, there were questions
and answers, *What did you see then? And what were you thinking?*
But after a while, the story would come out of its own accord
and there were the details they wanted, the smells and the sounds,
memories that had never made sense, for once locking into each other.

The first place they took you. At Wilhelmshaven that winter,
when every afternoon repeated the frost of that morning
and at night there was only hail to cut into the tracks
of their lights, they bundled me with a couple of dozen
newcomers into one of the big huts, my feet touching
the ground for the first time since the court-martial in Jersey.

How many in this hut? There were nearly a thousand,
crammed three to a bed, head to toe in the bunks and making
barely a sound. Near enough a thousand men. Packed
that tightly, you soon learn how to sleep without moving,
and you learn not to speak, you learn to lie still and say nothing
when there are guards on hand to force up the value of silence.

It was part of Neue Gamme, and I'd been brought over
from France with the others – Jean De Frotté, Bernard
Depuy, just to give two names as examples: the first one
tall, wispy-haired and delicate, the son of a Marquis,
then Bernard with his square head screwed down on to his shoulders,
though they have their own stories, parts of mine and still different.

We had three things to think about: food, sleep and work,
but no real need to think, for they were all taken care of,
especially the last. Once a day, there was thin turnip soup
and a crust of bread, a few hours of motionless sleep,
then the hard tramp through frost out to the Kriegsmarine
Arsenal, a day's work hearing the punch and clang of the riveters,

avoiding the welders' blue clouds of sparks; sweat and iron;
then our convicts' shuffle back to the camp in the dark,
their searchlights tailing us and filling in the distance
back to the gates, our hut with its three hundred bunks.
I mentioned guards: there were guards of course, but worse
were the Chiefs, one to each hut. Ours was called Omar.

You might ask me to describe, explain him, but I can do neither,
I can tell you his build, his features, even mimic his voice,
but that would add up to nothing, or nothing more really
than just a man in a story, maybe a bit of a monster,
a dead man anyhow. Yes, by now he'll be safely dead.
It might be easier, really, for you yourself to explain him.

Omar, it turns out, had once, like most of the others,
been a prisoner himself, a young man when they caught him
in 1933, some kind of radical journalist.
He'd been through worse than this in his time, worse beatings,
work, cold and the rest, and he was in for a lifetime.
Drop by drop, I suppose, the fight just bled out of him.

So by the time the camps were getting busy they made him an offer,
to serve his time as an *Alteste* in places like Neue Gamme
with at least enough freedom there to do as he pleased
and get on with the job. Yes, the words apply, brutal, sadistic,
just like the others, inhuman. And yes, there are stories.
I try to remember my friend Bernard's straight talking,

'There's no point in judging a place like this by the standards
of what we've all left behind: it has a code of its own,
a lunatic code, I know, but you just have to learn it.
Lie still and say nothing.' So what is there for me to say now
about Omar? Just the truth, just what I remember?
But I couldn't call it the truth then, and now that I tell you

the stories, does that make them all true? does it make them
happen, happen properly for the first time? It's harder,
watching the sea relax under the first mild summer evening
and waiting for dinner, too, harder to force those things
to happen again, and here, than just to keep silent. And lie?
Here by the bay, there's really no such thing as silence,

what with the waves breaking all night, and the seabirds
carrying on as usual each day. On the wireless, they tell me,
you can do wonders, but the one thing you can't get away with
is silence, the fretful noise of empty spaces, the worrying
gaps bare of music or talk, with just the sound of the atmosphere
coming into your very own room. I can give you two stories

concerning Omar, though whether or not they go well together
I myself couldn't say. The first happened only a few weeks
after we arrived at the camp: an Alsatian boy of sixteen
had been caught making off with some scraps of food from the plates
of patients dying in the infirmary (though that was hardly a hospital
as you'd understand the word – a dirty, crowded tin hut).

He came up before Omar, of course, who glared and let his face buckle
in on itself with disgust, then brought out the worst of his voices,
the fabulously wicked giant, to himself above all.
'You, boy,' he thundered down, 'you have committed
the one unforgivable crime; you have gone out and stolen
not only from your comrades, but from your sick comrades.

I'll tell you exactly how you can expect to be punished:
you're going to be made to learn the real meaning of hunger,
but you'll dread the food in your mouth; and when you leave us
you'll be raving mad, boy, gibbering away somewhere to die.'
He was perfect. Large as life and more monstrous than any
caricature. We kept quiet; the boy cringed, was carried away.

The usual stamping, shouting and beating. Then the wet blankets
to sleep in as well, for nights on end. They starved him,
then force-fed him salted food, served up on a scalding
hot spoon, day after day, all the while refusing him water.
By the time they finally lost interest, he looked like a skeleton;
unable to eat for the burns on his mouth, his scarred lips and tongue,

he would scream at the sight of a spoon. He died soon, of course,
raving mad, as Omar had promised. Now I can barely imagine
such things happening at all, but they did, and do still
in theory, in places far removed from this island,
the standard horrors, common knowledge now more than ever,
more than just hearsay these days: newsreels, words on the air.

And then of course there's the second *vignette*: the very same Omar –
who was, needless to say, cultured, had once been a classical
musician, to add to his attributes, always a lover of Mozart –
in the Christmas of '44, Omar's treat for the prisoners.
Imagine one of the huts that's been specially cleared for the purpose,
with benches there now and a stage, the audience all silent

(though you'd hardly mistake that silence for hushed expectation,
it being clearly enough the schooled silence of fear)
and then you make out a Christmas tree just to the right of the stage,
a piano likewise, the feeling of something about to begin.
Then suddenly Omar and the six other *Altesten*
troop on like schoolboys, heavy, bloated, all with straight faces.

For this is the carol service, and these fat men are the carollers.
Listen and you'll pick up easily Omar's gentle booming
among all the voices here. In fact I myself was arrested
for 'communal listening'; the whole thing happens again for the
              wireless,
but no actor alive could reproduce the sound of this memory,
that music in the hungry air, *Stille nacht, Heilige nacht.*

On clear evenings, I watch those rocks on the near side of the bay,
a circle of broken teeth, finally blotted out by the tide.
I listen to seabirds roosting for miles along the whole coastline,
and then there's just the sea noise and the evening programmes
with the bad and the good news, the music of Victor Sylvester,
the Epilogue, the King, the whisper and fizz of the atmosphere.

Some nights I almost see the dead and the living stand in a circle,
naked but for their memories, and in full view of each other,
immobile as those rocks crumbling gradually into the bay,
as though they were trying to speak, or cry, or scream in the silence,
to hear each other and understand; but the dead weight of stone
holds us all down, makes us stand still and say nothing.

But not when they call me to dinner, and I laugh with the children
over this or that story, though sometimes I'll catch myself thinking,
not of the past exactly, but more of that programme,
my voice and the voices of actors, and somewhere among them
Jean and Bernard alive; Omar's Christmas carol; the last
winter of a bad war; a boy with a horror of spoons.

Glyn Maxwell

MOHRA CONWAY

Selection from: *Tale of the Mayor's Son* (1990), *Out of the Rain* (1992) and *Crushed Velvet* (1994).

GLYN MAXWELL was born in 1962 in Welwyn Garden City, where he works as a freelance writer, poet and verse dramatist. His precocious talent has earned him every accolade from 'England's brightest new poet for a decade' and 'The Complete Modern English Poet' to 'The Shakespeare of the Suburbs'. His first collection, *The Tale of the Mayor's Son* (1990), was a Poetry Book Society Choice; his second, *Out of the Rain* (1992), a Poetry Book Society Recommendation.

'Glyn Maxwell's originality lies in his astonishing ability to orchestrate asides, parenthetical quips, side-of-the-mouth ruminations into a formal verse with a bravura not dared before' – Derek Walcott. 'He covers a greater distance in a single line than most people do in a poem' – Joseph Brodsky. ●

Drive to the Seashore

We passed, free citizens, between the gloves
of dark and costly cities, and our eyes
bewildered us with factories. We talked.

Of what? Of the bright dead in the old days,
often of them. Of the great coal-towns, coked
to death with scruffy accents. Of the leaves

whirled to shit again. Of the strikers sacked
and picking out a turkey with their wives.
Of boys crawling downstairs: we talked of those

but did this: drove to where the violet waves
push from the dark, light up, lash out to seize
their opposites, and curse to no effect.

We Billion Cheered

We billion cheered.
        Some threat sank in the news and disappeared.
It did because
        Currencies danced and we forgot what it was.

It rose again.
        It rose and slid towards our shore and when
It got to it,
        It laced it like a telegram. We lit

Regular fires,
        But missed it oozing along irregular wires
Towards the Smoke.
        We missed it elbowing into the harmless joke

Or dreams of our
        Loves asleep in the cots where the dolls are.
We missed it how
        You miss an o'clock passing and miss now.

We missed it where
        You miss my writing of this and I miss you there.
We missed it through
        Our eyes, lenses, screen and angle of view.

We missed it though
        It specified where it was going to go,
And when it does,
        The missing ones are ten to one to be us.

We line the shore,
        Speak of the waving dead of a waving war.
And clap a man
        For an unveiled familiar new plan.

Don't forget.
        Nothing will start that hasn't started yet.
Don't forget
        It, its friend, its foe and its opposite.

Sport Story of a Winner
(for Alun and Amanda Maxwell)

He was a great ambassador for the game.
                    He had a simple name.
His name was known in households other than ours.
                    But we knew other stars.
We could recall as many finalists
                    as many panellists.
But when they said this was his Waterloo,
                    we said it was ours too.

His native village claimed him as its own,
                    as did his native town,
adopted city and preferred retreat.
                    So did our own street.
When his brave back was up against the wall,
                    our televisions all
got us shouting, and that did the trick.
                    Pretty damn quick.

His colours were his secret, and his warm-up
                    raindance, and his time up
Flagfell in the Hook District, and his diet
                    of herbal ice, and his quiet
day-to-day existence, and his training,
                    and never once explaining
his secret was his secret too, and his book,
                    and what on earth he took

that meant-to-be-magic night in mid-November.
                    You must remember.
His game crumbled, he saw something somewhere.
                    He pointed over there.
The referees soothed him, had to hold things up.
                    The ribbons on the Cup
were all his colour, but the Romanoff
                    sadly tugged them off.

We saw it coming, didn't we. We knew
                something he didn't know.
It wasn't the first time a lad was shown
                basically bone.
Another one will come, and he'll do better.
                I see him now – he'll set a
never-to-be-beaten time that'll last forever!
                Won't he. Trevor.

The Sarajevo Zoo

Men had used up their hands, men had
offered, cupped or kissed them to survive,
had wiped them on the skirts of their own town,
as different men had shinned up a ladder and taken
        the sun down.

One man had upped his arms in a victory U
to a thousand others, to show how much of the past
he did not know and would still not when he died.
Another's joke was the last a prisoner heard:
        'Oh I lied'

which did win some applause from the bare hands
of dozing men. And others of course had never
fired before then fired, for the work of hands
was wild and sudden in those days
        in those lands.

For men. For the women there was
the stroke, the ripping of hair, the smearing of tears,
snot, and there was the push of a shaking man,
or with fused palms the gibbering prayer
        to the U.N.

The nothing they had between those palms was
hope and the yard between surrendering palms
was hope as well. Far off, a fist in the sky
was meaning hope but if you prised it open
        you saw why.

The hands of the children here were wringing themselves
Hot with the plight of animals over there,
and drawing them in their pens with the crimson rain
of what men do to each other on television
     crayoned in.

But hands continued to feed the demented bear
who ate two other bears to become the last
bear in the Sarajevo Zoo. And they fed him
when they could, two human Bosnian keepers
     all autumn.

Today I read that that time ended too,
when fifteen rifles occupying some thirty
hands got there and crept in a rank on knees
towards the smoke of the blown and stinking cages
     and black trees.

Trees were what you could not see the starving
beasts behind, or see there were now no beasts,
only the keepers crouching with their two lives.
Then winter howled a command and the sorry branches
     shed their leaves.

Lines on a Tycoon

Known by the shortest of three Christian names,
He rolls his sleeves and goes the distance. Laws
Like two commissionaires let him through, his claims
A fraction over half-convincing both,
And money opens the doors that open doors
As sure as gut and throat make way for vomit.

Nothing stands in the way of the whole truth,
His readers know, so when he comes to the rim
Of the whole truth there'll be nothing to speak for him,
Let alone save him from it.

Sylva Fischerovà

KAREL CUDLÍN

Selection from: *The Tremor of Racehorses: Selected Poems* (1990), translated by Jarmila and Ian Milner.

SYLVA FISCHEROVÀ was born in 1963 in Prague. 'She is unmistakably a poet of her Czech, more precisely Moravian, homeland, though distinct from her contemporaries, of whatever generation. Nowhere are her Czech roots more apparent than in her poems of social comment and protest. Her eye has fixed on a special aspect of repression: the occupation of her country by the Soviet-led Warsaw Pact armed forces in 1968. Poems such as *Necessary* and *Am I My Brother's Keeper?* stand, and will stand, as classic expressions of that traumatic phase of Czechoslovak history' – Ian Milner. 'An underlying satirical vision of considerable edge' – John Lucas. ●

Am I My Brother's Keeper?

That was what he asked then
and there was a sudden heaviness upon earth like
　　　　　when a bird spits
　　　　　when a woman in bed turns her back
　　　　　　　　　　on a man.

We shall guard our brothers, you said
in that night of the valkyries, fires and songs from Valhalla.
But even then you knew you were lying.
Even then you knew your love
was scarcely more than
　　　　　'not to lose self-esteem'.
Even then you knew that you were too many
for Him to condemn all.

　　　No one wanted that oath
　　　from you. And the eyes of the valkyries
burn on in the darkness
　　　　　like gilded spittle
　　　　　like the Inquisition.

Necessary

What was necessary
    we did

The fields lay fallow
    and we ploughed them,
    sowed the grain
        and waited.
Our women lay fallow
    and we did what was necessary
        and waited

When foreign riders came
    we did what was necessary
    fenced off the fields and houses,
    sharpened axes and knives.

But at night the riders
               jumped the fences
               on their high horses
               and played the flute
               under our bedroom windows.
We put up higher and higher fences
but the horses grew
        as fast as the fences
        and the flute played on.

Then our women left us
    and took the children with them.
We did what was necessary
burnt the remnants of their dresses,
        the flowers behind the windows,
    and waited.

But no one has come.
        The stoves are cold
        we go on waiting.

Maybe we've done less
        than was necessary?
        Or more?
And what if earlier,
before the riders came,

we had done less or more
and now we've done
                    enough,
but that's why
we can't wait to see,
since only the one
who does less
                    or more
reaches the end of waiting?

We don't know what to do
or whether to wait,
for by waiting
                    we're doing something.
Or aren't we?
We don't know what's necessary
                    And the stoves are cold.

The Tremor of Racehorses

Sometimes it's enough to put out the light
and sit
        in the night blue
        as the tremor of racehorses
            But what if the tremor of racehorses is green?
            What if it's brown?

They said: Is yellow more red than white?
        Is a curtain more a table than
                            shoe?
        Is tobacco more pipe than
                            matches?

Really, stupid questions
and how they jeered.
        Only because they don't know
            the tremor of racehorses.
        That tremor of racehorses!

Chris Greenhalgh

MOIRA CONWAY

Selection from: *Stealing the Mona Lisa* (1994).

CHRIS GREENHALGH was born in 1963 in Manchester, did a Ph.D. on Frank O'Hara at Hull University, and now lives in Kent. He won a Gregory Award in 1992.

His first book *Stealing the Mona Lisa* is remarkable for its lightness of touch and a restless comic energy. Inner and outer worlds come together in poems charged with vivid imagery and narrative excitement. His poems explore modern media society and personal experience, playfully conflating accurate satire and sensuality, eroticism and tenderness. Yet often beneath the glittering surface there is a sour, unsettling subtext as well as intimations of a darker tone. ●

The Night I Met Marilyn

*Ask not what your country can do for you, ask
what you can do for your country.*
      JOHN F. KENNEDY

The night I met Marilyn it was raining
for I remember her petulantly shaking
her hair free from a scarf,
                          and that pampered animality
in response to the cold – part come-on, part disdain,
the dangerously volcanic glamour of a mouth that
lured you to the lip, and caused you to fall in.

She had us all mesmerised, resembling a stack
of televisions in an electrical store
all receiving the same programme;
yet behind the lazy sensuality and insouciance,
the gloved white finger quizzical against the chin,
it was obvious – to me anyway – there lay
a quiet centre of hurt, an abject vulnerability.
As she looked at me, I recognised
the management behind her smile, and
she seemed to understand that I understood.

I registered in her a terrible need for love,
and what happened later that evening I have never related.
It would have been like stealing the Mona Lisa.

I promised Marilyn that in her all-too-public life
the privacies that we, at least, shared
                              would be respected.

Then that last calamitous August night:
coming home, I heard the phone
insistent behind the locked door.
By the time I had found my key
and made a grab for the receiver,
the phone was dead.
                    As at the ripple-ends
of an earthquake, the shock
came some time after the event,
yet it remains a painful, intractable thought even now,
and one which I have kept secret for over thirty years.

I will say no more, other than that the oblique details
and veiled portrait of the woman I knew
and understood – feisty, ardent, marketable –
can be found in the eponymous heroine
of my latest novel, *Marilyn Runmoe*, published tomorrow:
hardback £16.99, paperback £7.99 with 20 b/w photos.

The Big No-No

The erotic tension is almost palpable
as they stand jiggling brandy loin-high

in warm circles: the corpulent older man
with the bonhomie of a department-store Santa,

his right arm draped round a young man's shoulders,
his left arm circling a younger woman's waist.

His glasses, at an oblique angle to the camera,
have whited-out, while the pupils of the other two

are pink as rabbits' eyes from the flash –
and if I tell you that the older man

happens to be my boss, the girl his mistress,
the other me, and that several times

her labia have given me less trouble
than a milk-carton, then perhaps you will

understand why I'm no longer employed
and why I finger this photograph with

three parts nostalgia, one part regret.

A Song for Europe

> ...*he that travails weary, and late towards a*
> *great city, is glad when he comes to a place of*
> *execution, because he knows that is neer the town.*
>
> JOHN DONNE: Sermons II

The hotel's complimentary can of rapidshave
said GOOD MORNING in four languages,
but no one could change a large note
before 9 am
the Spring morning in Paris after
it was decided there were
too many pigeons in the city.

I had caught an early flight
that Friday,
flying through clouds that looked like
explosions slowed a thousand times
and the tongue upon tongue of
mist over the city,
into a white municipal silence.

The birds had become a public menace –
discharging themselves over citizens,
veering myopically
into oncoming cars.
Poison was laid in the basins overnight,
and as they preened themselves and sipped
at the early morning water

soon the boulevards were strewn
with their bodies:
urban, grey, stringy,
their glaucous throats twitching.
Couples shuffled through them
thinking autumn had come early
or the binmen were on strike,

and in the *Champs de Mars* the park attendants
raking them in
enjoyed the delusion of being croupiers.
A boy scraping the railings with a stick
stopped to look
at the river as it slopped and gulped and hiccoughed up
the dead birds into a soupy litter.

You could have knocked me over with a feather.
I thought of
the morning after a general election, the boredom
God felt on the seventh day, a butcher
wiping blood on his apron as an affectation.
I entered a café where a mulatto
waitress brought my English breakfast:

tomatoes, eggs and two quotation marks of bacon,
then plied me with
the slow vengeful poisons of the colonies –
coffee, sugar, tobacco. I returned to my
unbirdlimed balcony. On the TV yellow-
vested marathon runners swarmed at the starter's gun
like bees smoked out of a hive.

Stephen Smith

DAVID HUNTER

Selection from: *The Fabulous Relatives* (1993).

STEPHEN SMITH was born in 1964 in Stourbridge and moved to Wales in 1978, later living in Japan and now Croydon. He won a Gregory Award in 1991.

The fabulous relatives of his book title are both real and imagined: his Ulster Protestant forebears slip back into tribal history as even more phantasmagorical characters emerge from the murk of legend, dream and fantasy to haunt him in the present.

'*The Fabulous Relatives* is a truly auspicious debut. On this evidence, Stephen Smith may well become what we so desperately need – a poet capable of acting as a moral barometer for the age' – John Osborne. ●

On the Exhumation of Seamus Heaney 2220

Visceral investigations revealed
important aspects of his diet. Seed gruel
showed he was careful of cholesterol.
Several Martian scientists

argued certain stains upon his fingers
were vegetable extracts compatible with ink.
He was a possible disseminator
of knowledge to an age before telepathy.

Learned treatments were called for, extending
sympathies between these physiological
discoveries; conjecture catalogued
him in the end as having been

an agronomist, whose portfolio
was educational instruction of the mass.
Mildewed papers, his illegible grave-goods
found buried with him settled this.

The Death Shop

The Death Shop had relocated
to a bright shopping mall. UNDER NEW MANAGEMENT
said a sign picked out in neon. Gaudily
furbished like a souvenir grotto it was doing
brisk trade. A marketing drive to "up-tempo"
image dispensed with old fashioned regalia
at rock bottom prices. Attractive part-exchange
on discontinued lines of memorial urns
was a winner. 'Anything considered' involved
one assistant in off-setting costs
of stabling horses from a Victorian hearse
against synthetic coffins. Sentimental morality
was a no-no. Several far from tubercular
ladies flounced over tills registering cash-sales.
Customers browsed Pic'n'Mix buckets of pills
labelled 'Go for it Sucker'. Speakers played
muzak by Bach. There was something for everyone:
corners devoted to baroque demises,
a D.I.Y. section on kitchen euthanasia.
Really there was too much to see. I said I'd call back.
Management assured me there'd be no need,
already they had teams of trained salesmen
out in the provinces. I could expect a knock soon.

Danegeld

I saw North derelict: counties abandoned to rain,
the towns left to investigation by wolves,
factories beached by the longshore drift of money South.
Migrants appeared on our borders, men with strange accents.
Reports said the crossroads were blocked.
We waited their visit, trussing accounts of our learning
into sacks. We slept scarcely,
and then dreamt of precedent endings: Rome's collapse
into squalor, camp fires lit with our churches.

Bargains must have been struck at the top,
a Danegeld paid. The Barbarians never arrived.
Now we have cultural exchanges with them.
We teach in their schools and they show us new
ways to trim gold in elaborate patterns.
The current vogue is to give children their names,
a fetish believing they will not slay their own.

The Mosquito Country

For twelve hours it has rained without variation,
a heavy warm flood. First sun makes the street giddy
with steam, wavers the contours of buildings to liquid.
The mosquito understands this floating world best,
is a native inured to water-born sickness.
We sweat under netting and dream like opium
eaters poisoned by small incisions in the skin.
The mosquito transmits his knowledge to us,
returns us to primary sensations, fevers
of heat, torpors of cold.   For three days I became
the mosquito: saw a land swivel under my eyes.
I fed off its body with greedy insistence,
digested the blood of small-traders loading fruit
on the water-fronts, tasted the plumpness of commerce
in their veins; bit into warrior and Emperor;
was sick on the slack blood of vegetarian
priests; sucked at the nipples of geishas. I was tight
with the sweetness of life. I squatted on their backs
till they grew thin with my drinking, feverish
with my unfamiliar contagions.

Sara Berkeley

Selection from: *Facts About Water* (1994).

SARA BERKELEY was born in 1967 in Dublin, has lived in America, and now lives in London. Her first collection – published when she was 19 – was shortlisted for the Irish Book Awards and the *Sunday Tribune* Arts Awards. Her Bloodaxe selection *Facts About Water* (published in Ireland by New Island Books) includes some of the best work from *Penn* (1986) and *Home Movie Nights* (1989) as well as a whole collection of new poems. Her book of stories *The Swimmer in the Deep Blue Dream* was published by Raven in 1992.

Sara Berkeley's poetry evokes a personal world with – as Eavan Boland has said – 'a great sense of expansion and eloquence'. ●

Man by his life

Near the end of blue Tuesday
he wrote himself a note
about how miserable he felt;
put on clean socks, laced his boots,
went out to face the weather.

He sat on his step in the sun
until the fog rolled in;
fat fog rolls sat on the hills
and blew across his road.
He went inside, turned the wind down
and knelt by his life, blowing for a spark.

When it grew dark,
he crouched in the dark, fiddling with the dials
listening to the voices fade in and out
spreading the weather.
But news on the hour increased the interference
the hair on his neck rose
he turned from the news through a snatch of songs,
liquorice tunes he once whistled to.
He rocked and rocked in his white board house
head in his knees, casting around for himself.

It came unexpectedly, like the truth
right at the end – a silence that stilled his hand –
he passed through every station on earth
and in the end, face down, head first,
the hissing silence held him.

Man chopping wood

Man chopping wood
looks up to see
the helmeted boys go over,
he can hardly believe –
men in their khaki fatigues, running hard
across the no-man's-land of his back yard.

The whistles are screaming,
he drops his axe; the wood smells
warm, sweet, as it should;
the men going over
throw up their arms as they did
on the old news reels,
just as he had always pictured
Great Uncle John
who was lost on the Somme.

He thought it was all
black and white in the war,
all hands on hearts, flags in the breeze,
he's never seen men sink to their knees
he's never seen them torn limb from limb
he was just
getting the woodpile in.
His wife's in the kitchen, baking pies,
his kid's on the green
playing football with the neighbours' kids,
he tries to scream
but his voice won't come
and quick as they came, they're gone,
it's quiet again,

smell of new wood and raw air
and no knowing if history was played
or statistics made, if pain was real
or death hard
in the no-man's-land of his back yard.

Evidence

They came to the end of them
nettles took hold, the roof fell
thistles grew right down their hall
she listened to his doubtful thoughts,
gathering evidence.

Into other people's homes
he made his curious way
kept his bones in their stone jars
put his hot cheek to their flagstone floors
heard only echoes there.

She lay under a mountain ash
keeping count of the seconds that passed
with her free hand she traced a root
circled and circled the heavy doubt
cut his name in the dark.

Didn't he see the end of time
chasing minutes across the face
the gloomy cast of early June
fell too smartly on her pain
would she ever be safe?

She lay counting them to a close
in her vessel was bitter blood
truth flooded her deepest canals
truth found its own level
close to the bone.